Public Library Collections
in the Balance

PUBLIC LIBRARY COLLECTIONS IN THE BALANCE

Censorship, Inclusivity, and Truth

Jennifer Downey

Foreword by James LaRue

LIBRARIES UNLIMITED™

An Imprint of ABC-CLIO, LLC

Santa Barbara, California • Denver, Colorado

Library of Congress Cataloging-in-Publication Data

Names: Downey, Jennifer, author.
Title: Public library collections in the balance : censorship, inclusivity,
   and truth / Jennifer Downey.
Description: Santa Barbara, California : Libraries Unlimited, an imprint of
   ABC-CLIO, LLC, [2017] | Includes bibliographical references and index.
Identifiers: LCCN 2017027252 (print) | LCCN 2017004285 (ebook) |
   ISBN 9781440849657 (ebook) | ISBN 9781440849640 (acid-free paper)
Subjects: LCSH: Public libraries—Censorship—United States. | Public
   libraries—Collection development—United States. | Libraries and
   community—United States.
Classification: LCC Z711.4 (print) | LCC Z711.4 .D69 2017 (ebook) |
   DDC 025.2/13—dc23
LC record available at https://lccn.loc.gov/2017027252

ISBN: 978-1-4408-4964-0
EISBN: 978-1-4408-4965-7

21 20 19 18 17   1 2 3 4 5

This book is also available as an eBook.

Libraries Unlimited
An Imprint of ABC-CLIO, LLC

ABC-CLIO, LLC
130 Cremona Drive, P.O. Box 1911
Santa Barbara, California 93116-1911
www.abc-clio.com

This book is printed on acid-free paper ∞

Manufactured in the United States of America

In memory of Wendy Summers Lewis-Rakova

CONTENTS

FOREWORD

In theory there is no difference between theory and practice; in practice there is.
—Unknown, though often attributed to Yogi Berra

For many of us in the field, librarianship is less a job than a calling. There is a moment of recognition, an awareness that the profession speaks to our deepest internal values. Most often, that value is "intellectual freedom." We have a fierce belief in the fundamental dignity of human inquiry. We believe that all human beings have both the right to express themselves and unfettered access to the expressions of others. We stand proudly against the forces of censorship.

That's the theory.

In practice, things can sometimes be very different. As Jennifer Downey relays in the opening of her book, the collision between theory and practice can be as pointed and immediate as a reporter looking for a quote. Or, in the many realistic, uncomfortable vignettes at the end of each chapter, we may find that our values are not universally accepted, may falter, or have unintended consequences.

I suspect that American librarians are entering a time of new and greater challenge. On the one hand, we see a parenting style that has moved from helicopter to Velcro—no longer hovering, now bound close to the offspring's skull, to and through high school Advanced Placement English classes. On the other, as witnessed by the 2016 presidential election, we see growing anger and fear about Islam, globalization, and diversity in all its manifestations. We are, at this writing, still a nation divided, which means that half our population is poised to take instant offense, even outrage, at virtually anything the other half says or does.

Collecting what everyone says or does, then letting people know they can come and get it, is pretty much the job description of librarianship. That puts us smack in the middle.

So Downey's book comes at just the right time, with just the right information and tone. The theory is here, with clear, succinct explanations. But the practice is here, too, provided with the same unflinching directness. For instance, library principles hold that young people have First Amendment rights, just like adults. Yet the majority of (adult) Americans disagree. The majority can be wrong, of course. But whether they're wrong or not, it's a potent recipe for conflict.

So what do we do in this fractious time?

Answer: be professional. Think it through. Own our values. Understand and adopt the best practices in the field. Maintain courtesy and respect to all. Know where you can find help when you need it, because you will.

Public Library Collections in the Balance exemplifies the balance we strive for. In this survey of some of the key issues and players now current in American librarianship, Downey finds genuine poise, a perspective that is neither too naive nor too cynical.

The work we do continues to be important. It continues, in fact, to be transformative both for individuals and our communities. This book is a handy guide, and a good reminder.

James LaRue
Director, Office for Intellectual Freedom
American Library Association

PREFACE

The patron called the reference desk in the late afternoon, all blustery tone and sharp manner, asking me to put the book *Rabbit Is Rich*, by John Updike, on hold for her to pick up later, but first, she had a question: Was the book housed in the children's department or in adults'? "It's in adult fiction," I replied.

An hour later, there she was, having retrieved the book and handing me her business card. She was a reporter from a local news affiliate. A local 12-year-old girl, it seemed, had checked the book out from her middle school's library a few days earlier, seemingly not deterred by its more than 400 pages of dense text, including several sex scenes. The girl showed the book to her mother, who promptly contacted the local news station.

I wondered aloud why the reporter had come to the city's public library with a concern about a middle school's collection. It was late in the day, she explained, and the school had already closed. She wanted to get to the bottom of this right away so her piece could air the next morning, and that meant interviewing me on camera, right then and there, about how books containing adult content shouldn't be available to children. I refused, and she countered by asking if anyone would consent to an interview. Our director had gone home for the night. There was just myself and my coworker, Jessica, who quietly shook her head at the idea of an interview.

I tried to clarify our reticence. "We're all about promoting access, not restricting it," I explained. "We're not authorized to make reading decisions for other people's children." As I kept speaking, I realized that there was an unspoken word hanging in the air between us—a word I didn't want to use for fear of escalating the situation. I tried to stammer it out, but I knew it would upset the reporter, so I tried, and failed, to think of an acceptable synonym.

"Censorship," said Jessica, calmly and clearly, without looking up from her papers. I breathed a sigh of relief, nodded, and then I said it, too, out loud: "Censorship." Why had I been so afraid to say it?

When the news story came out the next day, there were several clips of the reporter interviewing parents with young children about *Rabbit Is Rich.* Those who made it on the air expressed the correct combination of horror, shock, and disappointment. The clip was dramatic, outrage-provoking sensationalism, and much of it took place right under our public library's sign, making it appear that we had agreed to such a thing. I was saddened and horrified but also glad I'd said it—that loaded word—the one Jessica said so coolly while I could not manage it. As I watched the news report, I wished I'd had the courage to say it first, and I admired Jessica for her straightforwardness.

I had begun thinking, and then writing, about censorship back in library school, quickly realizing it was a cause close to my heart. We all know (don't we—please?) that book-burning, book-banning, and all those obvious, in-your-face instances of censorship are adversaries of true librarianship. But so many other occurrences fall under the radar and out of our consciousness.

The day-to-day work of librarianship can be challenging to our convictions. All but the most sheltered or lucky of us will someday have to make at least one hard decision, be it about the safety of children, the sanctity of the First Amendment, the benefits and limitations of technology, or the overriding purpose of our collections. Separating our own strong feelings from our work can be so automatic that we might not even notice it happening—but when we honestly examine our points of view and confront our biases, we are practicing true, honest librarianship. In these moments, we can say with sincerity and integrity that we are proud to stand by our professional convictions.

We are professionals, and we use our minds to do our important work. In that spirit, please know that the point of this book is in no way to preach or moralize but to simply lay out the facts as they are and allow the reader to come to his or her own conclusions about difficult issues.

ACKNOWLEDGMENTS

My most sincere and heartfelt thanks go out to Lise Dyckman, who initially reached out to me about writing for Libraries Unlimited, and to Barbara Ittner, who picked up the reins. Both of you offered advice, patience, and encouragement as I slogged my way through this endeavor.

Thank you a million times, James LaRue, for your inspiration and support, and for the work you do every day at the Office for Intellectual Freedom. You bring inclusivity and justice to our profession, and that makes me proud to be a librarian. Kristin Pekoll, that goes for you, too.

Jessica King, you spoke up when I was afraid to, and not for the first time. Thank you for your friendship, sweet nature, and bravery in the important work you do. You are an inspiration to so many.

Many thanks to Lynne T. Díaz-Rico for showing me how it works.

Special thanks to my husband, Michael Downey, for patiently listening to my computer keys clack away, and for your never-wavering support of not only this project, but of everything we do in this life as spouses, partners, and best friends.

Diane Fly, your eagle-eye and effortless perfect grammar kept me from publishing countless embarrassing mistakes. You're almost as great an editor as you are a mother.

Finally, infinite thanks and love to my father, Richard Fly, who has spent decades quietly and tenaciously teaching me through example that the written word has the power of no other form of communication to break down walls and open minds.

INTRODUCTION

At first glance, librarianship appears to be more democratic, socially responsible, and egalitarian than most professions. After all, a quick Web search reveals that the American Library Association (ALA) boasts its own Bill of Rights (ALA, 2006a), an office dedicated to the preservation and defense of intellectual freedom (ALA, 2008), and a progressive-minded round table group that works in support of social responsibilities such as equity of access, economic parity, and human rights issues (ALA, 2012). Librarians do indeed work hard and sacrifice greatly in defense of intellectual freedom and the fight against censorship, and due credit should be given to those who make these efforts.

As of this writing, the ALA has accredited 59 graduate schools of library and information science throughout the United States and Canada (ALA, 2006b). In addition to the LIS master's degree, many also offer doctorial level studies. Distance learning is becoming a common option among these universities as well.

One might assume, given the democratic and socially responsible nature of librarianship and the small yet substantial number of universities where a LIS graduate degree may be obtained that an education in library and information science would include a good deal of study in the areas of intellectual freedom, censorship, equity, and diversity. And one might be correct, depending on what school is chosen and what electives are selected. On the other hand, depending on these same circumstances, one might be considerably mistaken.

Fewer than half of the 59 LIS graduate programs accredited by the ALA offer any courses at all in intellectual freedom, censorship, or ethics of librarianship. Those universities that do have courses on these topics almost always categorize them as electives. Some universities offer the courses regularly in the schedule so students have a chance to work them into their schedules should they choose to do so; but at other institutions, it can take up to two years for even one to come around.

PURPOSE OF THIS BOOK

The purpose of this book is fill in the gaps left in library education and to help spark the idea that censorship and intellectual freedom are important topics that should be more prevalent in LIS education. Whether as a professional reading, a textbook or as supplemental reading, librarians and students can use this book to examine both the professional guidelines of librarianship and their own personal feelings about topics that can be difficult to think about.

The main reason this book was written was to encourage readers to think about issues that are not always easy to think about and to be prepared for the inevitable. The objective is not to change minds but to open them. Whether it serves as required or supplemental reading for LIS coursework or as professional reading for anyone who works in public libraries or simply cares about their role in society, it is hoped that this book offers new insight and challenges readers to explore delicate topics with open and curious minds.

SCOPE OF THIS BOOK

This book deals primarily with issues that arise in public libraries. Because partnerships and collaborations between different types of libraries is a growing phenomenon, there is some mention of school, academic, and other types of libraries, but public library collections are the core of what is addressed. It should be mentioned here that school libraries bear a larger burden when it comes to community challenges to materials than do public libraries. As noted in Chapter 7, partnerships between public libraries and school libraries are becoming more and more common, as school libraries often have more limits on collecting than do public libraries. These partnerships provide a chance for public libraries to offer children and teens in a community the books they desire without school librarians having to take unnecessary risks of offending parents and administrators. Therefore, school librarians may benefit from this book as well.

While an exploration of censorship and intellectual freedom issues in libraries across both time and the globe would be fascinating in its complexity, this book deals with American libraries. That said, the ALA is closely affiliated with the Canadian Library Association, and libraries in these two countries are quite similar in both purpose and intent (ALA, 2007). For that reason, it is anticipated that those involved with Canadian public libraries could benefit from this book as well.

After an exploration of the history of censorship in American libraries, common intellectual freedom and censorship concerns such as the filtering of public computers, the benefits and perils of community assessments, and questions of quality and demand in collection development are examined. In addition, the ins and outs of community challenges are explored in depth throughout the book—from examining what types of elements make a book or other item susceptible to being challenged to the writing of strong policies and the training of staff in order to prevent or quell challenges to what steps to take when a challenge does occur or get out of control. Only the most fortunate of librarians will never have to speak with irate patrons about books or other items that are seen as offensive. For those who have not yet dealt with such situations, it is hoped that this advice will be useful when it is needed. For those who have been there and done that, it is hoped that new skills or at least the comfort of solitarily will come in handy the next time around.

There are two appendices in this book. One contains a source list of lesbian, gay, bisexual, and transgender (LGBT) resources for librarians to use in collection development. The other offers a list of small and alternative presses, also to assist in collection development. Because LGBT-themed books are uniquely vulnerable to censorship from both the public and from librarians themselves, it was deemed important to include resources for this demographic, as they seldom turn up in mainstream review sources. The same goes for small and alternative presses. In building comprehensive, well-rounded collections, librarians need as many places to turn as possible.

INTENDED AUDIENCE

While this book is chiefly intended for professionals in public librarianship and those studying to work in public libraries, it may also be used in training activities for librarians, library support staff, trustees, and stakeholders. Libraries often respond to the surprise and unpleasantness of a challenge by providing training and support and by changing policies in order to fill in whatever gaps were missing that could have helped tame the challenge more effectively. In cases like these, librarians and library managers can turn to this book for guidance and support.

Hopefully, this book will appeal to librarians and their allies in all stages of life and career—from the young student exploring ideas of intellectual freedom for the first time to the retiree volunteering at the local public library and wanting to learn more about the issues at the root of the profession.

Finally, those who issue challenges to materials at their public libraries may benefit, directly or indirectly, from this book. Challenges, despite the turmoil they create among library staff, are almost always the result of good intentions: the protection of children, the betterment of the community, the sanctity of great literature. This is not an "us-versus-them" book. Although challengers and librarians are so often at odds, this book aims to help readers understand that the two camps have more in common than they might know.

HOW TO USE THIS BOOK

This is not a "do this, don't do that" manual. While professional guidelines are in place to help librarians navigate delicate situations involving censorship and intellectual freedom, these are not simplistic subjects and there are no easy answers. When situations that involve these topics arise, they are almost guaranteed to be taxing, confusing, and even divisive.

Censorship, especially, is a topic that brings up difficult questions with no obvious right-or-wrong answers. It's probably fair to assume that most librarians would agree with the simple statement that censorship isn't a good thing, but what one person sees as absolutely right is very often seen by another as absolutely wrong. Throw in technology, children's rights, parents' concerns, and societal expectations of what the public library's role is, and you've got so many differences of opinion that coming to any kind of consensus would be not only a misguided endeavor but an impossible one.

Perhaps, reading this book will change your mind about some of your convictions, and perhaps it won't—but a conviction that hasn't been examined is really just a bias. It is through the examination of previously held notions of what is good and what is bad that people come to learn what they truly believe. It's a difficult process and not a particularly comfortable one, but, hopefully, coming out wiser and stronger in the end makes it worth the struggle. With this in mind, it is recommended that this book, especially the vignettes and "what would you do" questions be carefully explored with open minds and a commitment to critical thought.

All in all, it is hoped that reading this book will raise important questions and help guide the way to finding the answers. What those answers may be is entirely up to you.

REFERENCES

American Library Association. (2006a, June 30). Library Bill of Rights. Retrieved from http://www.ala.org/advocacy/intfreedom/librarybill.

American Library Association. (2006b, August 3). Alphabetical List of Institutions with ALA-Accredited Programs. Retrieved from http://www.ala.org/accreditedprograms/directory/alphalist.

American Library Association. (2007, April 19). Canadian Library Association. Retrieved from http://www.ala.org/groups/affiliates/affiliates/cla.

American Library Association. (2008, June 9). Office for Intellectual Freedom. Retrieved from http://www.ala.org/offices/oif.

American Library Association. (2012, February 22). Social Responsibilities Round Table. Retrieved from http://www.ala.org/srrt.

Chapter 1

HISTORY OF CENSORSHIP IN AMERICAN PUBLIC LIBRARIES

BEYOND BOOK-BURNING

When thinking about censorship, book-burning—that long-despised and yet long-practiced activity of destroying books in a showy, fiery display of self-righteousness—tends to come to mind. Indeed book-burning has had its big moments in history, from the disastrous burning of the Alexandria Library's scrolls back in the third century (LaRue, 2007) to the ceremonial torching of the *Harry Potter* books for the theoretical sake of children in modern times (Cronin, 2003).

With a nod of thanks to Ray Bradbury, the destruction of books tends to evoke a feeling of revulsion in both librarians and nonlibrarians alike. But one does not need to build a bonfire of books to act as a censor. Censorship can be loud and raucous, or it can be so stealthy and quiet that it isn't even noticed when it's happening. While the presence of censorship often lurks around books and other materials involving political, social, sexual, or religious themes (Oppenheim & Smith, 2004), these or any other themes may compel a reader to react to a book in a censorious manner. *Suppression* is the key element in the practice of censorship (LaRue, 2007). Burning a book (or a pile of books) is a clear and malicious act of suppression, as one obviously can't read a book that has been reduced to embers. But neither can one read a book, listen to a CD, download an MP3, peruse an article, or access a website that has been hidden behind barriers, removed from a collection, blocked from sight, or otherwise made either unavailable or not easily available.

A review of censorship in libraries throughout world history would take up a whole book in and of itself. Therefore, this chapter will focus on censorship in American libraries. As a relatively new country, the United States hasn't suffered from book-burning or other forms of book destruction as much as other cultures throughout history, but it does have its own unique record of censorship and oppression struggles in libraries.

American Libraries in Their Infancy

Public libraries in the United States began mainly as private enterprises rather than the municipal institutions that are common today. While a few volunteer-run social libraries came along in the 1700s, based on an English model of creating gathering places for culturally minded community members and offering services almost exclusively to educated, wealthy white men (Valentine, 2011; Wiegand, 2015), the United States' public libraries began to sprout up in earnest during the mid-1800s, with rapid growth occurring through the 1930s. Not coincidentally, this was the same time period in which compulsory secondary school enrollment rates began to increase (Kevane & Sundstrom, 2014; Wiegand, 2015).

Several states attempted an experiment in the mid-1800s mandating the creation of township libraries. Over 1,500 township libraries were built in Michigan and Indiana, and other states quickly followed suit with their own township library plans. Despite all good intentions, these libraries ultimately failed to be of much influence, and the vast majority had closed their doors by 1876 (Kevane & Sundstrom, 2014). Township libraries were supported by the public through voluntary tax donations to build and fund libraries for specific school districts. These libraries were chiefly meant to support public school students, much like modern school libraries (Freeman & Hvode, 2003; Wiegand, 2015).

The township library model was an outgrowth of the United States' Second Great Awakening, an era marked by attention to education, religion, and temperance. The Young Men's Christian Association (YMCA) program and the American Home Missionary Society were other creations of the Second Great Awakening. It was a time of reform as well as revival of New England Protestant morals. Township libraries generally held collections of books dealing with ethics and religion, and the overall intention was to strengthen public literacy rates and build up society through education and the prevailing moral principles of the time (Freeman & Hvode, 2003).

Despite these efforts, township libraries didn't last long. Community members complained that the libraries were inefficiently run and that the books often failed to meet their wants or needs. Collections were criticized for being both too scholarly for the average reader and too lowbrow for the educated. The public also complained that the library spaces were too small, and that not enough was done to keep the classes of citizens separated. As the social climate changed, funding dwindled and townships began to divide, leaving many township libraries in disuse until their doors finally closed for good (Freeman & Hvode, 2003). As a social experiment, township libraries taught community leaders their share of lessons. While these libraries were meant to strengthen townships in order to meet certain assigned standards of literacy and temperance, the community members were unhappy with having a social agenda forced upon them. Outright censorship was not necessarily taking place, but its predecessor—the tone of assuming to know what is in the best interests of others—had taken hold, and the result was clear in people's rejection of township libraries.

From the mid-1800s to the 1930s, as the township library model was failing, public libraries and obligatory public education continued to move along the same track. Attention began to focus on municipally run public libraries (also known as free or general libraries), supported by the legislative work of state library associations (Kevane & Sundstrom, 2014). These new Progressive Era public libraries were still primarily considered to be places of education (Kevane & Sundstrom, 2014), complimenting new compulsory schooling standards and continuing to support the importance of education throughout adulthood. As the printing revolution reduced the cost of producing books, libraries became more and more commonplace, and increasingly began to be run by municipalities rather than by volunteer groups (Valentine, 2011). Libraries were considered a place for forward thinkers, for those who read not for escape, but for virtue, with a goal of advancing society through knowledge and lifelong education (Battles, 2003). The task of librarians was seen as supplying quality reading material to an assortment of people in an efficient manner within this same spirit of societal advancement (Battles, 2003).

Early Censorship: Good Books and Bad Books

As municipally funded libraries grew in popularity, censorship concerns began to take root. Reading fiction books for pleasure was a common leisure activity, although doing so was often frowned upon by civic leaders. Librarians found themselves torn between supplying the public with what it demanded and satisfying community leaders' demand for quality nonfiction reading meant to educate, not entertain. Children and single women were considered to be especially susceptible to the romanticized ideals that were assumed to arise from reading popular fiction (Wiegand, 2015). The fact that public taxes paid for the establishment of libraries worked for both sides of the argument. While it could be said that the public's tax dollars should be spent on what was most popular, it was also often argued that public libraries were established for the betterment of the public, not to maintain the status quo or to encourage the reading of materials that were considered dangerous (Wiegand, 2015).

As these concerns grew, librarians began to get creative. At the Boston Public Library, which pioneered the creation of local taxpayer-based library services run by communities rather than larger governmental entities, librarians made frequent use of a room known as the Inferno, where they stored popular fiction. Patrons wishing to have a book retrieved from the Inferno were required to supply a character reference and a reason for wanting to read the book in question. It was then up to the librarian on duty to decide whether or not to supply the patron with the book (Wiegand, 2015).

Anytime a library item is placed behind a barrier, a phenomenon known as the chilling effect becomes likely to occur. The discomfort and embarrassment of having to ask a supposed authority figure for an item that is obviously considered distasteful, as evidenced by its removal from the general collection, is often enough to stop a patron from asking for it at all (Pinnell-Stephens, 2012). The Inferno may or may not have been intended to cause embarrassment to individuals—and in fact, it may very well have satisfied civic leaders' concerns about certain books being too visible—but the message was clear, and its very existence was certainly enough of a rationalization for keeping what the Boston Public Library staff—and many others—considered to be the wrong books out of the wrong hands.

Even in libraries that didn't have Infernos or other methods of concealing unsavory books, policies were frequently put in place to discourage the reading of fiction. Libraries were known to come up with rules such as a two-book limit per checkout, one of which was required to be nonfiction (Wiegand, 2015).

TIMELINE OF IMPORTANT EVENTS IN CENSORSHIP AND INTELLECTUAL FREEDOM

- **1700s** Volunteer-run social libraries, promoted by Benjamin Franklin and modeled after English institutions, begin to appear in American communities, predominantly open only to wealthy white men.

- **1800s** Township libraries, financially supported by tax donations, begin to spring up, with the intention of bettering communities and supporting school districts through literature. The model ultimately fails due to townspeople's sense that their wants and needs are not being met.

- **1890s to 1930s** Compulsory education laws and the printing revolution result in the creation of municipally run public libraries. In the spirit of societal advancement, public librarians are expected to decide what patrons should and should not read—an assumption that is not always appreciated by the public.

- **Mid-1800s** Boston Public Library opens its doors to the public, supported by municipal taxes. The library is known for the practice of sequestering popular fiction and other books deemed lowbrow in its Inferno, causing patrons to have to go to great efforts to retrieve books.

- **1886 to 1919** Philanthropist Andrew Carnegie awards $40,000 in grants to build 1,679 community libraries around the county, although many Southern cities decline the grants for fear of being required to admit African Americans. Those who do accept often go on to demand that the libraries be white-only establishments, sometimes with small branches for black patrons. Activism slowly begins to assimilate Southern public libraries.

- **1939** John Steinbeck publishes *The Grapes of Wrath*, leading to a conflict over whether libraries should purchase the book. The American Library Association (ALA) responds by creating the Library's Bill of Rights, later renamed the Library Bill of Rights.

- **1940** The ALA creates the Committee on Intellectual Freedom to Safeguard the Rights of Library Users to Freedom of Inquiry, later renamed the Intellectual Freedom Committee.
- **1967** The ALA establishes the Office for Intellectual Freedom (OIF) to help librarians deal with censorship and intellectual freedom challenges.
- **1969** the Freedom to Read Foundation is incorporated. Although not affiliated with the ALA, the two agencies work in partnership on censorship and intellectual freedom issues.
- **1974** The OIF publishes the first edition of the *Intellectual Freedom Manual* as a handbook for dealing with challenges and censorship concerns.
- **1982** The OIF introduces the first Banned Books Week to celebrate the freedom to read and to quell censorship and book-banning in libraries.
- **2000** The Children's Internet Protection Act is introduced and eventually declared constitutional. The ALA and OIF both oppose the act to this day.

The Carnegie Era

American libraries rapidly expanded and changed scope after the philanthropist Andrew Carnegie, having taken note of the success of public libraries in Boston, Chicago, and New York, came up with the idea of using a share of his fortune to create public libraries throughout the country and beyond (Wiegand, 2015). Beginning in 1886, Carnegie (and, later, the Carnegie Corporation) gave away approximately $40 million in grants to build libraries. By 1919, the United States was home to 1,679 Carnegie-funded public libraries (National Park Service, n.d.).

Carnegie was not particularly demanding of his grantees. His conditions simply stated that each municipality receiving a library grant was expected to donate the land for the building, and that building plans were to be reviewed by Carnegie's secretary prior to the grant being formally awarded. The municipality also had to agree to dedicate an annual tax revenue equaling 10 percent of the grant to the library. Beyond that, Carnegie didn't make any specific demands or requests about how his libraries should be operated or used, preferring to leave these decisions to the individual municipalities (Kevane & Sundstrom, 2014).

The combination of grant opportunities, compulsory schooling, advances in printing, and rising literacy rates pushed the building of new public libraries into overdrive. As this happened, libraries slowly began to shed their affectations and adopt a new, more democratic model of service. Recreational reading became more socially acceptable, and, while libraries were still seen as places of education and industriousness, their overall atmosphere began to feel less preachy. Soon, communities with public libraries were seen as prosperous and inviting places where families would wish to settle in and join the community (Kevane & Sundstrom,

2014). The stuffiness and uninviting air of township and social libraries began to give way to openness and democracy in public libraries.

North and South

If it seems reasonable to say, with the benefit of hindsight, that early American public libraries throughout New England and the rest of the North came with their share of snobbery or pretense, then it would surely be appropriate to say that libraries in the South were experiencing more socially complex problems. Compulsory public school attendance became the norm throughout the South around the 1860s, but by 1895, nine Southern states were still getting by with no public libraries at all—and even when they did begin to crop up, they were almost always subject to de jure, or legal, segregation. In short, these libraries were intended to be used only by wealthy, educated, white members of the communities they served (Fultz, 2006). By 1917, construction of buildings was moving along faster, with 144 new Carnegie-funded grants resulting in the creation of new public libraries at rapid speed. In 1902, Atlanta opened the doors of its stately public library, albeit only to white patrons (Fultz, 2006). Race and class worries led many Southern communities to turn down lucrative Carnegie grants for fear of being required to admit those they wanted to keep out (Wiegand, 2015).

In protest of Atlanta's Carnegie Library segregation, the scholar and writer W.E.B. DuBois and a group of fellow African American activists challenged the library to allow blacks representation on the library board and entrance to the library, or, at the very least, entrance to certain, specified branches (Wiegand, 2015). This activism ultimately came to naught. In a sardonic twist, Carnegie had given the city of Atlanta a grant to build an African American branch library along with the main building, but the money wasn't put into use by the city until 1923, when the first of the city's three African American branch libraries was opened (Atlanta-Fulton Public Library System, 2016).

While much of the activism leading up to the eventual desegregation of the South's public libraries didn't happen until the 1950s and beyond, DuBois and other early activists set the stage for the next wave. For example, in 1939, more than a decade before the beginning of the civil rights movement, six African American men participated in a peaceful sit-in at an Alexandria, Virginia, library. The men sat outside the building in silent protest after being denied library cards and were subsequently arrested for disorderly conduct (Library Marks 75th, 2014). Despite the arrest, this activism ultimately led to Alexandria's creation of a small branch library for African Americans (Wiegand, 2015)—sadly, not quite the intended outcome of integrating the main branch.

At their onset, as the 20th century began, library services for African Americans in the South tended to take place in annexes or add-ons to either black schools or white libraries—in essence, a bit of space for a small collection complimenting the school's curriculum, plus access for African American students and nonstudents alike, and the limited services of a librarian. Known, in the vernacular of the time and place, as Negro branches, these libraries suffered greatly from understaffing and meager budgets (Graham, 2001). Louisville, Kentucky's Western Colored Branch consisted of three rooms in a private home, a not-unusual venue at the time (Fultz, 2006). This sporadic mishmash of slow expansion continued as the 20th century advanced and came to a head in the 1950s, with the Supreme Court's landmark *Brown vs. Board of Education* decision (Fultz, 2006).

African American Southerners reported mixed feelings about the branches created for black patrons only. On one hand, the smack of segregation was offensive, but on the other hand, these branches supplied community centers where like-minded associates could gather and engage in an open environment—sadly, a rarity in the Jim Crow–era South. Branch libraries also created opportunities for training in the library field, and many African American women throughout the South received training and became skilled librarians during this era (Wiegand, 2015). Despite the pros, though, the cons of segregated library services couldn't be ignored.

Public libraries in the South saw their share of post-*Brown* civil rights activism and social unrest. In 1963, two African American ministers were badly beaten for their part in a movement that was intended to desegregate public libraries in Anniston, Alabama. Integration came to public libraries more easily than it did to swimming pools, buses, and other types of public venues, but change was nevertheless slow going (Fultz, 2006).

There are a few noteworthy exceptions in the history of resistance to segregation that bear mentioning. The Houston Public Library, for example, voluntarily desegregated in 1953, a year before the *Brown* decision and seven years before the desegregation of the city's school system, which was, at the time, the largest segregated public school system in the country. Houston in the 1950s was home to a large and prosperous black middle class. The Houston Public Library, a Carnegie grant-funded building, opened its doors to white Houstonians in 1903 and was joined in 1913 by the Colored Carnegie Library, which operated as a separate institution until 1921, when it officially became a branch of the main library. By the 1950s, spawned by a series of Texas court cases foreshadowing *Brown*, a group of prominent African American activists in Houston wrote a letter to the library board asking for voluntary desegregation, while implying that they felt quite confident that they would win a lawsuit should it come to that. It took a few years of back-and-forth, but the library was eventually—quietly and peacefully—desegregated, and the old, hardly used Colored Carnegie Library, by then considered a relic of the Jim Crow era and an embarrassing reminder of a gloomy time in Houston history, was closed for good (Malone, 2007).

Desegregation moved along in fits and starts, and censorship often came along for the ride. During the read-in movement of the 1960s, which was aimed at integrating public libraries once and for all, Southern segregationists went so far as to challenge and attempt to ban books with racial themes going against the grain of the pre-*Brown*-era South (Graham, 2001).

As desegregation gained momentum throughout the civil rights movement, so did censorship concerns. During a 1961 speech at the Waldorf-Astoria before the American Newspaper Publishers Association, President John F. Kennedy addressed the issue of censorship and libraries, declaring, "If this nation is to be wise as well as strong, if we are to achieve our destiny, then we need more new ideas for more wise men reading more good books in more public libraries. These libraries should be open to all—except the censor. We must know all the facts and hear all the alternatives and listen to all the criticisms. Let us welcome controversial books and controversial authors, for the Bill of Rights is the guardian of our security as well as our library" (John F. Kennedy Presidential Library and Museum, n.d.).

A BACKGROUND AND HISTORY OF CENSORSHIP IN THE UNITED STATES

Up until the 1930s, censorship didn't gain a great deal of mainstream attention in American public libraries. It was often assumed that a central task of librarians' jobs was to judge for readers which books were tasteful and which were not, and little fuss was made about this position (American Library Association Office for Intellectual Freedom [ALA OIF], 2010). While selection was seen as important, censorship and exclusion, whether by refusing to purchase certain books due to their potentially inflammatory subject matter or by deciding to place them behind barriers or in some version of the Boston Public Library's infamous Inferno, were regularly encouraged by leaders in the library world (Wiegand, 2015). This began to change, however, when John Steinbeck's 1939 novel *The Grapes of Wrath* gained attention, both positive and negative.

The Grapes of Wrath was a new kind of book, a distinctly American book, filled with coarse language and rough imagery, and fueled by an alarmingly matter-of-fact plot. The dust bowl classic follows the Joad family, led by son Tom, who is fresh out of jail and on parole for a deadly act of self-defense, as they leave the desecrated farm in Oklahoma they had sharecropped for years for the promised land of California with little more than an unreliable jalopy and a sense of optimism that would eventually become their downfall. As they experience death, desertion, and a constant foreshadowing of the cruel fate awaiting them in the West, the Joads attempt to maintain their humanity, only to have it squelched by the brutal realities of government camps, hunger, poverty, and the prevailing control of ruthless farm owners. In the end, Tom, jaded and angry, is insinuated to be on his way to becoming a union organizer, while his angelic sister, Rose of Sharon, gives birth to a stillborn baby in a boxcar (Kardolides, Bald, & Sova, 2005; Steinbeck, 1939). To sum it up brutally, the promised land of California didn't quite provide the prosperity and happy ending the Joads had in mind.

The Stomping of the Grapes

The Grapes of Wrath was quickly banned from the shelves of libraries across the country. The Library Board of East St. Louis, Illinois, created a commotion in the press when they declared their intention to burn three copies of the novel on the courthouse steps—although, in an odd compromise, they later decided to place the same three copies in an adults-only section of the library in lieu of setting them on fire. So widespread was the controversy that *The Grapes of Wrath* was no safer at sea than on dry land—the chaplain of the *U.S.S. Tennessee* was so offended by the novel that he had it removed from the ship's library (Kardolides et al., 2005).

The Kern County, California, Board of Supervisors was especially not amused by *The Grapes of Wrath*. Kern County is home to the San Joaquin Valley city of Bakersfield, Steinbeck's obvious symbol of the villainy of the agricultural West. The board presented Gretchen Knief, the head librarian of Kern County's Free Library, a resolution banning *The Grapes of Wrath* from all Kern County schools and libraries. Among other objections, board members were offended by the depiction of the county's citizens as uneducated and profane and of its civic officials as heartless vigilantes (Lingo, 2003).

Despite Knief's protests, the uproar in Kern County raged on. The president of the Associated Farmers of Kern County publically decried *The Grapes of Wrath* as propaganda and ceremoniously burned a copy in front of photographers. An image of the book-burning incident famously ran in *Look* magazine. The Associated Farmers had been formed only a few years earlier for the purpose of rallying against strikers, picketers, and union organizers (Kardolides et al., 2005), groups that are, paradoxically, central motifs of goodness and progress as depicted in *The Grapes of Wrath*.

As is so often the case, controversy and curiosity became interlinked. Despite its many challenges, *The Grapes of Wrath* quickly became a bestseller with a record-breaking waiting list, and it wasn't long before a movie deal was in the works. The Kern County Board of Supervisors, in addition to their many other demands, insisted that Twentieth Century Fox abandon the film, which was already in production (Kardolides et al., 2005). This, as any film buff can attest, did not happen.

The Grapes of Wrath was not the first or last book to be challenged and censored in American history, but its influence as a classic novel which was simultaneously praised and maligned helped to usher in a new age of American librarianship. Some librarians fell on the side of suppression, and others fell on the side of access. The ALA found itself in the middle of a great argument and, in a history-making move that would help define its role in the struggle against censorship, quickly and forcefully came down on the side of access.

THE LIBRARY BILL OF RIGHTS

In 1939, the ALA responded to the new demands and expectations surrounding librarianship by implementing the Library's Bill of Rights, later renamed the Library Bill of Rights, which became, and remains, the organization's official stance against suppression and censorship.

The Library Bill of Rights has gone through several revisions, amendments, and official interpretations over the years but has held tight to its central message of unbiased book selection, open meeting spaces, and balanced collections (ALA OIF, 2015). The current Library Bill of Rights is short and sweet and gets straight to the point:

The American Library Association affirms that all libraries are forums for information and ideas, and that the following basic policies should guide their services.

  I. *Books and other library resources should be provided for the interest, information, and enlightenment of all people of the community the library serves. Materials should not be excluded because of the origin, background, or views of those contributing to their creation.*

 II. *Libraries should provide materials and information presenting all points of view on current and historical issues. Materials should not be proscribed or removed because of partisan or doctrinal disapproval.*

III. *Libraries should challenge censorship in the fulfillment of their responsibility to provide information and enlightenment.*

 IV. *Libraries should cooperate with all persons and groups concerned with resisting abridgment of free expression and free access to ideas.*

  V. *A person's right to use a library should not be denied or abridged because of origin, age, background, or views.*

 VI. *Libraries which make exhibit spaces and meeting rooms available to the public they serve should make such facilities available on an equitable basis, regardless of the beliefs or affiliations of individuals or groups requesting their use* (ALA, 2006. Used with permission from the American Library Association).

The establishment of the Library Bill of Rights made it clear that censorship and exclusion were unacceptable in librarianship, but specific instructions or advice about how to handle censorship and challenges weren't made as apparent. In the mid-20th century, a time known for blacklisting of many types of professionals, the ALA considered the idea of banishing librarians who were found to practice censorship from the profession (Wiegand, 2015). This idea, with its uncomfortable shades of McCarthyism, was ultimately rejected, although it did help the ALA begin to decide how to go about helping librarians who refused to censor and who strove to adhere to the Library Bill of Rights in their daily work.

THE OFFICE FOR INTELLECTUAL FREEDOM

In 1940, very shortly after the adoption of the original Library's Bill of Rights, the ALA established the Committee on Intellectual Freedom to Safeguard the Rights of Library Users to Freedom of Inquiry, mercifully renamed the Intellectual Freedom Committee (IFC) in 1948. The IFC's main objective was to tend to library users' concerns in respect to the Library's Bill of Rights (ALA OIF, 2010). The IFC remains in place and active to this day and is made up of a chair and nine members, all of whom are selected by the ALA president-elect and the ALA's Council Committee on Committees (ALA OIF, 2010). The IFC currently serves as an oversight group for the OIF.

The OIF, in turn, was established in 1967, in response to mounting community challenges too numerous and time-consuming for the IFC to effectively manage. Once the OIF was in place, the IFC was able to work more efficiently on developing policies, while the OIF took on the role of educating librarians and the public on issues concerning intellectual freedom (ALA OIF, 2010; ALA, 2008). Because the ALA has never created a specific definition of intellectual freedom or decided upon a framework of issues to work on, the OIF is free to work case-by-case on librarians' needs as they arise (Jones, 2015). The OIF also provides support to the ALA's Intellectual Freedom Round Table (ALA OIF, 2015).

Philosophy and History of the OIF

The OIF has been very firm in its assertion that suppression of library materials runs in direct opposition to the First Amendment. The stress and anxiety of dealing with a community challenge can be extremely taxing for a librarian, and, therefore, the office seeks to provide advice and support to librarians dealing with the pressure of challenges to their collections. While librarians, for their part, must understand that library patrons have the right under the First Amendment to petition the government for a redress of grievances, this in no way means that library collections are beyond defense by those who develop them—in fact, it is a principle of the OIF to help librarians gather the information they need to shield their collections from challenges and other efforts at suppression (Morgan, 2010).

Throughout the years, the prominent reasons behind library challenges have shifted, but a few central themes have endured: the rights of minors, concerns involving the Internet and digital information, privacy and confidentiality of library patrons, and service to diverse populations.

Rights of Minors

Both the OIF and the ALA have strongly asserted that minors share the same First Amendment rights as adults and, therefore, have the same freedom to use their public libraries as they see fit. It is not the role of librarians to interfere with minors' selections or activities. For example, if a librarian were to witness a child accessing information about alternative lifestyles, sexualities, or religions, that librarian would not be justified in any attempt to act as a stand-in parent or supposed protector of the child by restricting or denying access to the material in question. The OIF stresses that it is a librarian's role to help minors learn to think critically, evaluate informational sources, and select materials of use to them. The OIF and the ALA both attest that it is the role of a parent, and only a parent, to allow or limit the use of a child's library materials (Morgan, 2010).

The Internet and Digital Information

Since the inception of the OIF, the digital age has changed the playing field of librarianship in ways one could never have anticipated. The amount of information that can be accessed on the Internet is enormous—and that fact alone gives many people pause. The vast amount of information at any person's fingertips has been known to bring up concerns for library patrons about the safety of children. Fears about minors accessing sexually graphic or violent content at their public libraries has led to pressures on public libraries to use filtering software, with the reasoning being that whatever harm or inconvenience this causes is superseded by the importance of protecting children from accessing inappropriate online material. The Children's Internet Protection Act (CIPA), which was declared constitutional by the Supreme Court of the United States in 2003, mandates that all school and public libraries receiving certain federal funds must apply filtering software to all public and staff computers. However, both the ALA and the OIF are openly opposed to the use of filtering software in public libraries, emphasizing that they block access to legitimate educational sites while failing to block access to truly pornographic sites. Both agencies also stress that librarians' time would be better spent educating both minors and adults about how to safely and effectively access and search the Internet and by offering classes as well as one-on-one learning opportunities for minors, their parents, and adult patrons (Morgan, 2010). CIPA and Internet filtering are examined in greater detail in Chapter 3.

Privacy and Confidentiality

The OIF attests that privacy is at the core of any library patron's constitutional right to read and access information without interference. If readers feel at all in danger of having their choice of reading materials exposed, it cannot be maintained that they are accessing information freely. Patron privacy wasn't a hot issue until shortly after the terrorist attacks of September 11, 2001, which spawned a national sense of distrust and suspicion about everyday people's motives. In 2012, the ALA adopted an interpretation on privacy in reaction to this new and lasting air of suspicion. The interpretation states that library users' personal information, circulation records, and database searches are strictly private matters. There have been numerous examples, both pre- and post-9/11, in which patrons have had their library information sought by the FBI, Internal Revenue Service, and other federal agencies, including under the auspices of the USA PATRIOT Act and Homeland Security regulations. These actions go against the ALA and the OIF's philosophy that patrons can and should expect complete privacy and confidentiality from their libraries. Both the ALA and the OIF actively seek out opportunities to educate library patrons about their rights to privacy during this age of mistrust (Morgan, 2010).

Service to Diverse Populations

Diversity has been an important component of the OIF's efforts for decades. The office has spent a great deal of time exploring, analyzing, and interpreting policies to ensure that its language is free of discriminatory overtones. The OIF has worked diligently to ensure open service to diverse populations, including any and all groups affected by discrimination. These groups are identified as those potentially facing economic discrimination as well as discrimination based on religion, citizenship status, and national origin. Anti-immigration discrimination is not tolerated by the OIF nor is discrimination based on religion or any other factor that may cause library patrons to feel prejudged or discriminated against (Morgan, 2010).

Current OIF Projects

The OIF has come up with several initiatives and campaigns over the years intended to increase awareness of censorship and library users' rights. In addition, the office has published a book, *The Intellectual Freedom Manual*, for librarians to use as a reference guide. The office also offers free, confidential legal advice to librarians dealing with challenges and related issues.

Banned Books Week

Current projects of the OIF include the well-known and widely celebrated Banned Books Week. This nationwide event, usually held during the last week of every September, unites librarians with teachers, publishers, booksellers, and readers of all genres in celebration of the freedom to read whatever one chooses (ALA, 2012). Libraries, schools, bookstores, and others celebrate Banned Books Week by creating displays of frequently challenged and banned books, holding special events such as inviting notable speakers to talk about book-banning, and hosting public discussions dealing with issues of overcoming censorship, as well as hosting art exhibits, readings, and more (Long, 2006). Promotional items, ranging from whimsical to serious, are available from the OIF for libraries to use in promotion of Banned Books Week events (ALA, 2012).

Over the years, libraries have become extremely creative and have had a great deal of fun with their Banned Books Week events. The popular website YouTube hosts a channel called Virtual Read-Out in honor of Banned Books Week, which features videos of famous authors as well as readers from across the globe reading aloud from their favorite challenged books (Perez, 2012). A library in Texas set up a makeshift prison in which staff members read a selection of frequently challenged books in a spoof on the popular story-time format for children they dubbed "prison-time" (Prison-Time Reading, 2011). Other out-of-the-box ideas have included speaking at library board or city council meetings, hosting mock debates, and posting about banned books on social media sites such as Pinterest, Facebook, and Twitter (Pekoll & Davis, 2015). The Freedom to Read Foundation (FTRF) offers grants to libraries and other organizations to help fund their Banned Books Week activities through their Judith F. Krug Memorial Fund (FTRF, n.d., a).

> Banned Books Week is a time to celebrate our freedom and our love for books that have made an impact on us . . . It doesn't have to be a controversial or negative experience.
> —Kristin Pekoll, Assistant Director, American Library Association Office for Intellectual Freedom, former Young Adult Librarian, West Bend Community Memorial Library

It's Everyone's Job

In 2011, in keeping with the spirit of Banned Books Week, the OIF launched a new awareness campaign called Defend the Freedom to Read: It's Everyone's

Job, in hopes of encouraging librarians to feel confident enough to report challenges to books and other library materials more often. This came about after it was discovered that only 20 to 25 percent of formal challenges ever went reported (Campaign Urges, 2011). The campaign included the creation of special downloadable artwork designed to promote the reporting of challenges. It was stressed that reporting challenges can be done anonymously, and that doing so helps the OIF keep accurate statistics (Defend the Freedom to Read, 2012).

Choose Privacy Week

In the spring of 2010, the OIF launched the first Choose Privacy Week, which has been held annually every spring since. This campaign, which came into existence after research found that privacy matters were of great concern to patrons and librarians alike (Maycock, 2013), was created to bring attention to digital age privacy concerns facing library patrons and also to promote open, honest dialogue regarding privacy issues. The OIF accomplishes this by providing tools for libraries to use in developing community conversations about privacy concerns (ALA, 2016).

Concerns such as the use of security surveillance and software-based monitoring of patrons' Internet use at public libraries have been found to be of considerable importance to library users, and privacy needs are an integral tenet of librarianship in general (Maycock, 2013). A 2012 survey found that privacy rights are a major concern for librarians, with 95 percent agreeing or strongly agreeing that all library users should have the freedom to control who is allowed access to their personal information. Virtually 100 percent agreed that libraries should never share their patrons' circulation records, Internet use information, or other personal information with third parties unless specifically authorized to do so by either the patron or by a court of law. Almost 80 percent of those surveyed felt that libraries can and should play an important role in educating the public about privacy issues (Survey Confirms, 2014).

Intellectual Freedom Manual

The *Intellectual Freedom Manual* was first published by the OIF in 1974. The book's most recent edition, the ninth, was published in 2015. The *Intellectual Freedom Manual* is intended to be used as a resource for librarians to confidently apply the standards of intellectual freedom to their work. The manual provides interpretations of the various sections of the Library Bill of Rights in order to help librarians apply them to real-life situations, and it serves as a useful reference in dealing with such issues as community challenges to materials, gaining assistance from the ALA to help fight against suppression, and learning to assertively contact legislators with intellectual freedom concerns (Morgan, 2010).

Other OIF Projects

In addition to Banned Books Week, Choose Privacy Week, and other campaigns, the OIF has dedicated its efforts to presenting programs at library conferences and other forums in order to bring attention to intellectual freedom concerns. The office also provides free online learning classes and offers legal assistance to libraries dealing with intellectual freedom issues and challenges (ALA, 2008).

The OIF provides oversight and staff support to the IFC, as well as to other member groups including the Committee on Personal Ethics, the Intellectual Freedom Round Table, and state-level intellectual freedom chapter committees (ALA, 2008). The OIF also oversees the LeRoy C. Merritt Humanitarian Fund, which provides assistance in the form of support, welfare, and medical care for librarians who have been denied employment rights or who have been otherwise discriminated against based on race, color, creed, place of national origin, age, religion, or disability, as well as those who have been discharged from employment or threatened with such action due to their stance in support of the defense of intellectual freedom rights in the workplace (ALA, 2007).

The OIF also works closely with the FTRF, which, although closely affiliated with the ALA, has a separate membership procedure and is officially a separate organization (FTRF, n.d., b).

THE FREEDOM TO READ FOUNDATION

Closely tied with the OIF and the IFC is the FTRF. Incorporated in 1969, the FTRF is a nonprofit organization which deals with legal and educational issues affecting libraries. While the FTRF is closely affiliated with the ALA, it is, in fact, a separate entity. In addition to its educational efforts, the FTRF distributes grants to help individuals and groups involved in legal disputes around First Amendment rights. The FRTF also often involves itself in court cases regarding freedom of speech and freedom of the press (FTRF, n.d., b). While the FTRF was initially established, and still remains, outside the realm of the ALA, the two are closely connected, with the FTRF frequently coming to the defense of ALA members in need (Asato, 2014).

TIPS AND TRAPS: LESSONS FROM HISTORY

Tips

- Public libraries are intended to be open and accessible to all, regardless of income, race, or socioeconomic status.
- Censorship issues have often gone hand in hand with cultural shifts such as civil rights and desegregation.
- When in doubt regarding issues of censorship, refer first to the professional guidelines put forth by the ALA and OIF, and your library's policy manual.

Traps

- Beware of classism and exclusion—when developing a collection, remember to include books appealing to a variety of tastes and interests.

- While they may seem controversial at the time of publication, books that challenge readers often become classics or pave the way for new genres.
- It is never advisable to act against the tenets of the Library Bill of Rights in the daily work of librarianship.

QUESTIONS TO CONSIDER

- Do you feel that librarians still have a role in determining which materials are quality reading and which are lowbrow?
- If you saw a child under 12 accessing graphic information in a public library about sex that you considered above his or her age level, how would you respond and why?
- If the local police came to your library with a request to access a patron's checkout record and record of database searches, how would you proceed?
- Do you feel that the practice of placing certain books in hard-to-find areas, such as behind desks or in drawers helps protect children from reading books their parents might disapprove of, or do you find it unethical? Why?

REFERENCES

American Library Association. (2006, June 30). Library Bill of Rights. Retrieved from http://www.ala.org/advocacy/intfreedom/librarybill. Used with permission from the American Library Association.

American Library Association. (2007, April 19). The LeRoy C. Merritt Humanitarian Fund. Retrieved from http://www.ala.org/groups/affiliates/relatedgroups/merrittfund/merritthumanitarian

American Library Association. (2008, June 9). Office for Intellectual Freedom. Retrieved from http://www.ala.org/offices/oif

American Library Association. (2012, December 20). Banned Books Week: Celebrating the freedom to read. Retrieved from http://www.ala.org/bbooks/bannedbooksweek

American Library Association. (2016). Choose Privacy Week. Retrieved from https://chooseprivacyweek.org

American Library Association Office for Intellectual Freedom (2010). *Intellectual freedom manual*. Chicago: American Library Association.

American Library Association Office for Intellectual Freedom (2015). *Intellectual freedom manual*. Chicago: ALA Editions, an imprint of the American Library Association.

Asato, N. (2014). Librarians' free speech: The challenge of librarians' own intellectual freedom to the American Library Association, 1946–2007. *Library Trends, 63*(1), 75–105.

Atlanta-Fulton Public Library System. (2016). 100 years of library service. Retrieved from http://afpls.org/history/166-100-years-of-library-service

Battles, M. (2003). *Library: An unquiet history.* New York: W.W. Norton & Company.

Campaign urges book challenge reporting. (2011). *American Libraries, 42*(11/12), 13.

Cronin, B. (2003). Burned any good books lately? *Library Journal, 128(3)*, 48.

Defend the freedom to read: it's everybody's job. (2012). *Newsletter on Intellectual Freedom, 61*(1), 8.

Freedom to Read Foundation. (n.d., a). Judith Krug Fund. Retrieved from http://www .ftrf.org/?page=Krug_Fund

Freedom to Read Foundation. (n.d., b). About FTRF. Retrieved from http://www.ftrf .org/?page=About

Freeman, R. S., & Hvode, D. (2003). The Indiana township library program, 1852–1872: A well selected, circulating library as an educational instrumentality. In R. S. Freeman & D. Hvode (eds.), *Libraries to the people: Histories of outreach.* Jefferson, NC: McFarland & Co.

Fultz, M. (2006). Black public libraries in the south in the era of de jure segregation. *Libraries & the Cultural Record, 41*(3), 338.

Graham, P. T. (2001). Public librarians and the Civil Rights Movement: Alabama, 1955–1965. *Library Quarterly, 71*(1), 2.

John F. Kennedy Presidential Library and Museum. (n.d.). John F. Kennedy speeches. Retrieved from http://www.jfklibrary.org/Research/Research-Aids/JFK-Speeches/ Willow-Grove-PA_19601029.aspx

Jones, B. M. (2015). What is intellectual freedom? In American Library Association Office for Intellectual Freedom, *Intellectual freedom manual.* Chicago: ALA Editions, an imprint of the American Library Association.

Kardolides, N., Bald, M, & Sova, D. (2005). *120 banned books.* New York: Checkmark Books.

Kevane, M., & Sundstrom, W. A. (2014). The development of public libraries in the United States, 1870–1930: A quantitative assessment. *Information & Culture, 49*(2), 117–144.

LaRue, J. (2007). *The new inquisition: Understanding and managing intellectual freedom challenges.* Westport, CT: Libraries Unlimited.

Library marks 75th anniversary of first sit-in. (2014). *American Libraries, 45*(11/12), 17.

Lingo, M. (2003). Forbidden fruit: The banning of *The Grapes of Wrath* in the Kern County Free Library. *Libraries & Culture, 38*(4), 351–377.

Long, S. A. (2006). Banned Books Week: A celebration of intellectual freedom. *New Library World, 107*(1/2), 73–75.

Malone, C. K. (2007). Unannounced and unexpected: The desegregation of Houston Public Library in the early 1950s. *Library Trends, 55*(3), 665–674.

Maycock, A. (2013). Privacy, libraries, and engaging the public: ALA's Choose Privacy Week initiative. *Indiana Libraries, 32*(1), 35.

Morgan, C. D. (2010). Challenges and issues today. In American Library Association Office for Intellectual Freedom, *Intellectual freedom manual* [Foreword]. Chicago: American Library Association.

National Park Service. (n.d.). Carnegie libraries: the future made bright. Retrieved from http://www.nps.gov/nr/twhp/wwwlps/lessons/50carnegie/50carnegie.htm

Oppenheim, C. & Smith, V. (2004). Censorship in libraries. *Information Services & Use, 24*(2), 159–170.

Pekoll, K. & Davis, M. (2015, September 1). Before the mud flies: Conversations for Banned Books Week [webinar]. American Library Association Office for Intellectual Freedom. Retrieved from http://www.ala.org/advocacy/before-the-mud-flies

Perez, N. (2012). Banned Books Week: Celebrating 30 years of liberating literature. *SRRT Newsletter Social Responsibilities Round Table, 181*, 1.

Pinnell-Stephens, J. (2012). *Protecting intellectual freedom in your public library.* Chicago: American Library Association.

Prison-time reading. (2011). *American Libraries, 42*(11/12), 15.

Steinbeck, John (1939). *The grapes of wrath.* New York: The Viking Press.

Survey confirms librarians' commitment to privacy rights. (2014). *Newsletter on Intellectual Freedom, 63*(3), 78–105.

Valentine, P. M. (2011). America's antebellum social libraries: A reappraisal in institutional development. *Library & Information History, 27*(1), 32–51.

Wiegand, W. (2015). *Part of our lives: A people's history of the American public library.* New York: Oxford University Press.

Chapter 2

WHAT GETS CHALLENGED AND WHY

It is impossible to predict exactly what materials may end up being challenged, but certain genres and topics tend to be seen as more controversial or provocative than others and are therefore more prone to challenges and complaints. Knowing ahead of time what types of books are more susceptible to challenges helps in policy writing and preparedness—however, it is never a good reason to gloss over these types of titles in collection development, no matter how strong the urge might be. Deciding to omit certain materials because of the perceived threat of a potential challenge constitutes self-censorship. Collecting a well-rounded assortment of materials for all tastes, while being prepared to speak to complainants about the importance of comprehensive collection development, is an imperative part of unbiased librarianship.

According to the Office for Intellectual Freedom (OIF), the reasons most often given for challenges and banning attempts are:

- Sexually explicit materials
- Offensive language
- Materials deemed unsuited to age group
- Violence
- Homosexuality
- Occult or satanic themes
- Religious viewpoint (American Library Association [ALA], 2013a)

It's rare for a book to be challenged for only one reason. Most often, a single book will be challenged for a variety of reasons. For example, the popular young adult (YA) book *Looking for Alaska* by John Green has received complaints for being sexually explicit, unsuited for its age group, containing offensive language, and for its references to drugs, smoking, and drinking alcohol.

Certain genres, such as graphic novels, street lit and romance fiction, tend to come under fire and are more subject to censorship from both inside and outside sources.

SEXUAL CONTENT

If may be difficult to believe, considering the popularity of sexually explicit books like E. L. James's *Fifty Shades of Grey* trilogy, but sexual content is still a major reason reported for challenges in libraries. Between 2000 and 2009, the OIF received reports of 1,577 challenges citing sexually explicit material, making it the most often-cited reason for challenges and banning during that decade (ALA, 2013a). However, when one considers that parents and other concerned adults are the primary complainants in this area, it becomes clear that it's not simply the sex in the books that these complainants object to but the idea that minors could find and read them (ALA, 2013a).

Sexual Content and Adult Books

Even classic adult literature such as Vladimir Nabokov's *Lolita* and Maya Angelou's *I Know Why the Caged Bird Sings* consistently make the list of challenged books due to sexual content (Connelly, 2009). Even *Fifty Shades of Grey*, while selling millions of copies, was one of the top 10 most frequently banned books in 2013, with reasons ranging from "unsuitable to age group" (the age group in question presumably being children and teens, though the book was clearly written for an adult audience) to the idea that teenagers might be compelled to try the sex acts depicted in the book (ALA, 2013b). In fact, the "unsuitable to age group" rationale has been applied to adult books with such frequency that one might wonder if there is any perceived discrepancy at all between children's, YA, and adult books in the eyes of complainants. The fact that they might land in the hands of minors seems to override the fact that these books were written for adults and belong in the adult section of public libraries, with corresponding catalog records indicating such. Nevertheless, the "unsuitable to age group" rationale has been applied to classic adult novels such as Toni Morrison's *The Bluest Eye*, memoirs like Jaycee Dugard's brutally honest account of her kidnapping and years of sexual abuse in *A Stolen Life*, and contemporary bestsellers like Khaled Hosseini's *The Kite Runner* (ALA, 2013b), all of which are categorized as adult books.

This brings up an odd dichotomy that exists when it comes to adult books in public libraries. Even those books clearly cataloged and shelved in the adult section can, of course, end up in the hands of minors, just as they can in bookstores and school hallways as they are stealthily passed from one hand to another. But it seems that libraries bear a stronger expectation for keeping books with sexual themes out of minors' hands than do bookstores or other corporate entities.

While schools are legally responsible to act in the place of parents under the *in loco parentis* doctrine, and therefore bear the responsibility of acting in place of parents when they are not present (Walker, 2014), public libraries operate under no such premise. Not only are public libraries not to be held responsible for deciding what minors may and may not read, the Library Bill of Rights states in no uncertain terms that minors have the same rights as adults in libraries (ALA, 2006), meaning that any attempt to assume parental responsibility is not only unprofessional but goes against the professional guidelines of librarianship.

Sex Manuals and Imagery

Books with sexual images and nudity, including those meant to educate and empower, are often subject to challenges as well. Robie H. Harris's *It's Perfectly Normal: Changing Bodies: Growing Up, Sex, and Sexual Health* has been challenged numerous times since the publication of its first edition in 1994, for reasons including it being perceived as child pornography (ALA, 2013b). Similar books with a more adult readership in mind, from Alex Comfort's classic *The Joy of Sex* to Emily Dubberley's whimsical *Sex for Busy People: The Art of the Quickie for Lovers on the Go*, have landed on most frequently challenged lists in recent years. Even when the reasons given for banning these books are their supposed inappropriateness for children, the idea is often to remove them from public libraries altogether, not just children's and teen areas (Doyle, 2010).

Parents and other adults who do not want the children in their care to see, touch, or read adult books in a public library have a responsibility to visit the library with them and steer them toward the books they want them to read. This is a heavy burden, and, as many would attest, simply not reasonable. Older children and teens very often visit public libraries without their parents or guardians, who must understand that the employees of the library, without *in loco parentis* status, are neither legally nor professionally bound to make decisions in place of parents—and furthermore, their profession prohibits them from doing so for reasons that are well thought-out in a spirit of fairness and access.

Sexual Content and YA Books

Sexual content is the most often–cited reason found for censorship, both from internal and external sources, when it comes to YA books (Whelan, 2009b). More than even graphic violence, books dealing with sex raise the hackles of parents and other adults (Heller & Storms, 2015).

It has often been pointed out that attempting to shield teens from books containing sexuality might actually do more harm than good. During the teen years, many young people stop reading for leisure—and, whether adults like it or not, books with sexual content are often exciting for teens and can help get them back into the habit of reading for fun (Heller & Storms, 2015). Making the public library a safe place for teens to explore new subjects in YA books may ultimately help with their development into adulthood and keep them in the habit of reading (Forman, 2015).

Labeling YA Books

Attempts to label YA books that contain sexual content have been met with various responses. The St. Louis County Library in Missouri, after considerable pressure from a group known as Citizens against Pornography, agreed to attach labels to YA books containing sexual content and to check them out only to patrons in ninth grade and up (Censorship Dateline, 2009). Other public libraries, such as Guilderland Public Library in New York, have refused to cave to pressure groups and have kept their teen books label-free (Board Rejects, 2005). While it may seem innocuous, the practice of labeling books with categories outside of their catalog records (which may include such value-free labels as mystery, historical fiction, and so on) creates a situation in which subjective value judgments, rather than mere subject identifiers, are placed on library materials.

Public Libraries and Sex Education

Debates rage on and on about how best to educate teenagers about sex and reproduction, with some parties insisting that abstinence is the only method of sex education that should be taught, and others stressing that teens need as much knowledge as possible in order to make wise decisions and steer clear of unplanned pregnancies and sexually transmitted diseases. What type of sex education young people receive depends very much on where they live and what local pressure groups exist in their communities (Creel, 2013). Public libraries answer to their own authorities and professional guidelines, though, and are not subject to regional or political trends. The ALA Policy Manual on Services and Responsibilities of Libraries, in its section on sex education materials in libraries, states:

> ALA affirms the right of youth to comprehensive, sex-related education, materials, programs, and referral services of the highest quality; affirms the active role of librarians in providing such; and urges librarians and library educators to reexamine existing policies and practices and assume a leadership role in seeing that information is available for children and adolescents, parents, and youth-serving professionals. (ALA, 2010)

In other words, public libraries have a responsibility to provide accurate and useful sex education information to anyone who seeks it. Because the Library Bill of Rights states that the information needs of minors are equal to those of adults, teens can and should expect to find a range of information on sex, reproduction, pregnancy, contraception, and relationships at their public libraries.

Diversity and YA Book Banning

An unfortunate side effect of challenging and banning YA books has recently been recognized. There appears to be a correlation between YA books that get challenged and the racial, ethnic, LGBT (lesbian, gay, bisexual, and transgender) status, and disability status of the characters in challenged books. Looking at commonly challenged books, such as Sherman Alexie's *The Absolutely True Diary of a Part Time Indian*, Toni Morrison's *Song of Solomon* and *Beloved*, and Rudolfo A. Anaya's *Bless Me Ultima*, it's hard to deny that diverse characters and censorship commonly correlate. While the rationales for challenging these books are often categorized as "religious viewpoint" or "sexually explicit," it has been theorized that these categories are little more than smoke screens concealing the real issue of discomfort with diverse characters (Lo, 2014).

Sexual Content and Children's Books

Children's books dealing with sexuality, from picture books to chapter books, are just as susceptible to censorship attempts as YA and adult books. Frequently seen on the chopping block for their frank portrayals of sex and reproduction are Robie Harris's children's book (the cover clearly states "For Age 7 and Up") *It's so Amazing: A Book about Eggs, Sperm, Birth, Babies, and Families*, and Dori Hillestad Butler's *My Mom's Having a Baby!* Both books explain in words and pictures how babies are conceived, how pregnancies progress, and how babies are born (ALA, 2013b; Butler, 2005; Harris, 1999).

Preteens and teens have been reading Phyllis Reynolds Naylor's series of *Alice* books, beginning with *The Agony of Alice*, for over two decades now, sometimes with the blessings of their parents and often without. Alice, whose mother had died, lives in a house full of boys and men, and struggles to grow up without a female adult to help her navigate her awkward teen years. As the series progresses, Alice and her friend giggle over *Arabian Nights*, albeit with some confusion, and leaf through a *Playboy* magazine. Alice engages in some explicitly written heavy petting with her boyfriend and discusses homosexuality with her father. Beloved though they are, the *Alice* books have been challenged consistently throughout the years for their language and sexual content (O'Brien, 2013; Chinn, 2007).

The 2007 Newbery Award-winning children's book *The Higher Power of Lucky*, by Susan Patton, famously includes the word "scrotum" on the first page, in reference to a dog being bitten by a rattlesnake. The main character, Lucky, didn't know what a scrotum was, other than a secret thing. Countless librarians opted not to buy the book for their collections (Stager, 2007) because of the uproar. For what it's worth, *The Higher Power of Lucky* is not a book about scrotums or about the correct terminology of anatomical parts at all, but about a 10-year-old parentless girl who eavesdrops on 12-step recovery meetings and worries that her guardian might leave her alone without her beloved dog (Patton, 2006). While *The Higher Power of Lucky* has not weathered any official challenges, it has been self-censored countless times by librarians across the country over that one word (Whelan, 2009a).

It is in no way the purpose of this book to assume how to best raise children. How families handle issues of sexuality with their children is entirely up to them, not their public libraries. When libraries come into play in these matters, it should be assumed that they are places of information, not suppression.

LGBT-THEMED MATERIALS

A mere 50 years ago, if one could find LGBT materials in a public library at all, they tended to be skewed dramatically toward presenting homosexuality and transgender conditions as either medical or psychological problems—dangerous perversions best kept repressed if not extinguished through therapies that would now be considered outmoded and barbaric (Oberg & Klein, 2003).

Public opinion regarding LGBT issues has changed significantly over the past several decades. The percentage of Americans supporting the legalization of same-sex marriage has risen from 35 to 52 percent since 2001, while those in opposition have fallen from 57 to 40 percent. For the first time in the country's history, the majority of Americans now support same-sex marriage (Pew Research Center, 2015).

Despite recent gains in LGBT issues, culminating in the Supreme Court's historic striking down of the nation's same-sex marriage ban in the case of *Obergfell v. Hodges* in June 2015 (Supreme Court of the United States, 2015), LGBT-themed library materials remain an almost-constant target for challenges, especially by parents and other adults who object to LGBT content in children's and YA books. LGBT-themed materials for adults tend to be somewhat safer, although challenges occur in that area as well. Jodi Picoult's *My Sister's Keeper* and Alice Walker's *The Color Purple* are prime examples of popular, well-received adult books that have been challenged and banned (ALA, 2013b).

LGBT Teens and Libraries as Safe Spaces

Even in this day and age, being an LGBT teen can be tough. LGBT teens experience significantly higher levels of violence, including harassment and physical assault, as well as suicide-related behaviors, than their straight peers. Over 60 percent of LGBT teens report feeling unsafe or uncomfortable in their usual surroundings. All of this exclusion and peril ultimately results in LGBT teens disproportionately experiencing depression and acting out in the forms of substance abuse and truancy, plus engaging in risky sexual behaviors all too often resulting in the contraction of HIV and sexually transmitted diseases. Between physical health concerns and psychological ramifications, it is no exaggeration to say that bullying of LGBT teens is dangerous at best, deadly at worst (Centers for Disease Control and Prevention, 2014).

Public libraries can be sanctuaries for LGBT teens, as well as children and adults. The ALA provides strong and clear guidelines about equal access of services to LGBT patrons in a proactive manner, and it has been maintained that public libraries have a responsibility to provide not just sufficient materials but also programming, displays, and public events in support of LGBT patrons (Albright, 2006).

The likelihood of coming out as an LGBT individual with confidence is partly determined by how taboo the topic seemed during one's teen years. Books with LGBT characters and content can do more than just open one's eyes to various sexual identities; they can also be a beacon of hope for those struggling with coming out to their friends and families. These books, therefore, can have a tremendous impact on people's lives. Unfortunately, they are also among the most commonly censored books, while also being those that tend to raise the most curiosity (Heller & Storms, 2015).

Teens coming to terms with their sexual orientation or gender identity have very specific information needs, and the public library is often their first stop on the road to self-discovery. It is therefore imperative that libraries not only supply the materials this demographic needs but that they do so in a welcoming manner (Helton, 2010). LGBT teens and their allies require books and materials featuring positive examples of LGBT characters, as well as materials explaining how to connect with others experiencing the same concerns, and how to successfully navigate the world with an LGBT identity. They also need solid, frank information about sexual health (Rauch, 2011). Libraries can serve as places of learning and personal growth for LGBT teens simply by having resources with this type of information on hand, offered in a nonjudgmental, friendly, and open manner.

Operating as a proactively LGBT-friendly library even helps avoid community challenges to library materials. When community members have the opportunity to meet and mingle with people outside of their usual circles, stereotypes, assumptions, and fears about LGBT people are likely to give way to acceptance.

It's also difficult for those who disapprove of LGBT-themed materials to assume that their communities don't have any LGBT people if they have the chance to experience otherwise at their libraries (Rauch, 2011).

Protecting LGBT teens' privacy is also important, as it's a common worry for LGBT teens that their parents, guardians, teachers, or other adults might be able to access their library records (Parks, 2012).

> What does safe space mean? It means that all staff, security, and volunteers have been trained in how to help someone if an issue relating to mistreatment as a result of gender or sexuality arises. . . . Create an atmosphere of acceptance.
> —Jessica Jupitus, Central Library Manager, Sacramento Central Library

Children and Families

Openness to LGBT patrons includes offering services to children with LGBT parents or caregivers. This important, but often overlooked, demographic can benefit greatly from such services as a well-rounded collection of picture books with LGBT family themes, LGBT-themed story-times and other children's programs, lists of parenting books for LGBT families, plus book discussion groups for LGBT caregivers (Naidoo, 2013). If these tasks seem daunting, partnering with community organizations such as PFLAG (Parents, Families and Friends of Lesbians and Gays) and local LGBT Pride groups can help immensely with developing new programs (Naidoo, 2013).

LGBT-Themed Picture Books

Children's picture books with LGBT themes are extremely vulnerable to censorship attempts. A couple of common examples are the books *And Tango*

Makes Three by Justin Richardson and Peter Parnell and *Uncle Bobby's Wedding* by Sarah S. Brannen.

And Tango Makes Three is based on a true story of two male penguins, Silo and Roy, who happily share a nest at the Central Park Zoo in New York City. The two penguins enjoy cuddling and nuzzling together, and they wish to add a baby penguin to their family. One day, their keeper discovers an extra egg, and he offers it to Silo and Roy. The penguins devotedly take care of their precious egg until it hatches and their adorable little ball of fuzz is born. The zookeepers know it takes two to tango, so they name their beloved baby penguin Tango. Silo, Roy, and Tango live happily ever after as a family (Richardson, Parnell, & Cole, 2005).

Uncle Bobby's Wedding tells the story of Chloe, a young guinea pig who is worried that her favorite uncle, Bobby, won't have time for her anymore after he marries his fiancé, Jamie. Bobby helps Chloe understand that she's not losing an uncle, but gaining one, and assures her that he and Jamie both love her and will always remain close with her. Chloe has a blast serving as her uncles' flower girl and choosing their wedding cake (carrot, of course—these are guinea pigs, after all) and learns that no matter how her family changes, she will always be deeply valued by Bobby and Jamie. The fact that Bobby and Jamie are both male is as much a non-issue as the fact that the characters are guinea pigs (Brannen, 2008).

If purchased at all, *And Tango Makes Three* and *Uncle Bobby's Wedding* often fail to make it to the picture book shelves, instead landing behind barriers and roadblocks. There is no coarse language or sexuality in either book, just warm, age-appropriate depictions of caring relationships; yet in each case, the pairing of two male animals is enough to render the books controversial, leading them to either being censored by omission or sequestered behind barriers in astounding numbers across the country (Whelan, 2009a).

These examples could go on and on, but the point must surely be clear by now—LGBT-themed books are often deemed controversial, edgy, or downright inappropriate even when devoid of the slightest hint of the practice of LGBT sex. Even guinea pigs and penguins aren't safe from the glare of censorship.

Professional Guidelines Regarding LGBT-Themed Materials

Both the ALA and the OIF have strongly supported the inclusion of LGBT-themed materials in public library collections. The ALA was ahead of its time when it established the country's first LGBT professional organization. Formed in 1970, the ALA's GLBTRT (Gay, Lesbian, Bisexual, and Transgender Round Table), then called the Task Force on Gay Liberation, began as a home base for librarianship's LGBT community and its allies. Since then, the GLBTRT has expanded to offer mentorship, networking opportunities, and the chance to experience greater representation and involvement in the ALA community (ALA, 2009).

As part of a 2004–2005 policy review process, the OIF revised its official interpretation of the Library Bill of Rights, using the new interpretation title of Access to Library Resources and Services Regardless of Sex, Gender Identity, or Sexual Orientation. In 2009, the OIF worked with the GLBTRT to reword the interpretation to Access to Library Resources and Services Regardless of Sex, Gender Identity, Gender Expression, or Sexual Orientation, making it clear that the Library Bill of Rights protected all groups falling under the LGBT umbrella (ALA OIF, 2010).

Issues in LGBT Collection Development

Collection development of LGBT materials often comes with a unique set of challenges for librarians. Fortunately, with proper tools and professional support, it's not difficult to build and maintain a quality collection of LGBT-themed materials.

Finding Sources

When relying primarily on standard, mainstream review sources for collection development activities, it's easy to become frustrated with the lack of LGBT-themed materials and even to abandon the idea altogether. With a bit of searching, though, building a well-rounded and inclusive collection of LGBT-themed materials is not as complicated as it may seem at first. Including proactively built collections of relevant LGBT-themed materials in the library's collection development policy is a wise starting point. The GLBTRT suggests using the ONE National Gay & Lesbian Archives' collection development policy statement as a template to follow in writing an inclusive and fair collection development policy reflecting openness to LGBT materials (The ONE National Gay & Lesbian Archives, 2011). A list of LGBT-themed review sources is provided in Appendix A.

Hesitation and Fear of Judgment

The proverbial elephant in the room for many librarians when it comes to collecting LGBT-themed materials is an overriding culture of hesitation. Despite the many gains made over the past decades in the LGBT rights movement, a sense of apprehension regarding building an LGBT collection still exists for many librarians. Fear of controversy, fear of challenges, and even fear of being judged can cloud decision-making resources to the point of consciously or unconsciously making the decision to self-censor (LaRue, 2012). Even when LGBT-themed materials are purchased, they often wind up sequestered behind roadblocks—a common example being the practice of keeping children's LGBT-themed books behind the reference desk or in a parents-only section so they need to be specifically requested (LaRue, 2012). Having to ask for an item that is kept behind a roadblock often creates a chilling effect among patrons who might not be comfortable approaching a librarian for this purpose. A book on a shelf is much more likely to be perused, checked out, and read than one that is kept behind a barrier of any kind (Naidoo, 2013). The same phenomenon occurs when an item is placed in an area away from its intended audience. This may take the form of shelving a YA novel in the adult section of the library where it is less likely to be found by its intended audience (Whelan, 2009a).

The West Bend Challenge

During the 1990s and 2000s, a new wave of YA novels hit the market, and they introduced more diverse protagonists and other characters than ever before, including those who were openly LGBT (Gaffney, 2014). This new trend in YA fiction eventually came to the attention of conservative individuals as well as formal groups who opposed LGBT-themed books, such as the American Family Association, Family Friendly Libraries, and Focus on the Family. These groups had strong opinions on the LGBT characters portrayed in this new era of YA literature, going so far as to label the books as everything from propaganda to pornography (Gaffney, 2014).

In 2009, upon learning that their community's public library, West Bend Community Memorial Library, held many books dealing positively with LGBT themes, West Bend, Wisconsin, parents Ginny and Jim Maziarka wrote a letter to the library protesting the collection of LGBT-themed books, and later filed a formal complaint regarding 37 specific books, almost (although not all) of which were YA titles. The Maziarkas met with West Bend's YA librarian to discuss their concerns and the library's policy regarding the collection of YA books. However, this meeting did not result in any common ground being found, as the Maziarkas' concerns turned out to go beyond the 37 protested books to include any books with positive LGBT themes for young adults (Gaffney, 2014). The Maziarkas also objected to a list on the West Bend Community Memorial Library's website of recommended LGBT-themed books. In a subsequent meeting with the library director, the Maziarkas requested that the YA book *The Perks of Being a Wallflower*, by Stephen Chbosky, be banned from the library, along with the other books they disapproved of, some of which had LGBT themes and others that did not (Zimmer & McCleer, 2014). Before long, another 11 books were added to the couple's list of titles they wanted to see banned from the library.

As the challenge raged on, the Maziarkas began to involve the greater community, holding a town hall meeting and urging West Bend citizens to sign a petition for the library staff to reconsider their policies. They collected over 700 signatures and brought them to a board meeting, but it was later announced that the board had decided to maintain the current collection in its original location, without restrictions of access (Zimmer & McCleer, 2014).

Greatly displeased with the board's decision, the Maziarkas, along with other critics of the West Bend Community Memorial Library and the ALA's policies, began writing and using social media to condemn the ALA and its adherents as being dangerous to children and undermining to parents (Gaffney, 2014).

Throughout and after the challenge, the Maziarkas insisted that the library staff were the true censors, as indicated by the amount of LGBT-supporting books versus the number of faith-based books about conversion therapy and the ex-gay movement. This discrepancy, the Maziarkas stated, made it clear that West Bend's collection was not inclusive of all points of view, but skewed toward LGBT-affirming materials while failing to collect an equal number of materials representing their views on LGBT issues. This point may have been better received had the Maziarkas claimed that the books they promoted about the ex-gay movement should be sequestered, banned, or hidden, as they wished books with positive LGBT characters to be (Gaffney, 2014).

As the West Bend controversy gained momentum, it also gained publicity. Ginny Maziarka started an inflammatory blog, and soon the blogosphere was teeming with posts, comments, and arguments for both the West Bend Community Memorial Library and the Maziarkas, along with allies on both sides.

The West Bend Community Memorial Library was the recipient of the 2009 Robert B. Downs Intellectual Freedom Award for its commitment to advocacy and refusal to compromise its ethics in the face of controversy (Graduate School of Library and Information Science, University of Illinois at Urbana-Champaign, 2009).

The Aftermath of West Bend

After the challenge, the West Bend Community Memorial Library revised its collection development policy to provide greater clarity in the face of challenges (Zimmer & McCleer, 2014). Ginny Maziarka's blog is still active and includes a prominently placed post describing the ALA's involvement as a hijacking of the West Bend Community Memorial Library, along with links to Family Friendly Libraries and Safe Libraries for others who share her concerns (Maziarka, 2014). Both the Maziarkas and West Bend Community Memorial Library have large numbers of supporters.

> When I think back to the West Bend Library challenge, I know things would have turned out differently if we'd had more conversations about intellectual freedom before the challenge occurred. The library director and Board were knowledgeable and supportive, but when the complainant took her concerns to City Council and the mayor, I was shocked by their lack of knowledge about libraries, our policies, and the First Amendment.
> —Kristin Pekoll, Assistant Director, American Library Association Office for Intellectual Freedom, former Young Adult Librarian, West Bend Community Memorial Library

RELIGION AND ATHEISM

Religion is rightfully a hot topic in collection development, as most public libraries are municipally run and therefore subject to the First Amendment mandate of separation of church and state. Whelan (2009b) reports that 16 percent of librarians surveyed reported that books with religious themes make them wary and prone to instances of self-censorship. Outside censorship is also extremely common, creating an even lower chance of books with religious themes landing on public library shelves.

The *Harry Potter* Series

A discussion about censorship and religion would be remiss not to mention the *Harry Potter* series and its many challenges. School libraries took the brunt of the *Harry Potter* challenges, but public libraries and even, in one odd case, a YMCA in Pennsylvania that offered an after-school *Harry Potter* reading program (Boston,

2002) had to answer to parents and community groups claiming *Harry Potter* was introducing children to witchcraft and the occult. Public libraries felt the pressure as well, and *Potter* events were frequently cancelled after complaints came in (Boston, 2002). In addition, it has been suggested that self-censorship of *Potter* books has been very common due to fear of challenges (Scales, 2005).

A pastor in New Mexico made headlines for starting a *Potter* bonfire, and another pastor in Maine attempted to do the same, but was denied a fire permit and ended up slicing a single book with scissors and ceremoniously throwing it in a garbage can. Religious Right leaders across the country condemned the *Potter* books and even insinuated that the books were part of a larger movement to lure young children into the occult and that reading them could even lead to children becoming unrepentant murderers (Boston, 2002; Harry Potter Foe, 2007).

Occultism and the Question of "Religious Viewpoint"

The *Harry Potter* witchcraft debacle did a great deal of damage, while the *Potter* books and movies were being released during the 1990s and early 2000s, and it resonates to this day. Between 2000 and 2009, 274 complaints about occultism came to the attention of the OIF, while another 291 cited "religious viewpoint" as the reason (ALA, 2013b). In 2011, Suzanne Collins's *Hunger Games* series had landed on the top 10 most challenged books, as reported by the OIF, for reasons including its supposed promotion of satanic and occult themes. Other books that have been challenged for these reasons include Rudolfo Anaya's *Bless Me Ultima* and Katherine Paterson's *Bridge to Terabithia*, both well-known and well-reviewed books for young readers (ALA, 2013b).

Aside from challenges to books due to their assumed link to Satanism or the occult, other books bearing the stigma of "religious viewpoint," don't seem to be about religion at all. Modern adult novels such as *The Curious Incident of the Dog in the Night-Time* by Mark Haddon and *The Kite Runner* by Khaled Hosseini, and nonfiction such as Barbara Ehrenreich's *Nickel and Dimed* have made the OIF's list of challenged books. As far as children's books fare, even *And Tango Makes Three* has been challenged for its alleged religious viewpoint. The odd thing is that these books, by and large, are not about religion. *The Kite Runner* takes place partly in a Muslim country but deals primarily with human relationships (Hosseini, 2003). *And Tango Makes Three* is about a penguin family at a zoo in which both parents are male (Richardson et al., 2005), and *Nickel and Dimed* is an exposé of low-wage workers in the United States (Ehrenreich, 2001). Looking at the synopses of these books, one may well wonder exactly what religious viewpoint is at stake. From there, it isn't much of a leap to also wonder if "religious viewpoint" might be a catchall phrase used in challenges to books that present anything other than conservative Christian ideals.

Atheism and Attitudes across the United States

A study conducted in 2010 revealed significant geographical differences among American public libraries, comparing those in the New England area to the East

South Central Region. The New England libraries were found to have much more balanced collections in terms of items dealing with atheism and its philosophies and books of a religious nature, with close-to-equal numbers of books being found in each area. The southern states, meanwhile, tended to hold about twice as many books dealing with religious philosophies than atheist ones. After careful analysis of the data and the specific titles under investigation, the researchers concluded that a combination of self-censorship and community expectations played a considerable role in this disparity, although whether the self-censorship aspect was due to librarians' fear of challenges or personal discomfort couldn't be determined (Sloan, 2012).

LANGUAGE

Coarse language and sexuality seem to go hand in hand when it comes to book challenges, in that books written for adults are often challenged for profanity and considered unsuitable for younger readers, without the intended audience of the book being taken into account. This is certainly the case with such adult books as *The Glass Castle*, *The Catcher in the Rye*, and even *To Kill a Mockingbird*.

YA books are often challenged for language as well. In the past decade or so, rough language has become more common in YA literature, to the dismay of parents who aim to shield their children from swearing (Campbell, 2007). School librarians and public librarians specializing in YA literature are often called upon to walk a fine line between giving teens the gritty drama they desire and keeping worried parents placated. In the end, of course, trying to please everyone often leads to a scenario in which nobody feels fully content with the result. Public librarians do enjoy more freedom than school librarians in this area, although challenges to YA materials are often quite common at public libraries as well—and wherever fear lurks, so lurks the potential for censorship.

VIOLENCE

Between 2000 and 2009, the OIF received reports of 619 challenges to books due to violent content. Books challenged for violence have included those clearly meant for an adult audience such as Alison Bechdel's *Fun Home* graphic novel, as well as those meant for teens and children such as Sherman Alexie's *The Absolutely True Diary of a Part-Time Indian* and Dav Pilkey's *Captain Underpants* series.

In YA books especially, but also in adult titles, violence, even when well within the context of a larger story, can cause a book to be vulnerable to both internal and external censorship. One recent example is Markus Zusak's 2005 YA/adult fiction crossover bestseller *The Book Thief*, famously narrated by Death himself, which tells the story of a young, book-loving girl struggling to survive the Holocaust while helping the Jewish man hiding in her foster family's basement (Zusak, 2005). *The Book Thief* has been subjected to a great deal of criticism for its realistic depictions of cruelty, violence, and death during the Holocaust. The violence and horror in the book are often disturbing, as the subject matter certainly calls for, but to label it as gratuitous would be a stretch. Despite the historical accuracy of *The Book Thief* and other books geared toward YA readers, parents and other adults often object to their violent themes (Hill, 2013).

GENRE FICTION AND ALTERNATIVE PRINT FORMATS

Librarians and community members alike have endured a reputation of snobbery when it comes to certain genres of fiction, such as romance fiction and street lit. While the days of librarians taking on the role of purveyors of taste are long gone, some echoes of that attitude remain. Many librarians proudly refuse to collect romance novels, claiming this constitutes not self-censorship, but well-intentioned intellectual discrimination (Isaacson, 2006), and many that do collect them don't create catalog records for these books. Street lit often faces a similar fate—while some street lit books have been challenged, many others never even make it to the library shelves. In these areas, self-censorship is most likely occurring at least as often as external censorship. While patrons may or may not object to romance and raciness, librarians often make the choice for them either by failing to purchase the books or by making them hard to find (Isaacson, 2006), leaving readers to either purchase or go without the books they desire rather than check them out from public libraries.

Romance Fiction

Romance novels have long been objects of derision for librarians, some of whom have gone so far as to deem the genre pornographic and misogynistic. Despite the enduring popularity of romance novels, many libraries rely solely on donations to collect romance fiction, choosing not to add the genre to their standard collection budget (Adkins, Esser, & Velasquez, 2006). Because of their less-than-serious reputation, romance paperbacks often get shelved without corresponding catalog records in public libraries (Wiegand, 2015), leading to an understandable frustration among patrons searching for particular authors, characters, or series.

Romance fiction has changed quite a bit in the past few decades. The passive damsels in distress of the 1970s and 1980s have given way to empowered women with satisfying careers, sizeable bank accounts, and plenty of rewarding hobbies—including sex. Despite these changes, the genre suffers from a stigma so injurious that readers are often embarrassed to read romance novels in public, much less obtain them from their public libraries. A 2006 survey revealed that a mere 14 percent of romance readers check their books out from public libraries (Adkins et al., 2006). The stigma of reading romance fiction combined with inadequate collections and the attitudes of disapproving librarians make the odds of romance readers becoming regular library patrons quite slim.

Street Lit

Street lit is a genre of adult fiction featuring mainly urban African American characters, bluntly violent story lines, and profanity-laced text. Moreover, street lit has traditionally been published by small presses, and proofreading isn't as strict or common as it is in other genres—meaning street lit books are often published with blatant spelling and grammatical errors and inaccurate punctuation (Pattee, 2008).

Despite the roughness of its presentation, or perhaps in part because of it, street lit has evolved from a small group of pulpy novels published in the 1960s and 1970s to a full-fledged genre of fiction. Sister Souljah's *The Coldest Winter Ever*, which was published by Simon & Schuster's Atria Publishing Group imprint in 1999, was the first work of the genre to be backed by a major publishing house. Since that publication and the subsequent commercial success of Souljah's novel, street lit has taken off and benefitted from more mainstream success than ever before (Pattee, 2008).

The Coldest Winter Ever tells the tale of Winter Santiaga, the teenage daughter of a wealthy drug kingpin in Brooklyn, New York. Winter lives a life of enviable luxury until her father is arrested and imprisoned. Prideful Winter quickly undergoes an undesired change in lifestyle and is eventually sent to a group home as a ward of the state. Violence, crime, and an unplanned pregnancy follow, culminating in Winter's incarceration (Souljah, 1999).

Street lit, when it is purchased by public libraries, often ends up not cataloged and hiding out in odd spots—hidden in desk drawers or locked display cases—for fear of upsetting patrons. Again, as with romance fiction, self-censorship often precludes or overrides external censorship (Morris, 2012).

Between the bluntly told stories and rough grammar, it's not difficult to see why street lit strikes fear in the hearts of public librarians to such an extent. But this is an area where it may be wise to take a moment and consider what other genres of not-quite-literature tend to be included in public library collections. Librarians who collect such authors as Danielle Steel and Nora Roberts, with their steamy storylines and over-the-top characters, may very well find themselves having difficulty explaining the lack of street lit in their collections, and the rationalization that reality isn't represented in street lit doesn't hold much water for those who collect fantasy or science fiction.

Reader's Advisory and Gateway Reading

While low reading levels, imperfect grammar, unrealistic storylines, and steamy plots may cause librarians to turn up their noses at street lit, romance, and other types of genre fiction, many in the profession see books like these as gateway reading for teens, younger adults, and readers of all ages looking to expand their horizons. For those patrons who initially desire dramatic plotlines and plenty of sex in their books, gateway reading may eventually lead to more quality reading (Gutierrez, 2012)—and, then again, it may not, depending on an individual patron's wishes. This is where comprehensive collections and skilled librarianship come into the picture. With quality reader's advisory for those who desire to take their reading farther, public library users may very well begin to climb the proverbial ladder of literature (Honig, 2011).

The idea of gateway reading can apply to any genre that librarians might find unsavory. Keeping an objective in mind can be helpful. Is the goal of reader's advisory to provide library patrons with the materials they desire for enjoyment and education, or is it honestly for everyone in a community to read Sartre on the beach for fun?

Reader's advisory, when done competently and respectfully, focuses on the desires of the reader, not the librarian. Public library users read for a range of reasons: for education, for enlightenment, to expand their sense of the world, and, of course, for leisure. While some may work their way through the Modern Library's 100 best novels as leisure reading, many others will certainly just read what they feel like reading, be it cookbooks, thrillers, bestsellers, or whatever strikes them as interesting at the moment (Saricks, 2004). Different tastes abound, and it is common for readers to tailor their reading to fit with their circumstances. Whether it's labeled as escapist reading, recreational reading, or some other moniker, there is nothing wrong with enjoying it. Part of what makes librarianship so rewarding is connecting with patrons over the joy of reading. Whether it's *Wuthering Heights* or *Ghetto Superstar*, it feels good to send patrons home with books they are likely to enjoy.

As satisfying as it feels to introduce patrons to new and exciting genres beyond their current reading tastes, it is important to keep in mind a key element of librarianship: customer service. The service of helping patrons choose what to read is sometimes desired and sometimes not. When it is not, any suggestions, no matter how well-intended, may come across as insensitive or condescending. While it is imperative to provide quality service in a friendly manner, not everyone wants or needs help with deciding what books they truly want to read. The uniqueness and individuality of library patrons adds an enjoyable sense of community service to the job.

Graphic Novels

In 2014, Banned Books Week took a turn from the ordinary and focused on graphic novels, an often-challenged and commonly misunderstood type of media. Public librarians reported that this new focal point helped them enlighten a younger demographic about censorship issues, and also helped libraries partner with comic book shops, thus creating new allies (Shivener, 2014).

Graphic novels, like print novels, are written for readers of all ages—children, teens, and adults. Over the past 20 years or so, graphic novels have come into the mainstream, and their presence in public libraries has grown along with their popularity, despite the fact that they tend to be taken less seriously than print novels and are often considered overly violent or sexually exploitative (Pinkley & Casey, 2013).

The critically acclaimed *Bone* graphic novel series, by Jeff Smith, is consistently one of the most frequently challenged and banned items, due in part to its depictions of smoking, gambling, and various political viewpoints (Shivener, 2014). Written for readers in fourth grade and up (Success Stories, 2010), the *Bone* series follows the adventures of Fone Bone and his cousins Smiley and Phoney, who, having been cast out of Boneville, must make their way through the Valley, with its rat creatures, Lord of Locusts, and even the occasional human. Complaints and challenges about *Bone* usually center on it being unsuitable to its intended age group, mainly due to the fact that Smiley occasionally smokes cigars and all three Bone characters spend time in a tavern (Comic Book Legal Defense Fund, 2016; Success Stories, 2010).

Other graphic novels that have come under fire include Alison Bechdel's *Fun Home: A Family Tragicomic*, an autobiographical telling of Bechdel's growing up in her family home, which also served as a funeral home, as well as her coming to terms with her own and her father's homosexuality. Unlike the *Bone* series, which came under fire for being inappropriate for children, *Fun Home*, clearly intended to be read by adults, was criticized by college students. Crafton Hills College in California briefly agreed to apply a trigger warning to both *Fun Home* and Marjane Satrapi's graphic novel about her youth during post-revolution era Iran, *Persepolis*, after a student and her parents complained about the books, which were required reading for a course on graphic novels. The student likened both books to pornography and stated that they should be removed from both the course syllabus and the college bookstore. The college administration initially conceded to apply trigger warnings but eventually decided that doing so wasn't appropriate for a college campus (Censorship Dateline, 2015; Success Stories, 2015).

Librarians dealing with challenges to graphic novels may wish to turn to both the OIF and the Comic Book Legal Defense Fund (CBLDF) for assistance. The CBLDF keeps track of banning attempts and works to ensure that First Amendment rights are applied to graphic novels. The 2010 Robert B. Downs Intellectual Freedom Award was given to the CBLDF for their efforts to keep graphic novels and comics on library shelves.

HISTORY AND POLITICS

When perusing lists of frequently challenged books, the rationale of "political viewpoint" often appears. The aforementioned *Persepolis* graphic novel by Marjane Satrapi has endured this label, assumedly because it deals with Islam and the Middle East (Satrapi, 2003), as has the *Bone* graphic novel series for reasons that are less clear. Philip Pullman's classic fantasy trilogy *His Dark Materials* has been slapped with the "political viewpoint" rationale, although politics plays virtually no role in the books, while themes of religion and atheism do (Pullman, 2007). And, of course, the much-maligned *And Tango Makes Three* has been censored for its political viewpoint, again for reasons that seem to have little to do with politics and much to do with discomfort about LGBT themes (ALA, 2013b).

WHAT WOULD YOU DO?

Mary was a YA librarian at her small city's library for several years, and she had come to know some of her young patrons quite well. Stephen, a quiet 15-year-old, was one of her regulars. It took a while for Stephen to trust Mary, but after she noticed him reading *Boy Meets Boy* and handed him a printed list of LGBT-friendly YA books with a friendly smile, Stephen realized that Mary was on his side. It was a relief to have an adult who was comfortable with his being gay, especially considering his home life.

Stephen lived with his mother and stepfather, who made it clear that if they ever caught him with another boy, they would send him away and force him to undergo conversion therapy. Stephen kept his sexuality a secret from them, but his stepfather became increasingly suspicious, and one day while Stephen was at school, he searched his room. He found a few YA novels with gay main characters and a nonfiction book for gay teens called *It Gets Better*, all of which had been checked out from the public library.

Furious, Stephen's stepfather showed up at the library and demanded to see his stepson's circulation records. Mary intervened by pointing out that Stephen's stepfather wasn't his legal guardian. The next day, the stepfather reappeared, along with Stephen's mother, and the demand was made again. Mary and the rest of the staff checked their policies, but it was determined that, because they had not written minors' rights into their policies, they had no recourse but to hand over Stephen's circulation records. Feeling guilty and worried, Mary printed out the records, handed them over, and hoped for the best for her young friend. She never saw him again.

> What happens between the ages of 14 and 16 . . . they are starting to become sexual beings, and they start to test some of those values that the parents taught them. And, so really, what's going on . . . with the parents is not that they hate the library, not that they want to censor the books—they love their children, and they feel this moment of grief. . . . When the adolescent becomes a young adult, they fear for them and they want to hang on to them. They want them to remain their children. It's love and grief. It's not really anger. It's not really an ideological thing. It's a personal thing.
> —James LaRue, Director, American Library Association Office for Intellectual Freedom and former Library Director of Douglas County (Colorado) Libraries.

TIPS AND TRAPS: PROTECTING YOUR COLLECTION AND YOUR PATRONS

Tips

- Being proactive is key in creating safe spaces—take initiative by creating bibliographies, pathfinders, and website links to LGBT-themed materials and services.
- Have a policy in place regarding minors' rights, based on the Library Bill of Rights and the First Amendment statement, and update it regularly.

- Refer to the Library Bill of Rights when in doubt about a librarian's role in the lives of other people's children.

Traps

- It is important for anyone involved in collection development to be diligent in avoiding self-censorship in regard to LGBT-themed materials.
- Avoid meddling in the reading choices of children and teens—remember that they have the same rights as adults in how they use their public library.
- If a library is in the practice of keeping commonly censored materials hidden behind roadblocks, consider their reasons for doing so—and question them if they seem censorious.

QUESTIONS TO CONSIDER

- Do you feel that the West Bend Community Memorial Library was adequately prepared for a challenge of this magnitude? Why or why not? What could they have done better?
- Conversely, do you feel that the challengers in this case had a valid point about the items in the West Bend Community Memorial Library?
- If you, as a community member, felt offended by a book or other item in your local public library, how would you go about addressing your concern?
- Do you have biases about genres such as graphic novels, street lit, and romance fiction? If so, what can you do in order to keep them from affecting your collection development activities?

REFERENCES

Adkins, D., Esser, L., & Velasquez, D. (2006). Relations between librarians and romance readers: A Missouri survey. *Public Libraries, 45*(4), 54–64.

Albright, M. (2006). The public library's responsibilities in LGBT communities. *Public Libraries, 45*(5), 52–56.

American Library Association. (2006, June 30). Library Bill of Rights. Retrieved from http://www.ala.org/advocacy/intfreedom/librarybill

American Library Association. (2009, August 5). GLBTRT membership. Retrieved from http://www.ala.org/glbtrt/membership

American Library Association. (2010, August 4). B.8 Services and Responsibilities of Libraries (Old Number 52). Retrieved from http://www.ala.org/aboutala/governance/policymanual/updatedpolicymanual/section2/52libsvcsandrespon#B.8.6.2

American Library Association Office for Intellectual Freedom. (2010). *Intellectual freedom manual.* Chicago: American Library Association.

American Library Association. (2013a, September 6). Number of challenges by reasons, initiator & institution, 2000–1009. Retrieved from http://www.ala.org/bbooks/frequentlychallengedbooks/statistics/2000–09#reasons2000

American Library Association. (2013b, March 26). Top ten frequently challenged books of the 21st century. Retrieved from http://www.ala.org/bbooks/frequentlychallenged books/top10

Board Rejects Labeling Explicit YA Books. (2005). *American Libraries, 36*(7), 22–23.

Boston, B. (2002). Witch hunt. *Church & State, 55*(3), 8.

Brannen, S. S. (2008). *Uncle Bobby's wedding*. New York: G.P. Putnam's Sons.

Butler, D. H. (2005). *My mom's having a baby!* Morton Grove, IL: Albert Whitman & Co.

Campbell, P. (2007). The pottymouth paradox. *Horn Book Magazine, 83*(3), 311–315.

Censorship Dateline. (2009). *Newsletter on Intellectual Freedom, 58*(3), 78–79.

Censorship Dateline. (2015). *Newsletter on Intellectual Freedom, 64*(5), 145–150.

Centers for Disease Control and Prevention. (2014, July 22). Lesbian, gay, bisexual, and transgender health. Retrieved from http://www.cdc.gov/lgbthealth

Chinn, J. (2007). In your library: Do you have something to offend everybody? *Medium, 32*(1), 22–23.

Comic Book Legal Defense Fund. (2016). Case study: Bone. Retrieved from http://cbldf. org/banned-comic/banned-challenged-comics/case-study-bone

Connelly, D. S. (2009). To read or not to read: Understanding book censorship. *Community & Junior College Libraries, 15*(2), 83–90.

Creel, S. (2013). Talk dirty to me: Why books about sex and relationships belong in libraries. *Mississippi Libraries, 76*(2), 2–5.

Doyle, R. (2010). Books challenged or banned in 2009–2010. Retrieved from http:// www.ala.org/advocacy/sites/ala.org.advocacy/files/content/banned/bannedbooks week/ideasandresources/free_downloads/2010banned.pdf

Ehrenreich, B. (2001). *Nickel and dimed: On (not) getting by in America*. New York: Metropolitan Books.

Forman, G. (2015, February 6). Teens crave young adult books on really dark topics (and that's ok). *Time*. Retrieved from http://time.com/3697845/if-i-stay-gayle-forman-young-adult-i-was-here

Gaffney, L. M. (2014). No longer safe: West Bend, young adult literature, and conservative library activism. *Library Trends, 62*(4), 730–739.

Graduate School of Library and Information Science, University of Illinois at Urbana-Champaign. (2009, December 8). West Bend Community Memorial Library named Downs Award recipient. Retrieved from https://www.lis.illinois.edu/articles/ 2009/12/west-bend-community-memorial-library-named-downs-award-recipient

Gutierrez, S. (2012). Does street lit belong in middle school? *CSLA Journal, 35*(2), 20–21.

Harris, R. H. (1999). *It's so amazing: A book about eggs, sperm, birth, babies, and families*. Cambridge, MA: Candlewick Press.

Harry Potter foe loses challenge. (2007). *American Libraries, 38*(7), 21–22.

Heller, M. J., & Storms, A. (2015). Sex in the library. *Teacher Librarian, 42*(3), 22–25.

Helton, R. (2010). Diversity dispatch: Reaching out to LGBT library patrons. *Kentucky Libraries, 74*(2), 14–16.

Hill, R. (2013). Content without context: Context ratings for young adult books. *School Library Monthly, 29*(5), 35–37.

Honig, M. (2011). What should teen street lit fans read next? *Voice of Youth Advocates, 34*(5), 458–459.

Hosseini, K. (2003). *The kite runner.* New York: Riverhead Books.

Isaacson, D. (2006, December). Don't just read—read good books. *American Libraries, 37*(11), 43.

LaRue, James. (2012). Uncle Bobby's wedding. In V. Nye & K. Barko (eds.), *True stories of censorship battles in America's Libraries* (pp. 108–114). Chicago: American Library Association.

Lo, M. (2014, September 18). Book challenges suppress diversity [web log post]. Retrieved from http://www.diversityinya.com/2014/09/book-challenges-suppress-diversity

Maziarka, G. (2014, January 9). Your library: No longer a safe place [web log post]. Retrieved from http://wissup.blogspot.com

Morris, Vanessa Irvin. (2012). *The readers' advisory guide to street literature.* Chicago: American Library Association.

Naidoo, Jamie Campbell. (2013). Over the rainbow and under the radar. *Children & Libraries: The Journal of the Association for Library Service to Children, 11*(3), 34–40.

Oberg, L., & Klein, G. (2003). Gay-themed books in Oregon public and academic libraries: A brief historical overview. *OLA Quarterly, 9*(2), 8–12.

O'Brien, R. D. (2013, October 16). Growing up with Alice. *The New Yorker.* Retrieved from http://www.newyorker.com/books/page-turner/growing-up-with-alice

The ONE National Gay & Lesbian Archives. (2011). Collection policy statement. Retrieved from https://web.archive.org/web/20110803201455/http://www.onearchives.org/collections_policy

Parks, A. F. (2012). Opening the gate. *Young Adult Library Services, 10*(4), 22–27.

Pattee, A. (2008). Street fight. *School Library Journal, 54*(7), 26–30.

Patton, S. (2006). *The higher power of Lucky.* New York: Atheneum Books for Young Readers.

Pew Research Center. (2015). Changing attitudes on gay marriage. Retrieved from http://www.pewforum.org/2015/07/29/graphics-slideshow-changing-attitudes-on-gay-marriage

Pinkley, J., & Casey, K. (2013). Graphic novels: A brief history and overview for library managers. *Library Leadership & Management, 27*(3), 1–10.

Pullman, P. (2007). *His dark materials.* New York: Alfred A. Knopf.

Rauch, E. W. (2011). GLBTQ collections are for every library serving teens! *Teacher Librarian 39*(1), 13–16.

Richardson, J., Parnell, P., & Cole, H. (2005). *And Tango makes three.* New York: Simon & Schuster for Young Readers.

Saricks, J. (2004). Not just fiction. *Booklist, 101*(1), 56.

Satrapi, M. (2003). *Persepolis.* New York: Pantheon Books.

Scales, P. (2005). Core collection: Censorship and young readers. *Booklist, 101*(22), 2018–2019.

Shivener, R. (2014). How GRAPHIC are these NOVELS? *Publishers Weekly, 261*(22), 44–45.

Sloan, S. (2012). Regional differences in collecting freethought books in American public libraries: A case of self-censorship? *Library Quarterly, 82*(2), 183–205.

Souljah, S. (1999). *The coldest winter ever.* New York: Atria.

Stager, G. (2007). Good books and bad reactions. *District Administration, 43*(4), 86–87.

Success Stories. (2010). *Newsletter on Intellectual Freedom, 59*(4), 175–178.

Success Stories. (2015). *Newsletter on Intellectual Freedom, 59*(4), 160–162.

Supreme Court of the United States. (2015, July 28). *Obergfell v. Hodges* [web log post]. Retrieved from http://www.scotusblog.com/case-files/cases/obergefell-v-hodges

Walker, A. (2014, February). In loco parentis. *Learning & Leading with Technology, 41*(5), 7.

Whelan, D. L. (2009a). A dirty little secret [cover story]. *School Library Journal, 55*(2), 26–30.

Whelan, D. L. (2009b). SLJ self-censorship survey. Retrieved from http://www.slj .com/2009/02/collection-development/slj-self-censorship-survey

Wiegand, W. (2015). *Part of our lives: A people's history of the American public library.* New York: Oxford University Press.

Zimmer, M., & McCleer, A. (2014). The 2009 West Bend Community Memorial Library controversy: Understanding the challenge, the reactions, and the aftermath. *Library Trends, 62*(4), 721–729.

Zusak, M. (2005). *The book thief.* New York: Alfred A. Knopf.

Chapter 3

CENSORSHIP AND THE INTERNET: TO FILTER OR NOT TO FILTER?

Written works have been censored throughout history, but the digital age brought about new ways to both gain and suppress information. Books, being physical objects, can be banned, barricaded, burned, or hidden, but digital information from the Internet is different. Choosing which sites are acceptable and which are not would be impossible task, as the amount of information on the Internet is beyond enormous, plus it's constantly changing.

The impossibility of censoring websites with any amount of efficiency hasn't deterred censors from trying. Instead of picking and choosing good sites and bad sites, Internet censorship, by and large, depends on the use of filtering software. To complicate matters even more, money and legislation have become enmeshed in Internet filtering, culminating in the enactment and upholding of the Children's Internet Protection Act and its aftermath.

HISTORY OF THE CHILDREN'S INTERNET PROTECTION ACT

The Children's Internet Protection Act (CIPA) first came into play in 2000, enacted by Congress with the best of intentions—to prevent children from accessing obscene, pornographic, or otherwise harmful material via the Internet at schools and public libraries. Three types of content are specifically required to be blocked by CIPA's guidelines:

- Obscene material
  - that which appeals to prurient interests only and is offensive to community standards

- Child pornography
  - depictions of sexual conduct and or lewd exhibitionism involving minors
- Material that is harmful to minors
  - depictions of nudity and sexual activity that lack artistic, literary, or scientific value (Federal Communications Commission [FCC], 2014)

CIPA is enforced by the distribution (or lack thereof) of certain monies, funding opportunities, and discounts made available through the federally funded Universal Service program, known familiarly as the E-rate program—a program designed to make certain products and communication systems more affordable to public and school libraries. In order to qualify for E-rate benefits, public and K-12 school libraries must make use of Internet filtering software on all public and staff computers, regardless of whether their use is intended for children, teens, or adults. In addition to E-rate monies and discounts, libraries not in compliance with CIPA are ineligible for Library Services and Technology Act (LSTA) funding for technology-related purchases (FCC, 2014). CIPA requires each library to have a written Internet-use policy (Pinnell-Stephens, 2012) and allows for an authorized person at each location to disable the filtering software on a computer for any adult who requests it and is found to be conducting bona fide research (Jaeger & Zheng, 2009).

Pre-CIPA Cases

CIPA appeared on the heels of the Communications Decency Act (CDA) of 1996. CDA, if passed into law, would have made it illegal to post or send obscene material to minors over the Internet. CDA was, however, rejected by the Supreme Court as unconstitutional and in opposition to the First Amendment (Jaeger & Zheng, 2009).

The Child Online Protection Act (COPA) was passed by Congress in 1998 but never went into effect due to prolonged litigation. After nearly a decade of court cases, the District Court for the Eastern District of Pennsylvania ruled that COPA was unconstitutional on grounds of the First and Fifth Amendments. The Supreme Court allowed the Pennsylvania ruling to stand, effectively ending any further legal action. COPA would have made it illegal for commercially operated websites to display material that could be deemed harmful to minors unless they made use of an age-verification system (Jaeger & Zheng, 2009; Supreme Court Rejection, 2009).

The Neighborhood Internet Children's Protection Act (NICPA), closely tied to CIPA, remains law to this day. NICPA requires all public libraries and schools that choose to receive E-rate benefits to write an Internet-safety policy addressing the security of minors in e-mail and chat rooms, unlawful activities such as hacking by minors, access by minors to inappropriate material on the Internet, unlawful disclosure of personal identification regarding minors, and information on how the library in question intends to restrict minors' access to harmful materials. One or more public meetings must be held before the policy is enacted, in order to allow for community input (Pinnell-Stephens, 2012).

The CIPA Supreme Court Case

After President Clinton signed CIPA into law, the American Library Association (ALA) challenged it in court on the grounds that it infringed upon the First Amendment rights of library patrons (Cornell University Law School Legal Information Institute [CULSLII], 2003). In 2003, the Supreme Court rejected the ALA's challenge in *United States v. American Library Association* and upheld the law as constitutional.

Although school libraries, by and large, complied with CIPA's mandates right away, public libraries were not as quick to implement changes. However, in the years since the ALA lost the Supreme Court case, the majority of public libraries have chosen to follow CIPA's directives (CULSLII, 2003; Jaeger & Zheng, 2009). Some have compromised by including one unfiltered computer, often situated in view of a service desk so that library staff members may monitor the activities of patrons using the computer and ask for them to stop viewing sites they consider objectionable (Wiegand, 2015).

It should be noted that, prior to CIPA's enactment, many public libraries were already voluntarily filtering some or all of their computers. As of 2002, while CIPA was still tied up in legislation, 24.4 percent of public libraries filtered all of their public computers, while 17.5 percent reported filtering some (generally assumed to be mainly those commonly accessed by children), but not others, and 52.1 percent did not use filtering software at all. In an interesting side note, it was found that rural libraries were significantly less likely to use filtering software than urban libraries, which were found to filter quite heavily (ALA, 2015; Jaeger, McClure, & Bertot, 2005).

TURNING OFF THE FILTER

CIPA's guidelines state that a filter may be disabled in the case of an adult conducting bona fide research or another lawful purpose. Proponents of CIPA stress that this is key in keeping CIPA constitutional, as it allows adults to decide for themselves what they view on the Internet, while keeping children safe from potentially dangerous sites (Kniffel, 2003).

Opponents of CIPA note that it is unclear how it should be determined whether a particular patron is, in fact, an adult (e.g., whether library staff should ask for identification) and is truly conducting bona fide research or another lawful purpose (e.g., whether library staff should question the intentions of patrons or require some sort of proof in order to determine if their research is, in fact, bona fide and lawful). These matters are left to the judgment of an authorized person at each library, but the practicalities of determining who may and may not have a filter turned off remain vague (FCC, 2014).

It is also unclear how, if at all, adult patrons are meant to be advised that the filter on their computer may be disabled. Even if a patron does happen to be in the know about such policies, it has been argued that the process of approaching library staff, explaining that the filter is falsely identifying a website necessary for an act of bona fide research as obscene and asking for it to be disabled presents a potentially uncomfortable roadblock. Roadblocks, by their very nature, minimize the odds of this type of interaction taking place and maximize the odds of patrons abandoning their web searches and leaving in frustration without communicating the source of this frustration to the library staff (Stone, 2005). This phenomenon of making a decision to stop using the library's services due to lack of privacy or other personal discomfort is known as the chilling effect (Pinnell-Stephens, 2012).

HAND IN HAND: CIPA AND MONEY

Opponents of CIPA stress that while libraries do have a choice in whether or not to filter their computers, the reality remains that without E-rate benefits and LSTA grant opportunities, many school and public libraries, and, in turn, the communities they serve, would suffer greatly from lack of funding, as these benefits were in place for several years prior to the enactment of CIPA (Jaeger et al., 2005), thus often making filtering less of a choice than a circumstance to be dealt with (Kolderup, 2013). A 2014 ALA policy brief reported that this is especially true for libraries in underserved communities and rural areas, where patrons are less likely to have unfiltered Internet access at home, thereby adding another element of inequity to already-compromised communities (Batch, 2014).

E-rate monies accounted for over $250 million to public libraries and $12 billion to school libraries between 2000 and 2003, while the ALA was contesting CIPA in the Supreme Court. By 2005, virtually 100 percent of public schools had complied with CIPA's filtering and safety policies, and nearly half of public libraries had come into compliance by 2008 (Jaeger & Zheng, 2009). The fact that CIPA was established in the early 2000s, during a time of economic downturn in the United States, undeniably made the choice of whether or not to filter even more complex and politically driven.

DEPENDENCE ON FILTERING SOFTWARE

A 2014 ALA policy brief found that over-filtering beyond CIPA's mandates is extremely common, while the failure of filtering software to block objectionable sites is similarly widespread (Batch, 2014). Judging from this information, it appears that libraries are over-relying on filters, perhaps due to a lack of knowledge about the expectations of compliance, or perhaps to over-accommodate CIPA's mandates in the spirit of better-safe-than-sorry. Misunderstanding or misinterpretation of the law can easily lead to a decision to filter as much as possible in order to assuage the fear of losing necessary funding (Batch, 2014). However, as Deborah Caldwell-Stone, deputy director of the Office for Intellectual Freedom (OIF), points out, "The [FCC] has refused to establish specific criteria for what constitutes effective filtering and has never found a school or library out of compliance since CIPA first went into effect in 2001" (Caldwell-Stone, 2013).

Perhaps, then, the culture of over-reliance of filtering is for naught, as the FCC has never made a move to reprimand any library managers or revoke E-rate funding from even one library since the inception of CIPA. Or, to look at the issue another way, perhaps nobody wants to risk the embarrassment and hassle of being the first.

How Do Filters Work?

To simplify a complex algorithm, today's filtering software is typically either **keyword-based**, meaning certain words or phrases set off the proverbial alarms to block search results, or **URL-based**, meaning certain websites are deemed unsafe according to the software's parameters. Despite all good intentions, no technology is perfect, and filtering software is certainly no exception. It has been found that filtering software over-blocks legitimately non-explicit sites and under-blocks sexually explicit images 15-20 percent of the time, accounting for an accuracy rate of between 78 and 83 percent (Batch, 2014). Add this to the discomfort of approaching library staff and asking for the filter to be turned off, and the chances of a patron finding the information he needs dips significantly, immeasurably lower.

While this book focuses on public libraries, it is significant to note that school libraries are especially vulnerable to CIPA's rules, as schools are held to the legal doctrine of *in loco parentis*, or the assumption of parental duties, rights, and suppositions while children are in school (Walker, 2014). This heavy responsibility may certainly help explain why the practice of over-filtering is so common. For example, it has been found that over-filtering has led to instances of students being unable to access websites with information on foreign countries, despite the reality that students in Advanced Placement classes are required to conduct online research about world cultures (ALA, 2014). Another study found that several Rhode Island schools' filtering systems blocked 89 content categories, which led to students being unable to access sites including the American Civil Liberties Union, Planned Parenthood, People for the Ethical Treatment of Animals, and the National Organization for Marriage (Bayliss, 2004). While these sites may certainly contain information often considered controversial, it does not seem unreasonable to wonder how students are meant to gain critical thinking and debate skills without access to disparate points of view.

Public libraries are not held to the *in loco parentis* doctrine and therefore may write and enforce their policies with somewhat more flexibility regarding parental rights and obligations, although they are still bound by the rules of CIPA if they choose to comply and receive E-rate benefits (Bayliss, 2004).

Who Decides What to Filter?

One of the harshest criticisms against CIPA is the fact that relying on filtering software takes the decision-making responsibility regarding content out of the hands of those closest to their patrons—librarians and other library staff—and places it into the trust of for-profit filtering software corporations whose agendas may very well be vastly different than those of the schools and libraries with whom they contract (McCarthy, 2004). The overall agenda of a public library and that of a proprietary software company are likely to differ in a multitude of ways. For example, shortly after the Supreme Court ruled in favor of CIPA's constitutionality, it was found that at least 15.9 percent of public libraries in Indiana were making use of filtering software created by companies with connections to conservative religious groups, thus creating a strong possibility that the keywords or sites the filters would block out would be at least in part determined by the values of the company. With separation of church and state being such a strong component of the First Amendment, this type of situation can be quite troubling (Radom, 2007).

Filtering software was first produced, and continues to be heavily marketed, as a product for parents to install on their own home computers in order to prevent children in their care from accessing controversial sites. While CIPA was in its beginning stages, it was noted that most parents making use of these filters preferred over-blocking to under-blocking (Radom, 2007). Filtering software companies, therefore, have a history of overstretching in terms of blocking legitimate sites in order to provide the services desired by their customers. Filtering software has improved since CIPA first came into play in public libraries, but over-filtering and under-filtering are still serious concerns (Kolderup, 2013).

Before the enactment of CIPA, library staff, especially those working in public libraries, had the freedom and accompanying responsibility of deciding how and when to filter, if at all. Back then as well as today, a library that does not filter must depend on its staff to determine whether someone is using the Internet within a public building in a way that might offend other patrons (e.g., the viewing of a clearly offensive website in an area where young children can see the monitor), or perhaps even violates the law (such as the viewing of child pornography). Because of the imperfect nature of software filters, every library must make decisions about how to handle situations like these, regardless of whether or not the library has chosen to filter its computers.

The possible examples of "is-it-or-isn't-it-offensive" are endless: What about a pregnant woman viewing a childbirth video online in preparation for her baby's own delivery? Or a parent and teenage daughter viewing a body-positive sex-education website complete with photos or videos? What about a concerned and caring parent viewing websites about LGBT (gay, lesbian, bisexual, and transgender) issues in order to help learn how to best support his beloved child who has come out as gay? Some would see these as perfectly acceptable uses of technology, while others would likely be shocked and angered. Seemingly infinite potential reactions can be applied to every possible scenario.

Furthermore, when developing policies around Internet filtering, librarians must not forget to account for those instances of egregious, unmistakable viewing of obscene content that all but the most fortunate or most sheltered of library staff will have to deal with at some point. Even then, though, at what point should the patron be asked to stop? When a staff member notices? When another patron complains? When children are nearby? When the content in question is possibly illegal? Always? Never?

Filtering software, like any type of technology, takes the human decision-making responsibility out of the hands of library staff to a large extent. In doing so, however, it also removes the freedom to make informed, thoughtful decisions about what is and is not inappropriate in a library setting. This combination of blessing and curse would be less problematic if filtering was a perfect science, but it has been consistently proven to be anything but. For example, it has been found that filters have blocked content that many would consider appropriate. Among many others, these have included:

- Websites designed to educate users on Wicca and Native American spirituality
- Websites presenting information on teen use of tobacco and firearms
- Websites designed to support LGBT youth without promoting ministries offering ex-gay services to questioning young people. (Caldwell-Stone, 2013)

Wi-Fi and Other Connectivity Options

When CIPA was first enacted, Wi-Fi was a relatively new technology. Since then, Wi-Fi has become a common service available in libraries. A 2011–2012 survey found that 90.5 percent of public libraries offer Wi-Fi, adding up to a 4.7 percent increase since 2010–2011. Even in rural areas, only 5.6 percent of public libraries report that they do not provide, and do not plan to begin providing, Wi-Fi services, down from 8.2 percent in the previous year (ALA, 2012). It seems obvious that public libraries are routinely counted upon as places to access the Internet through a Wi-Fi connection.

While filtering software can be applied to a library's public-use computers, Wi-Fi does not offer the same protections. Library patrons accessing the Internet using the library's Wi-Fi on their own devices are not bound by filters. This was less of a concern in the early 2000s, when laptops were the main form of portable device. Since then, the market has exploded with smartphones, tablets, smartwatches, and other easily portable devices. Internet connectivity has changed dramatically as well. While Wi-Fi is still common, people now often have the choice of using a Wi-Fi connection or an alternative form of connectivity such as 4G. The more these choices continue to expand, the less impact filters are likely to have on library patrons' Internet usage.

Even with so many advances in portable devices and connectivity, the digital divide is by no means closed, and those who are able to enjoy access to the new world of portable devices and connectivity are in a position to find information that those who rely on their public library for both a device and connectivity may find themselves unable to access.

FINDING A BALANCE

None of this is meant to imply that the use of filtering software in public libraries is, in and of itself, a bad idea. Whether or not to filter is a judgment call made by countless library directors, boards of trustees, and city councils, all of whom must navigate the many pros and cons involved in deciding whether or not to filter, as well as legal and professional guidelines that surround CIPA. The controversial nature of CIPA and the fact that the gain or loss of funding is tied into the decision makes these choices even trickier. Within the profession as well as outside of it, disagreements abound about CIPA and its specific rules.

While it would surely be difficult to find a library professional who happily supports the viewing of truly obscene material by children, opinions differ greatly about who is ultimately responsible for keeping children safe, and even from what, specifically, they should be shielded. Public libraries are widely perceived as safe places, but the fact remains that they are, by their very nature, public, and therefore open to everyone, for better or for worse. In a perfect world, children could be safely left unsupervised or under-supervised while reading a book or accessing a computer at their local public library, but this simply isn't a reasonable expectation. Those who disagree with CIPA's mandates often tend to be quite clear that they absolutely do not object to the idea of keeping children safe. By and large, it is the methodology, not the intent, which they view as a First Amendment issue (Goldstein, 2002).

In this unfortunately unsafe world, reasonable precautions certainly seem like a wise idea. Having a well-researched and carefully worded Internet usage policy is highly recommended by the OIF, as is the encouragement of participation from both library staff and the public in the development of the policy. Thorough researching of filtering choices is also advisable, as is comprehensive training of staff on how and when to disable the filter for patrons who request it (Caldwell-Stone, 2013). Having a checklist of CIPA rules handy has also been recommended as a practical way to make sure compliance has been met (Don't Forget CIPA, 2014), as has keeping local elected officials informed and up to date on the policy in order to avoid any unpleasant surprises (Pinnell-Stephens, 2012). Notifying patrons that their library uses filtering software and giving adult patrons instructions on how to proceed if they would like a filter disabled are encouraged, as is having the Internet-use policy come up on the screen as the first thing a patron will see when she logs on to a library computer (Pinnell-Stephens, 2012). In general, offering the greatest possible amount of information up-front regarding CIPA's directives is strongly recommended in order to help avoid confusion and frustration.

School Libraries and CIPA

As stated above, while this book focuses on public libraries, the connection between CIPA and school libraries is important to note in the debate over CIPA. Especially in schools, societal pressures to keep children safe on the Internet are rampant and, of course, well-meaning. Combine this genuine concern with the potential loss of a significant amount of E-rate money, and it becomes easy to understand why schools choose to filter at a rate of nearly 100 percent. A discrepancy does come into play, however, when some students have to rely solely on the filtered computers available at their schools while others have the added benefit of unfiltered Internet access at home—a classic case of inequality among the haves and the have-nots (Batch, 2014). Will those students whose families have the means to provide unfiltered Internet access at home produce higher-quality work than their less-fortunate peers, thus leading to environments in which opportunities are not truly open to all students?

Adding to the complications of school libraries and CIPA mandates is the fact that some schools filter their computers more than others do—and some use human filtering on top of technological filtering. A 2006 study found that some school districts refused to allow for the use of search engines such as Google or Yahoo. Students in these districts were permitted to enter only URLs of websites from a preapproved list—no searching for other sites allowed. Librarians wanting students to access a site not on the list had to get written permission from the district's technical specialist. This lack of trust in librarians' expertise and reliance on the decisions of noncredentialed technical staff was seen as offensive and unprofessional by many school librarians (Bell, 2007). Websites assumed to be frivolous, such as those dealing with cars or the weather, were found to be not allowed in certain districts, and others simply didn't allow for any Internet use at all, by either students or teachers, thus suggesting that the Internet is inherently unsafe, even for trained educators, and thereby denying students the opportunity to learn how to safely and wisely search the Internet for useful information (Bell, 2007).

Public Libraries and CIPA

Public library employees, generally speaking, have been more vocal than school librarians about their concerns regarding CIPA, likely due to commonly held educational standards on top of pressures from parents and administrators. In addition to the confusion about how and when a filter should be disabled for an adult patron engaging in bona fide research or another lawful purpose, it is vital to note that roughly 11 million people in the United States rely on library technology due to their lack of a computer or Internet access at home or work (Goldstein, 2002). The high probability of patrons becoming frustrated by filtering software combined with either not knowing that they can ask for the filter to be disabled or not wanting to deal with the awkwardness of doing so is seen by opponents of CIPA as an issue negatively affecting an already-underserved demographic.

It has also been argued that, while CIPA purports to protect children, the result is that patrons of all ages end up being treated like children who cannot be trusted to navigate their own Web searches (Kolderup, 2013). Furthermore, while supporters of CIPA often cite the ease in which filters can be turned off upon request, it has been found that it can take days or even weeks for a patron request to disable a filter to be resolved.

Even deciding whether or not a certain website's material is truly obscene is a difficult task—so difficult, in fact, that librarians, library directors, and library boards are not legally qualified to make the determination. The word "pornography" and the term "harmful to children" have no legal definitions and a glance through a variety of dictionaries makes it clear that interpretations vary to a great degree. On the other hand, the word "obscene" and the term "child pornography" do have legal definitions. Individuals may decide for themselves, subjectively, what constitutes obscenity or child pornography; but without a court ruling, these determinations are merely opinion and remain open to interpretation (ALA OIF, 2015). What appears obscene to one librarian could very easily be seen by another as educational and valid. Standardization is highly unlikely to exist in any library setting and only a court of law can determine whether a website or any other material is legally obscene (Pinnell-Stephens, 2012). Librarians must be careful when using these subjective words and terms without legal documentation.

Public librarians who oppose CIPA argue that the impossibility of agreeing on a clear definition of obscenity and issues involving patrons' lack of privacy and confidentiality make the simple-sounding act of turning off a filter much more difficult in reality for patrons and librarians alike (Kolderup, 2013).

PROFESSIONAL AND LEGAL GUIDELINES

Whether librarians agree or disagree with CIPA's rules, the fact remains that CIPA has been found to be constitutional by the Supreme Court. However, this does not mean that libraries have no choices when it comes to filtering. Forgoing E-rate benefits and LSTA funding is still an option, though, some would argue, a loaded one. Those who disagree with CIPA's mandates while still working in systems accepting E-rate and LSTA benefits have options as well. Educating staff to thoroughly understand the law—what CIPA requires and does not require—can help library staff navigate the dos and don'ts with greater confidence. Providing a clearly written Internet-use policy and extensive staff training on when and how to disable filters also help take the guesswork out of the equation and can empower library staff to feel confident in their day-to-day work (Caldwell-Stone, 2013). The management and trustees at each library must also ultimately decide, when constructing policies, whether to take the stance of enhancing access in order to preserve the First Amendment, or the stance of denial in order to preserve the well-being and safety of children (Pinnell-Stephens, 2012). This is a difficult decision, as falling on either side may upset community members, staff members, and elected officials. Librarians, as information professionals, tend to feel strongly about their convictions, no matter where they lie. As gatekeepers to knowledge, librarians are entrusted with both the added responsibility and burden of holding fast to these convictions when challenges come along.

The ALA's Stance against CIPA

The ALA has been quite vocal about its dislike of CIPA. This dates back to 2001, when the ALA, along with the American Civil Liberties Union (ACLU), filed a lawsuit challenging the constitutionality of CIPA (CULSLII, 2003; ALA, 2010). At a press conference announcing the lawsuit, then-ALA president Nancy Kranich voiced her discomfort with the mandates of CIPA, claiming that they would force librarians to choose between funding and censorship at the ultimate peril of library users across the country and stating that the government was, in essence, attempting to force libraries to purchase technology that ultimately doesn't work (ALA, 2010).

Although CIPA was eventually upheld, the ALA continued to oppose it, stating in a 2014 policy brief that CIPA's directives have been widely misunderstood, that filtering software too often blocks legitimate educational sites, and that filters disrupt education by limiting what librarians can use as source material. This combination of issues can very well place limits on students' understanding of the digital world (Batch, 2014).

The ACLU's Stance against CIPA

Since the passing of CIPA into law, several states' ACLU chapters have filed lawsuits and complaints regarding CIPA's mandates. A 2006 case in Washington State in which the ACLU of Washington filed a suit against the North County Regional Library (NCRL) District, claimed that the library system refused to unblock filters when requested to do so by adults. The court case went on for six years, and it was finally determined in 2012 that NCRL was not violating the First Amendment rights of adult patrons by refusing to disable the filters due to the fact that its branch libraries were small and did not provide enough visual blockage between the children's and adults' areas (Chmara, 2012).

Shortly after the Supreme Court ruled in favor of CIPA's constitutionality, Rhode Island's ACLU chapter filed a report on their findings about CIPA's effectiveness in the state's public libraries. It was reported that some libraries' filtering systems over-blocked beyond the minimum standards of CIPA compliance, and that librarians did not often make patrons aware of their legal right to ask for the filter to be disabled. The report claimed that librarians who engaged in these practices were, in essence, acting as censors by keeping patrons from knowing or practicing their rights to access the information they desired without inconveniences, roadblocks, or flat-out refusals (Stone, 2005).

The Supreme Court's Stance in Favor of CIPA

During the ALA's court case challenging CIPA, Chief Justice Rehnquist emphasized the fact that adults are given the choice of asking for filters to be disabled without being expected to provide any explanations or justifications. It was also argued by Rehnquist, along with Justices O'Connor, Scalia, and Thomas that libraries provide a traditional role in society based on learning and cultural enrichment, and that just as librarians collect print materials with this role in mind, the online materials provided to patrons should meet the same standards. To paraphrase, one would not expect to visit a public library to browse pornography in books and magazines, so why should the same not be true for online materials (CULSLII, 2003)?

The Supreme Court's decision was also bolstered by the fact that complying with CIPA's rules, regardless of any inconveniences to library staff or patrons, is a voluntary act. If the management of a particular library does not care to comply, then that is perfectly legal, if not always economically practical. It simply means that the public funds making up E-rate benefits will not be made available to that library, as these funds are intended to assist libraries in acquiring appropriate materials based on their long-standing societal role (CULSLII, 2003).

Other Supporters' Stances in Favor of CIPA

Family Friendly Libraries (FFL), a conservative organization that favors CIPA's directives, asserts that while parents are responsible for practicing primary authority over the actions of their children while in public libraries, filtering nevertheless protects children by preventing them from being exposed as passersby to harmful images, and by helping to keep them from coming into contact with child pornographers. FFL leaders have also stated that filtering software helps prevent child pornography trafficking on public computers (Kolderup, 2013). FFL members emphasize the importance of libraries as publicly funded institutions reflecting the family-based values of the communities they serve. While FFL members recommend that parents work within library systems alongside trustees and library boards, they do recommend that parents engage in public debates with those who oppose CIPA, and they encourage going to the press and/or city council meetings when they have concerns about public library policies and procedures (Gounaud, 2016).

FFL and other supporters of CIPA argue that its opponents are unrealistically or even arrogantly ideological, to the point of disregarding the safety of children and the needs of the general public. Just as librarians aren't practicing censorship when they do not purchase every book or periodical on the market, supporters attest, they also are not required to provide open access to every site on the Web— and these acts of selection do not equate to censorship. Selection is a fundamental element of a librarian's job, and supporters of CIPA see filtering as merely one more example of this task (McCabe, 2003). It has also been suggested that the fact that CIPA's rules state that filters may be turned off when requested means that First Amendment rights are not being infringed upon. Finally, CIPA supporters strongly assert that the safety and well-being of children more than makes up for the inconvenience of having to ask a library staff member to disable the filter (Kniffel, 2003).

Ideals and Realities

A 2006 survey of Texas public librarians' attitudes about filtering revealed that it is quite common for librarians to change their minds about filtering as their careers advance. In a group of 300 public librarians, 80 percent of the group stated that they felt Internet filters have the potential to be useful, and 60 percent of those respondents reported that their views on filtering changed as they gained real-world experience. Many noted that observing problems such as children viewing websites and visiting chat rooms that were clearly pornographic and even predatory in nature led them to change their convictions about filtering. Those who didn't decide that filtering was the clearly better choice decided that it was at least a necessary evil, even when the filters failed to work ideally.

Some participants in the Texas study commented that they have decided that Internet filtering is best seen as a form of collection development—in the same manner in which librarians decide which books to purchase and which ones not to, they decide which websites to offer and which ones not to (Smith, 2006). Still, the filtering-as-collection-development debate has been a hot one. While books and other traditional library materials can be individually selected, cataloged, and checked out, the Internet, in its enormity, complexity, and dynamic nature, simply does not lend itself to site-by-site selection or cataloging. It could be argued that, even with the benefit of filtering software and attention to requests to have filters disabled, the Internet exists more as a whole than a series of sites, and therefore must be taken or left as a whole (Pinnell-Stephens, 2012).

The results of the Texas study indicate that perhaps concerns about filtering tend to be more ideological than logical, or simply easier to discuss and debate than to put into practice in the everyday life of a librarian.

ETHICS AND THE INTERNET

Librarians have long had to contend with difficult ethical dilemmas in their day-to-day work. A commonly cited example is whether or not they should allow hate groups to use their public spaces to hold meetings. Should they fall on the side of freedom of speech at any cost, or should they maintain that such actions fly in the face of community standards of decency? The ALA's Freedom to Read Statement (FTRS) could be cited as grounds for both choices (Bossaller & Budd, 2015).

Proposition Five of the FTRS states: It is not in the public interest to force a reader to accept the prejudgment of a label characterizing any expression or its author as subversive or dangerous (ALA, 2006. Used with permission from the American Library Association).

However, Proposition Six of the FTRS states: It is the responsibility of publishers and librarians, as guardians of the people's freedom to read, to contest encroachments upon that freedom by individuals or groups seeking to impose their own standards or tastes upon the community at large; and by the government whenever it seeks to reduce or deny public access to public information (ALA, 2006).

Proposition Five appears to imply that librarians should not take it upon themselves to decide on behalf of any individual what is innocuous and what is harmful. Therefore, it could be argued, the hate group has a right to use the library's public space to voice the ideas of its constituents, and members of the public must be trusted to use their own critical thinking skills to make decisions about what they will believe.

Proposition Six, in contrast, seems to be stating that librarians are meant to be counted upon to challenge those who attempt to impose their own views upon the greater community. Therefore, it could be argued that the hate group must be denied the use of the library's meeting space, as it is a group that seeks to deny, rather than support, critical thought while imposing its own standards on others.

Before the digital age came along, these ethical dilemmas were few and far between. Since then, however, ethics came to the forefront (Bossaller & Budd, 2015). The Clinton administration propelled the process of introducing Internet access into public libraries and other public spaces with the National

Telecommunications and Infrastructure Administration. The vice president at the time, Al Gore, was a vocal supporter of the idea that public libraries would make ideal settings for equity of Internet access to the public (Jaeger, Thompson & Lazar, 2012). These clearly good objectives have allowed libraries to progress and thrive in the digital age. But every new service comes with its own new set of challenges.

As is likely the case with every profession, change is often the only constant in librarianship. Whatever conveniences the digital age provides, it has also brought about new fears of the unknown, a common reaction to new and unfamiliar formats of media (Crump, 2012). Whatever one's personal ethics regarding the Internet age may be, it must be noted that the OIF has gone to great lengths to ensure that its statements and the Library Bill of Rights transcend changes and continue to remain relevant in the digital age (Pinnell-Stephens, 2012).

The age of the Internet changed patrons' and communities' expectations of their libraries. These days, librarians are expected to be technically adept, and the amount of information a patron can expect to find at libraries, in print and digital form, has exploded. What was historically a place to read, conduct research, and check out materials is now a place where Internet access and connectivity are expected to be provided as standard services (Jaeger et al., 2012). Despite the conveniences offered by new technology, when libraries introduce any new medium into the milieu, such as Internet services, eBooks, or downloadables, a rash of patron complaints tends to come along on its heels, and the safety of children is often cited as the reason behind these complaints (Pinnell-Stephens, 2012).

Now that public space can be viewed as not just the building in which a library is housed, but a place where the entirety of the Internet may be accessed, the hypothetical hate group may become quite real with only a few mouse clicks. If they should be denied of the use of a room, who is to say they shouldn't be prevented from popping up on the computer screens of unsuspecting patrons? And, if it is decided that such sites should be blocked in protection of the public interest, can librarians truly rely on filtering software to do the job for them? To stand back and allow technology to do the dirty work leaves librarians in the position of having to decide what to do when it fails at this task. Should they step in and ask the patron to leave the website or should they look away?

Defining Public Space

It has been argued that the *United States v. American Library Association* Supreme Court case would have served as an ideal time to officially decide what the status of library space is, legally speaking (Gathegi, 2005). Places such as public parks and sidewalks are legally considered to be public forums, where free speech cannot be barred except in cases of it being unreasonably disruptive. During the Supreme Court case, the ALA maintained that public libraries fall into the public forum category as well, and that filtering of computers was therefore unconstitutional under the First Amendment. The Supreme Court justices, however, maintained that public libraries are places of education and information. This disagreement about the overriding purpose of public libraries was never settled, and debates on the subject continue to remain widespread (Bossaller & Budd, 2015).

CONCLUSION AND FURTHER THINKING

Public libraries serve patrons of all ages—children, teens, and adults—and different age groups generally have different levels of what is appropriate, as do parents and guardians. But the decision of where these lines should be drawn is subjective and unique to each family and each child, making it impossible to develop public library standards that meet the needs, values, and expectations of each individual.

When strongly held professional guidelines clash with upheld laws, arguments on both sides of an issue are almost guaranteed to be especially strident. The ALA, along with many public librarians, bristled at the Supreme Court's ruling on CIPA, and many continue to oppose it to this day. The ruling was controversial and divisive, and it remains so. Any sort of compromise or other declaration of shared aims does not appear to be on the radar for the near future. Therefore, librarians, whether new or seasoned, must make their own personal ethical decisions about CIPA and its mandates.

In the end, whether or not to filter is not a decision with an obvious answer for every individual librarian, nor is it one that can possibly satisfy any entire community, let alone an entire profession. The individuality of children, families, and even software systems leaves the benefits and pitfalls of CIPA's mandates open to both constant defense and constant scrutiny.

TIPS AND TRAPS: WHEN FILTERING CROSSES THE LINE

Tips

- Regardless of any personal feelings for or against CIPA, it is a law upheld by the Supreme Court, and any library receiving E-rate benefits must be in compliance with its mandates.
- Whether or not to comply with CIPA's mandates is a choice, although the ramifications of choosing not to filter may impact libraries in negative ways.
- If choosing to filter, remember to research the companies offering filtering services, and be alert to any corporate interests that might interfere with the tenets of librarianship by researching the ideological, political, religious, or other potentially subjective stances of the companies in question.

Traps

- Being objective regarding CIPA's mandates can be difficult when dealing with issues of budgets, political pressure, and parental pressure—so take the time to think these matters through carefully.

• When writing policies and making decisions about filtering, remember to adhere to professional guidelines and laws but also to act based on ethical decisions.

• While it is common for librarians to change their convictions as their careers progress, it is advisable to periodically recall the tenets of librarianship throughout the span of a career in order to avoid giving in to convenience at the peril of strongly held beliefs.

WHAT WOULD YOU DO?

Wendy worked as librarian at a small public library in a conservative town. The library accepted E-rate benefits and therefore followed the mandates of CIPA. All of the computers in the building were filtered, but some patrons knew how to get around the filters, and would view photos and videos Wendy considered obscene in the computer room. Whenever she saw someone viewing sites she disapproved of, Wendy would tap the patron on the shoulder and ask him to either leave the site or leave the library.

As specified by CIPA, one staff member, Tricia, had the authority to turn off a filter when asked to do so, but there were no messages posted anywhere in the library stating that this was an option, so it rarely came up. Eventually, Tricia got wind of Wendy's method and confronted her. It was not Wendy's job to determine what was and was not pornographic or obscene, Tricia insisted. Wendy vehemently disagreed. She had been a proud member of this conservative town all her life, she knew smut when she saw it, and she was determined to keep the children in the library safe from stumbling across such images. Tricia, who outranked Wendy, told her to stop immediately. "Just let the filters do their job, and come to me if you have a concern," she said.

After their confrontation, Wendy began to contact Tricia several times each week with complaints about patrons viewing sites she considered obscene. Tricia came to believe that Wendy was somewhat prudish and overly reactive, and began not to take her concerns seriously. She allowed almost all of the sites to remain open, often without even taking a look.

One day, Wendy noticed a man viewing photos that appeared to be child pornography. She was horrified and shaken. Knowing Tricia would probably just side against her as usual, Wendy called the police. Within 30 minutes, the man was in handcuffs and the computer he had been using had been confiscated by the police. Tricia was furious that Wendy hadn't contacted her, and Wendy responded by simply stating that she had done what any decent person would have in her situation.

Tricia later explained to her supervisor that she would absolutely have reported an obvious crime like child pornography had she seen it, but stressed that Wendy didn't even give her a chance to assess the site in question. The supervisor was dismayed to learn that Tricia had been so passive in allowing the filters to be disabled, and transferred Tricia to another branch in order to make Wendy more comfortable. No compromise was ever reached, and the two employees simply avoided each other from then on.

QUESTIONS TO CONSIDER

- When coworkers disagree on what defines pornography, what do you feel is the best way to reach consensus?
- Do you support CIPA and its mandates? Why or why not?
- As a library user, have you ever come across difficulty accessing the information you needed at your library due to filtering?
- Aside from illegal activities, such as viewing of child pornography, what are your feelings on what patrons should be able to access at their public libraries?
- If, as a librarian, you saw a patron watching pornography in a private area of the library with nobody watching, would you intervene? How?
- If, as a librarian, you saw a patron watching pornography within eyeshot of a young child, would you intervene? How?

REFERENCES

American Library Association. (2006, July 26). The Freedom to Read Statement. Retrieved from http://www.ala.org/advocacy/intfreedom/statementspols/freedomreadstatement. Used with permission from the American Library Association.

American Library Association. (2010, April 6). APA files Lawsuit challenging CIPA. Retrieved from http://www.ala.org/advocacy/advleg/federallegislation/cipa/alafiles lawsuit

American Library Association. (2012, June 6). Public library funding & technology access study 2011–2012. Retrieved from http://www.ala.org/research/plftas/2011_2012

American Library Association. (2014, June 11). Over-filtering in schools and libraries harms education, new ALA report finds. Retrieved from http://www.ala.org/news/press-releases/2014/06/over-filtering-schools-and-libraries-harms-education-new-ala-report-finds

American Library Association. (2015). *Internet access and digital holdings in libraries* [fact sheet]. Retrieved from http://www.ala.org/tools/libfactsheets/alalibraryfactsheet26

American Library Association Office for Intellectual Freedom. (2015). *Intellectual freedom manual*. Chicago: ALA Editions, an imprint of the American Library Association.

Batch, K. R. (2014, June). *Fencing out knowledge: Impacts of the Children's Internet Protection Act 10 years later*. (American Library Association Policy no. 5). Retrieved from http://connect.ala.org/files/cipa_report.pdf

Bayliss, S. (2004). Research: Net filters limit education. *Library Journal, 139*(13), 18.

Bell, M. A. (2007). The elephant in the room. *School Library Journal, 53*(1), 40–42.

Bossaller, J. S., & Budd, J. M. (2015). What we talk about when we talk about free speech. *Library Quarterly, 85*(1), 26–44.

Caldwell-Stone, D. (2013). Filtering and the First Amendment. *American Libraries, 44*(3/4), 58–61.

Chmara, T. (2012). Why recent court rulings don't change the rules on filtering. *American Libraries, 43(7/8)*, 17.

Cornell University Law School Legal Information Institute. (2003). *United States v American Library Ass'n. Inc.* (02.361). 539 U.S. 194 (2003) 201 F. Supp. 2d 401, reversed. Retrieved from https://www.law.cornell.edu/supct/html/02-361.ZO.html

Crump, A. (2012). Respect of fear. In V. Nye & K. Barko (eds.), *True stories of censorship battles in America's libraries* (pp. 86–90). Chicago: American Library Association.

Don't Forget CIPA. (2014). *Technology & Learning, 35*(4), 26.

Federal Communications Commission. (2014, December 31). Guide: Children's Internet Protection Act. Retrieved from https://www.fcc.gov/guides/childrens-internet-protection-act

Gathegi, J. N. (2005). The public library as a public forum: The (de)evolution of a legal doctrine. *Library Quarterly, 75*(1), 1–19.

Goldstein, A. (2002). Like a sieve: The Child Internet Protection Act and ineffective filters in libraries. *Fordham Intellectual Property, Media, and Entertainment Law Journal, 12*(4), 1187–1202.

Gounaud, J. (2016). Family Friendly Libraries: Ten ways to create a family friendly library. Retrieved from http://www.ccv.org/issues/harmful-to-children/family-friendly-libraries

Jaeger, P. T., McClure, C. R., & Bertot, J. C. (2005). The E-rate program and libraries and library consortia, 2000–2004: Trends and issues. *Information Technology & Libraries, 24*(2), 57–67.

Jaeger, P. T, Thompson, K. M, & Lazar, J. (2012). The internet and the evolution of library research: The perspective of one longitudinal study. *Library Quarterly, 82*(1), 75–86.

Jaeger, P. T, & Zheng, Y. (2009). One law with two outcomes: Comparing the implementation of CIPA in public libraries and schools. *Information Technology & Libraries, 28*(1), 6–14.

Kniffel, L. (2003). Why we lost the CIPA case. *American Libraries, 34*(8), 36.

Kolderup, G. (2013). The First Amendment and internet filtering in public libraries. *Indiana Libraries, 32*(1), 26–29.

McCabe, R. (2003). The CIPA ruling as reality therapy. *American Libraries, 34*(7), 16.

McCarthy, M. M. (2004). Filtering the internet: The Children's Internet Protection Act. Legal update. *Educational Horizons, 82*(2), 108–113.

Pinnell-Stephens, J. (2012). *Protecting intellectual freedom in your public library.* Chicago: American Library Association.

Radom, Rachel. (2007). Internet filtering companies with religious affiliations in the context of Indiana public libraries. *LIBRES: Library & Information Science Electronic Journal, 17*(2), 1–19.

Smith, Arro. (2006). Internet filtering policy & attitudes in Texas public libraries. *Texas Library Journal, 82*(4), 149–151.

Stone, A. (2005). ACLU reports on use of filters in R.I. libraries. *American Libraries*, *36*(6), 18.

Supreme Court rejection Nixes COPA. 2009. *American Libraries, 40*(3), 18–19.

Walker, A. (2014, February). In loco parentis. *Learning & Leading with Technology*, *41*(5), 7.

Wiegand, W. (2015). Part of our lives: A people's history of the American public library. New York: Oxford University Press.

Chapter 4

MEDIA MATTERS

CONCERNS REGARDING MEDIA MATERIALS IN PUBLIC LIBRARIES

Public libraries' media collections, which often include CDs, movies, and games, as well as downloadable items such as eBooks and music, come with their own special concerns. For example, should public librarians allow minors to borrow R-rated movies or M-rated games? Should they collect music with potentially offensive lyrics or games with violence and sexuality at all, and, if so, who should be allowed to borrow them? At what point should the line be drawn between giving the people what they want and avoiding items that could be seen as truly tasteless? And how is it best to deal with potential theft of these expensive items?

Questions such as these have plagued librarians for decades, and different library systems have elected to deal with them in various ways. Some libraries have put special policies into place, such as the issuing of juvenile-only cards that limit what minors may borrow, while others have refused completely to get involved in the decision-making process, leaving these concerns to parents and individuals. Others simply do not collect items that might be deemed controversial, thus avoiding the chance for conflict to arise. This chapter explores the reasoning and subtext behind these decisions.

RIGHTS OF MINORS AND RESPONSIBILITIES OF ADULTS

The American Library Association (ALA) and the Office for Intellectual Freedom (OIF) have made it quite clear that minors in public libraries are entitled to the same First Amendment rights as adults. Despite this, the reality remains that a significant number of librarians, trustees, and community members consider it essential for public libraries to restrict their access when it comes to materials that contain violent or sexual content, regardless of organizational standards or libraries' lack of *in loco parentis* status (Morgan, 2010). In this way, limiting minors' borrowing privileges mirrors the practice of applying filters to public computers as discussed in Chapter 2, often becoming a contest of sorts, with one side promoting the protection of children and the other side promoting the protection of intellectual freedom.

Parents and guardians, of course, bear the ultimate responsibility of deciding what their children (and only their own children) may and may not access at a public library. But, knowing that each family and each child present unique needs and desires, is it truly reasonable, or even possible, for library policies to support one parent's right to restrict access to certain materials while supporting another's right to allow access to the same materials? When attempting to intervene in this area, librarians may very well create a slippery slope in which good intentions can lead to false ideas about libraries' roles in making decisions for children that only parents and those acting *in loco parentis* have the right and responsibility to make. Or, in other words, acting upon good intentions and a genuine desire to support parents and keep children safe may ultimately create more problems than it solves.

Juvenile-Only Cards

Some libraries have dealt with the issue of parental responsibility through the use of juvenile-only cards. At the discretion of a child's parent or guardian, a juvenile card may be issued to minors in place of a standard library card, limiting their access to certain materials or to items in the children's section only. The card might look the same, but these limits will be entered into the child's account. Even library systems that try to follow the Library Bill of Rights and the OIF's principles have found themselves going this route after facing or anticipating challenges from the community (Nojonen, 2012).

The Pros

The positive aspects of juvenile-only cards are clear and plentiful. Parents can control what types of materials their children may check out, thus exercising their parental rights and responsibilities without having to physically be at the checkout desk with them. This issuance of juvenile-only cards also helps children understand the limits their parents have set on their borrowing privileges. Librarians are given a choice in how to hold parents responsible for their children's borrowing limitations, thus freeing them from the burden of having to attempt to make judgment calls about other people's kids by themselves (Nojonen, 2012).

Issuing juvenile-only cards also conveys a message that parents and guardians, not library staff, must decide what is best for a child. Offering parents various options can serve as an empowering reminder of their responsibilities regarding their public libraries, and it highlights the importance of their decisions (Pinnell-Stephens, 2012).

The Cons

On the other hand, issuing voluntary juvenile-only cards can only do so much to keep a parent's rules in check. If a parent fails to supervise his child in the library, nothing and nobody can stop that child from looking at whatever she chooses while inside the building itself. Even in the juvenile collection, there may be certain items a parent could disapprove of, and the librarians on duty wouldn't have any way of gauging this. While a juvenile-only card might give a parent a sense of comfort and allow him to feel that his child is safe, it is in no way a guarantee that library staff will protect or supervise a child within the library's walls. While all of this may be made abundantly clear on the card application, the simple act of issuing these types of cards might create a situation resulting in an unspoken, but very real, belief that library employees will supervise children and make only those choices that their parents would (Pinnell-Stephens, 2012).

Similarly, public libraries that don't sequester certain books behind barriers will undoubtedly have books in their children's areas of which not all parents will approve—in fact, even those libraries that do sequester books will still very likely have something on the shelf a parent might disapprove of as well, considering the near-impossibility of predicting what might offend someone. Picture books with LGBT (lesbian, gay, bisexual, and transgender) themes such as *Uncle Bobby's Wedding*, detailed in Chapter 3, could be freely available to an unsupervised child. Birds-and-bees types of books and DVDs for children about sexuality and reproduction would very likely be openly available as well. Some parents would doubtless be fine with this, and others would certainly feel otherwise. An unsupervised or under-supervised child also has nothing stopping him from wandering into the adult section of the library and perusing such adult-themed books as *The Kama Sutra* or *Fifty Shades of Grey*—and again, it can't be a librarian's call to decide for anyone else whether this is acceptable or not.

The Reality

In a perfect world, all parents and guardians would have the awareness, energy, and wherewithal to supervise their children both in and out of the library at all times—and library workers would not be too busy to immediately notice and intervene when an unsupervised child wanders the stacks. But interventions such as juvenile-only cards exist because this is not a perfect world. They can be well-meaning and designed to keep children as safe (as defined by their own families) as possible, but caution must be taken to avoid making, or appearing to make, any promises that cannot be kept. At the end of the day, kids are library users, too. Any public librarian will come into regular contact with both adult and minor patrons—and that librarian has a responsibility to both groups to provide the best possible service without false promises but with honesty and integrity (Nojonen, 2012).

WRITING EFFECTIVE POLICIES REGARDING JUVENILE-ONLY CARDS

Whether a public library issues juvenile-only cards or not, an explanation for the decision should be reflected in the policy manual in order to clarify the library's reasons, as well as to prepare for and prevent challenges. Libraries that adhere to the ALA and the OIF's interpretation of the Library Bill of Rights and therefore do not issue juvenile-only cards are advised in the OIF's *Intellectual Freedom Manual* to adopt the Library Bill of Rights as a substantial part of their policies, citing references and official interpretations therein to minors' rights to use their libraries with the same privileges and rights as adults (ALA OIF, 2015).

Libraries that do choose to limit certain items to patrons of certain ages also have a responsibility to explain their decision and its rationale in their policies. In these cases, the policy should clarify the reasons for issuing juvenile-only cards, and should include a strong statement that the library ultimately considers parents and guardians responsible for the borrowing behaviors of their children. It should also be clearly stated that the library has no legal or ethical authority to prevent children from accessing whatever materials they wish within the library itself. If fitting, this is also a wise place to put a statement that the library does not engage in the practice of concealing any items behind barriers, as parents may have this expectation (Nojonen, 2012).

POINTS TO CONSIDER REGARDING JUVENILE-ONLY CARDS

Despite the protests of the ALA and the OIF, many public libraries issue juvenile-only cards. Should your library choose to go this route, be alert to these potential pitfalls:

- Whatever your library's policies may state, minors are legally entitled to the same rights as adults in public library settings—therefore, should a challenge or lawsuit occur, a minor patron would very likely be backed up by the First Amendment and the Library Bill of Rights.
- Parents are ultimately responsible for what their minor children check out—public libraries do not have *in loco parentis* status and therefore have no legal standing to make judgment calls when it comes to other people's children.

MOVIES AND RATING SYSTEMS

Parents Have Differing Ideas of What Is Acceptable

A juvenile-only card could limit a child's movie-borrowing privileges to only those housed in the children's area of the library, or to those with certain MPAA (Motion Picture Association of America) ratings. For example, PG and PG-13 movies might be fine with a parent, but R-rated movies might not be. Others might only be comfortable with a G rating, and others might not adhere to any hard-and-fast rules when it comes to movie ratings.

Ratings Change

At any given time, the MPAA Ratings Board is made up of 12 anonymous Los Angeles-area-based laypeople, all of whom must be parents. The demographics of the group's membership are constantly in flux, as each term lasts between one and five years. The group watches hundreds of movies each year, which are voluntarily submitted by filmmakers, and then reports back to the MPAA with their determination of each movie's rating. Movies may receive ratings of G, PG, PG-13, R, or NC-17 (Kniffel, 1999).

Rating Systems Have No Legal Standing in Public Libraries

While the movie industry and the MPAA have been involved in a voluntary partnership for decades, no such partnership exists between the MPAA and public libraries. The MPAA is a private organization and public libraries are governmental organizations. While movie theaters may or may not choose to prevent minors from entering movies of certain ratings, public libraries are not held to these private standards—and, in fact, the MPAA has made threats to sue public libraries for denying access to any movie based on its rating due to the fact that the MPAA system has no legal standing whatsoever as far as public libraries go (Pinnell-Stephens, 2012).

Rating Systems Do Not Cover All Movies

A similar issue arises where non-rated movies are concerned. Many foreign and some domestic films do not have MPAA ratings but may still contain coarse language, explicit sexual content, or graphic violence. Sometimes, these movies will come with a statement such as For Mature Audiences Only on the box, but even this is subjective—does that mean it would be rated PG in the United States, or perhaps R, or even NC-17 (Dean, 2012)?

Movie Ratings, Public Libraries, and Controversy: A Historical Overview

The ALA's Freedom to View Statement, which was written in 1979 and updated in 1989, affirms that access to audiovisual materials including film and video is protected under the First Amendment because they provide a means for the flow and discourse of ideas, much as reading does. Therefore, public libraries are expected to provide diverse and inclusive collections of media offered without prejudice or judgment, and librarians are expected to avoid the practice of labeling on the basis of perceived controversial content. The Freedom to View Statement was approved in both 1979 and 1989 by the American Film and Video Association Board of Directors (ALA, 2006).

Also in 1989, the ALA created an interpretation of the Library Bill of Rights called Access for Children and Young People to Videotapes and Other Nonprint Formats. This official interpretation made it clear that the ALA supports minors' unrestricted rights to use library materials, and states that only parents or guardians may restrict usage, as library staff cannot legally assume *in loco parentis* status. Setting age limits and other restrictions on certain materials was declared a form of censorship (ALA, 2004). Under this interpretation, then, the practice of issuing juvenile-only cards, as far as the ALA is concerned, constitutes censorship in and of itself.

During the first decade of the 2000s, pressure for public libraries to restrict R-rated movies to only adults was building across the country (Caldwell-Stone, 2004). The Cook Memorial Public Library District in Illinois made the news during this period when it began discussion about whether to adopt a policy forbidding minors from borrowing R-rated movies, or any movies housed outside the children's or designated family movie collection areas without expressed parental permission. Board members expressed frustration at what they saw as a failure to provide service to parents through the convergence of community standards and library policies (Cook Library Urges, 2008).

In response to these pressures, Deborah Caldwell-Stone, deputy director of the OIF, gave a presentation and released an accompanying article addressing the push for public libraries to restrict R-rated movies from minors. Caldwell-Stone highlighted the legal risks involved in applying MPAA ratings in government settings such as public libraries, stressing the fact that the MPAA is a private trade association and is not involved in any way with public libraries. MPAA ratings are meant simply as informative items of information for parents and guardians, not pieces of legislation. Because there is no legality behind MPAA ratings, even movie theaters are not legally required to follow the guidelines of the MPAA ratings when selling tickets, nor are stores legally required to follow them when selling or renting DVDs (Caldwell-Stone, 2004).

Movie theaters and retail venues that sell or rent DVDs have a choice in whether or not to sell movie tickets or DVDs with certain MPAA ratings to minors because they are proprietary, nongovernment organizations. Public libraries, asserts Caldwell-Stone, do not have this choice. As nonfederal government agencies, public libraries are expected and required to follow only the conditions of the United States Constitution and Bill of Rights. Therefore, public libraries are free to develop policies and rules as long as they do not violate these regulations. Caldwell-Stone attests that restricting library materials to specific age groups infringes upon the First Amendment rights of minors. In their constrained role, public libraries would be required to provide a hearing before of a court of law regarding the legitimacy of any restriction to access—meaning one hearing for each individual movie the library wishes to limit to adults only, resulting in that item being judged as legally obscene. This is highly improbable, if not completely impossible, stresses Caldwell-Stone, as the MPAA itself freely admits that its criteria for rating movies is subjective and constantly changing. To use MPAA ratings as policy, then, would be to grant authority over the library's regulations to an unregulated and uninvolved private agency, without any legislative rationalization, thus violating the Due Process Clause of the Fourteenth Amendment. Furthermore, using MPAA ratings as policy leaves public libraries at risk for lawsuits as well as the financial and time-management burdens involved in litigation. Finally, Caldwell-Stone encourages public library staff members to empower parents through activities such as providing resources to help guide children's borrowing choices and creating programs designed to help children develop critical thinking skills (Caldwell-Stone, 2004).

Echoing one of Caldwell-Stone's points about the arbitrariness of ratings systems, it has been found that a phenomenon known as ratings creep has been going on for decades. As time has moved on, greater leniency has been found in MPAA ratings of movies containing violence and sexually explicit imagery. In other words, a movie that would have been rated R by the MPAA 10 years ago could very well receive a rating of PG-13 or even PG today. This means that, depending on when a movie was released, minors borrowing a PG-13 movie from their public libraries could easily be viewing material that they are not permitted to see if their parents forbid them from viewing R-rated movies (Study Finds Film Ratings, 2004).

Despite the ALA's statements about MPAA ratings, the fact remains that many public libraries do allow parents and guardians to designate which types of movies their children may borrow, and this practice is rarely disputed (Procaro & Galloway, 2011). The current situation is that while many libraries support and follow the ALA and OIF's guidelines, many others have taken something of a don't-ask-don't-tell stance when it comes to their DVD lending policies regarding minors. Among other issues, this lack of consensus results in circumstances in which the rules of one public library may be completely different from another one within the same general geographic area.

WRITING EFFECTIVE POLICIES REGARDING MINORS AND MPAA RATINGS

Much like juvenile-only cards, many libraries have elected to restrict movies of certain ratings to minors whose parents request it. This choice often makes parents feel more secure, but it is not in any way supported by either the ALA or the OIF. Therefore, any policies about MPAA ratings should be carefully constructed, in order to make the library's stance clear before any complaints or challenges come along.

Public libraries that follow the ALA and the OIF's stance on MPAA ratings having no bearing on public libraries are encouraged to write policies that don't give any mention to MPAA ratings, while offering information for both minors and adults about the development of critical thinking skills, thus helping all age groups make well-considered decisions about what movies are appropriate for themselves and their families (Caldwell-Stone, 2015).

Conversely, libraries that do choose to allow parents and guardians to place limits on their children's movie selections need to write policies explaining this decision and the reasons behind it. As with juvenile-only cards, the policy should explain the reasons behind the decision, as well as a section explaining that the library does not have *in loco parentis* status, and that the responsibility ultimately falls upon parents and guardians. This educates and empowers adults with children in their care, and lessens the possibility of an irate parent issuing a challenge.

POINTS TO CONSIDER REGARDING MOVIES AND MINORS

If your library elects to restrict movies with certain ratings to minor patrons, be alert to these potential pitfalls:

- The MPAA is a private trade association and has no ties whatsoever with public libraries, or even movie theaters—therefore, minors are legally entitled to check out anything an adult would be permitted to check out.

- If your library has a policy about lending movies of certain ratings to minor patrons, be aware that there is no support from the MPAA, any legal entity, or the ALA to do so, and be prepared to write your policy in a manner that addresses this issue, as complaints are likely to arise.

- If your library has a policy about lending movies of certain ratings to minor patrons, check the other libraries in your geographic area—what one library doesn't permit, a library close by very well may permit, and be ready to speak to questions or concerns about this discrepancy.

GAMES AND RATING SYSTEMS

The same concerns that apply to movies also affect the collection of computer-based games, which typically come with ratings as well. The ESRB (Entertainment Software Rating Board), much like the MPAA, provides ratings including EC (Early Childhood, ages 3 and up), E (Everyone, ages 6 and up), E10+ (Everyone, ages 10 and up), T (Teen, ages 13 and up), M (Mature, ages 17 and up), and AO (Adults Only, ages 18 and up). Game packages also tend to contain information about why a certain game was given a certain rating. Reasons may include such categories as realistic-looking violence and use of tobacco or alcohol (Schmidt, 2000). Like MPAA ratings, the ESRB designations are developed by a private party, and therefore fall under the same legal status as movies in relation to public libraries (Caldwell-Stone, 2004). However, parents are often directed to give permission about which games a child may borrow based on the ERSB rating system when they apply for library cards for their children (Danforth, 2010). It has even been suggested that public libraries have a responsibility to restrict games to certain age groups because parents and guardians are perceived as being too out of touch with video games to be able to understand or make sense of the ESRB rating system (Procaro & Galloway, 2011).

Today's gaming consoles, by and large, have built-in parental controls, and many games offer parental options such as modifying the amount of violence and profane language a child may encounter while gaming (Procaro & Galloway, 2011). It is much simpler for a concerned parent to modify a child's gaming experience than it is to modify a movie-viewing experience. Again, this decision and the action necessary are the responsibility of parents or guardians—the owners of the console and overseers of the games in their homes—with the ability to monitor either in person or through parental control systems. These systems are far from perfect, and, of course, kids might always play computer games at friends' homes or learn how to hack the parental control system, but to insist that monitoring a child's whereabouts and activities while not at home is the responsibility of a public library's employees would be quite a stretch.

While it has long been assumed that ESRB ratings are based on expert analysis, the truth is that the rating system is imperfect at best, and deeply flawed at worst. For example, ESRB raters are not required to play the games they are responsible for rating. Rather, they are instructed to watch short videos of the games, which the creators provide (Kutner & Olsen, 2008). ESRB raters have had full-time employee status since 2007, although there is no set salary. Prior to 2007, they were permitted to work as freelancers, logging as little as one day a month. The raters are not required to have any training in child development, either on their own or on the ESRB's dime—in fact, being a parent is not a requirement for ESRB raters as it is with MPAA movie raters. Requirements are simply to have experience with children in any capacity, to be familiar and interested with video games, and to have good written and verbal communication skills (Kutner & Olsen, 2008).

Violence in Fantasy and Reality

The ESRB ratings are often assumed to have some resonance in the ongoing cultural debate about whether video games with violent themes are connected with youth violence. This became a serious concern for many parents in the 1990s, when video games began to push the envelope with violence-laden games such as the *Mortal Kombat* series (Kutner & Olsen, 2008). Teens and young adults involved in high-profile crimes such as school shootings are often assumed to have been compelled to carry out their crimes, at least in part, by playing violent video games and thus becoming desensitized to violence. The actions of the infamous Columbine High School shooters, Dylan Klebold and Eric Harris, were presented as examples of the appalling effects video games were assumed to have on young people's actions. This was an era when games became more common, more likely to be played in the home, more bloody, and more realistic. The first iteration of *Mortal Kombat*, which was created to be played in arcades, led to even more gruesome versions of itself designed to be played on home systems like Super Nintendo and PlayStation. Just when parents and other concerned adults were fretting over *Mortal Kombat 3*'s extremely violent content, other blood-and-guts games such as *Doom* came along as competition (Kutner & Olsen, 2008). By the time the 2000 presidential campaigns were underway, media violence had become big news, and many congressional initiatives arose regarding regulating, labeling and monitoring of video games, to the dismay of gamers, the Freedom to Read Foundation, and other groups dedicated to the preservation of free expression (Reid, 2000).

The problem with the speculation that video game violence breeds actual violence was that it ultimately turned out to be a disproven theory. Between 1994 and 2001, while violent games were on the rise, juvenile arrests for violent crimes including forcible assault, rape, and murder dipped lower than they had been in 18 years. As is so often the case when individual fears develop into national panics, these statistics did little to subdue the rising fear that video games could turn teens into soulless monsters capable of committing terrible acts of violence at any given moment. In truth, even quite young teenagers, except in very rare cases, are able to understand the difference between fantasy and reality. Teen gamers often explain that they play violent games for entertainment or stress relief, but they don't report any crossover between the things they do in a gaming environment and the things they could do in real life (Kutner & Olsen, 2008). None of this is to suggest that it is necessarily a good idea for parents to allow their children to play violent video games in their own homes or those of their friends, as this is a decision that can be made only by individual parents of individual children. Rating systems may help guide these decisions, but at the end of the day, for the majority of American families, the kids really are alright.

Legislation and Video Games

In 2005, a law was passed in California making it illegal to sell violent video games to minors. Retailers found to be in violation faced fines of up to $1,000 for each game sold. This law was brought before the California Supreme Court in 2011 in the case of *Brown vs. Entertainment Merchants Association* and was ultimately struck down on the grounds that it was found to be unconstitutional. The Free Speech Clause of the First Amendment, which works in protection of public discourse, was specifically noted as being a factor in the decision. In cases of written and visual works such as books and movies, the Free Speech Clause protects works from being censored due to their communication of ideas. Video games, it was decided, fell under the same First Amendment protections as these other works because they communicate ideas through players' decision-making actions, dialogue, and interactions with the digital world. Therefore, it was decided that the government did not have the authority to restrict video game sales. Although the court case was not about libraries, the resolution was obvious—if privately owned stores and other businesses could sell any video game to a customer of any age, then public libraries certainly could not restrict the borrowing of any video game due to a patron's age (From the Bench, 2011).

Sellers of video games saw the *Brown vs. Entertainment Merchants Association* decision as a victory over censorship, while opponents claimed that the California Supreme Court was acting in favor of corporate needs at the peril of the safety of children. On the other hand, proponents of the decision reasoned that it helped cement the authority of parents to make decisions for their own children without relying on outside parties to maintain this parenting responsibility (From the Bench, 2011).

WRITING EFFECTIVE POLICIES REGARDING MINORS AND ESRB RATINGS

The ALA and the OIF both attest that minors, having the same rights as adults, have the legal right to check out whatever items they choose, and this includes video games. The wording of a policy addressing this stance should be very similar to those addressing movies—that ESRB ratings have no legal bearing on public libraries and therefore don't belong in their policies at all. A policy of this nature would ideally state that a refusal to lend specific games to children violates the Library Bill of Rights.

It seems safe to assume that libraries that allow parents to limit their children's movie selections would most likely have a similar rule regarding video games. Therefore, any policies about this issue should be carefully constructed, in order to make the library's stance clear before any complaints or challenges might come along.

There are, however, many public libraries that do choose to allow parents and guardians to place limits on their children's game selections. These libraries need to write policies explaining the rationale for this decision and, once again, make it clear that the library has no legal rights or responsibilities to make decisions for other people's children. As with juvenile-only cards and movies of certain MPAA ratings, the rights and responsibilities regarding video games lie with the parents and guardians. A request to restrict certain items, in the end, is merely a request—and while requests should be honored to the best of the library staff's ability, there are always gray areas. A policy that places rights and responsibilities of children's lending choices squarely in the hands of parents goes a long way toward quelling potential challenges, and also provides an atmosphere of empowerment for parents (Danforth, 2010).

POINTS TO CONSIDER REGARDING GAMES

If your library elects to restrict games with certain ratings to minor patrons, be alert to these potential pitfalls:

- The ESRB, much like the MPAA, is a private organization, and it has been determined that the Free Speech Clause of the First Amendment protects video games from acts of censorship in public libraries and elsewhere.
- Attitudes about violent video games abound, but public libraries are neutral places where these judgments are not appropriate, and they have no place in policy writing.
- If faced with parents who have concerns about the video games their children play, it may help to remind them of the parental controls they have on their consoles—a little helpful communication can go a long way.

LABELS, RATINGS, AND VALUE JUDGMENTS

An overriding issue with labeling and restricting of movies and video games is the fact that public libraries do, in fact, use labels all the time. Items are regularly labeled into such categories as children's, young adult, mystery, science fiction, new releases, country music, Academy Award winners—the list could go on and on. Labels are routinely placed on items and in their catalog records, leading to these items being arranged in order to physically house certain subcollections in certain areas. While this practice is sometimes seen as dangerously tantamount to using non-library rating systems like those of the MPAA and ESRB, an important distinction exists. When labeling in areas such as intended age range or type of material, objective criteria are being used, free from implied moral judgments. When an outside party's subjective rating system is utilized, a gray area appears, innocuously or impertinently, and value judgments are implied about items offered in public library collections (Schmidt, 2000). The actions of adding a mystery label to an Agatha Christie novel, cataloging it with a subject heading of Mystery Fiction, and housing it in the library's mystery section don't imply anything about the book other than the fact that it's a mystery novel. Whatever value judgments might be assumed are those of the library users, not the employees. However, the action of adding an outside party's rating to a movie or video game implies that there is something about the item that makes it potentially unsuitable for certain library users, but fine for others. The label itself is not the issue—the implication assigned to it is where the trouble begins.

The ALA has offered its support to those dealing with this contentious issue through the website Questions and Answers on Labeling and Rating Systems, which can be found at www.ala.org/advocacy/intfreedom/librarybill/interpretations/qa-labeling. The information provided on this site makes it clear that any attempt to either restrict or endorse library users' decisions based on suggestions about the assumed morality or decency of any item is in direct violation of the Library Bill of Rights, and that using rating systems of any kind is clearly meant to influence viewpoints upon the public and is therefore antithetical to the tenets of intellectual freedom. This goes for all library items and specifically mentions games, movies, and music, all of which are often subject to ratings based on assumed decency. Furthermore, ratings, according to the ALA via this website, have no place in any public library item's cataloging record. To add outside ratings to catalog records implies that what one person finds objectionable or in need of noting in the bibliographic record matches exactly what any other person might find offensive. Because the entire decision-making process herein is subjective, no system is needed or warranted (ALA, 2007).

PROFESSIONAL REALITIES AND THE EXPECTATIONS OF THE PUBLIC

The Harris Poll is a popular survey of American attitudes and opinions on a range of topics, with the results often being used in market research. The 2015 Harris Poll results indicated that 28 percent of respondents felt that there are books that should be banned completely. In an odd twist, though, 40 percent of respondents stated that they would be more likely to read a book if it was considered controversial and 30 percent would be more likely to read a book if it was outright banned (Harris Poll, 2015), illustrating the phenomenon that tends to occur around banned books—the more they are publically criticized, the more interest they tend to generate.

The Harris Poll results also indicated that seven out of ten people in the United States believe that it is the responsibility of librarians to prevent minors from accessing and checking out materials that are inappropriate for their age group. However, perceptions of what constitutes inappropriateness were shown to vary greatly from person to person, with topics ranging from explicit language to evolution to vampires. According to the same poll, 71 percent of Americans polled stated that they felt that a ratings system for books should be put into place, similar to MPAA ratings for movies and ERSB ratings for video games (Harris Poll, 2015).

Although these findings may be upsetting to librarians and their allies, especially those who use the philosophies of the ALA and OIF as their means of professional guidance, the sheer number of people who believe that librarians can and should restrict, rate, and even ban books raises concerns that must be taken into consideration. Is it the responsibility of librarians to educate the public on their role, or is it to provide the services that communities want and expect? Public librarians are almost always employees of local governments, after all, working in a service capacity to communities.

In light of these poll results, it seems wise to ponder whether there is some middle ground between following the professional organizations' guiding principles and giving the public what it expects. It may be uncomfortable to even ask the question, but at least it is possible to know that, in the end, these convictions will be well thought-out and sincere.

THEFT AND THE PERCEIVED THREAT OF THEFT

Ideas and assumptions about who steals what aren't strictly censorship-based concerns, but censorship's partner—suppression—is very much a concern in this area. Whenever public librarians engage in acts of suppression, which may include refusing to collect certain materials for fear of them being stolen or monitoring these items so ruthlessly that patrons are made to feel uncomfort-

> Seven in ten Americans believe there should be a book rating system, like MPAA ratings. . . . MPAA ratings have absolutely nothing to do with educational value, and if you were to ask the people that made them, they would tell you that.
> —Millie Davis, Director, National Council for Teachers of English Intellectual Freedom Center

able, suppression is happening. No matter how much sense the rationale might appear to make, these acts leave libraries open to going one step further toward practicing acts of censorship.

Whether a certain genre of material is more likely to be stolen is a question that plagues librarians and often bears upon collection development decisions. While it seems to be true that media items such as DVDs and CDs are more vulnerable to theft, whether that takes the form of outright stealing or of being checked out and never returned (Nice, 2006), they are among many other types of items that tend to disappear from the shelves.

In 2001, the ALA e-mailed hundreds of libraries to determine what types of items are most frequently stolen. Books dealing with the occult, witchcraft, and astrology were reported as being commonly stolen, as were items that patrons might be too uncomfortable to check out in person, such as books about sexual abuse, attention-deficit disorder, and sex manuals (Epstein, 2001).

Media materials are often viewed as theft targets, due to both their cost and to their sometimes-controversial matter. Media items are generally more expensive to purchase and replace, and this fact often compels librarians to lock them up in anti-theft cases and to implement security increases and harsh signage to make it clear to library users that they are being monitored (Narciso, 2011). As much as these measures may seem warranted, creating a Big Brother type of atmosphere may, oddly enough, only result in higher rates of theft. Studies have found that theft is less likely to occur when library users feel like they are involved in a partnership with their library's employees and do not feel that they are being treated with an aura of suspicion or distrust. In general, when patrons feel that their libraries' media collections adequately represent their interests and priorities, theft decreases and patron satisfaction increases (Urban Libraries Council, 2016). This is no guarantee that theft will never occur, of course, but it appears that open communication and good customer service have much more to do with controlling theft than the genre of the items.

Assumptions and Actualities

Anecdotal data gained from browsing the blogosphere and social media points to a frequently held assumption that items such as rap or hip-hop CDs and fiction books in the urban or street lit genres are at greater risk of theft than other items. Librarians often house these materials in areas with greater-than-average visibility and increase video security around them. Adding threateningly worded signage is also common. It has even been suggested that it might be best to move certain subcollections away from large, urban branches and into smaller branches in order to deter theft (Collection Dilemmas, 2012; TheRedditPaperClip, 2014).

Unfortunately, the assumption that materials such as rap and hip-hop CDs and urban or street lit fiction books, which feature predominantly African American characters and plotlines heavy with sex, violence, and explicit language (Pattee, 2008) may lead librarians to develop subtle, or perhaps even blatant, racist ideas about theft and these genres. To combat this danger, it is wise to keep in mind that research has shown that while theft does occur across the board, it has been shown to diminish significantly when patrons feel welcomed, listened to, asked for feedback, provided with convenience of service, offered a wide array of choices in materials, and given the chance to develop an open rapport and friendly relationships with their library staff (Narciso, 2011; Urban Libraries Council, 2016). To put it more simply, making biased assumptions about certain patrons based either on their race or their preferred genres of library materials is likely to result in a sense of distrust, thus leading to more visual security measures and a feeling among patrons of being singled out—the very factors that act as antitheses to developing low-theft libraries.

DOWNLOADABLE MUSIC

As libraries move further into the digital age, downloadable music is becoming a commonly offered service. This is another area in which censorship concerns tend to lurk around the corners.

Not only does downloadable music eliminate the possibility of theft, it also eases worries about CDs being damaged due to misuse or age, and about the amount of space they take up. Vendors such as Freegal are able to offer a wide range of music genres along with apps for portable devices, making it simple for library users to add their weekly allotment of music to their personal digital music collections (Enis, 2012).

Although many strides have been made, public libraries are still in the in-between stage when it comes to providing music in desired formats, due to both the digital divide and personal preferences. Some patrons want the latest digital options for downloading music, and some still want physical CDs, meaning many public libraries must stretch their budgets to purchase both CDs and access to downloadable music.

eBOOKS AND ETHICS

eBooks have been big news for several years now, and for good reason. They are convenient, instantly available, and take up less space than print books. Devices for reading eBooks offer useful choices for readers in need of larger or differing text options, and they usually also provide services such as built-in dictionaries and online searching capability. Unfortunately for public library users, it is typically much less simple to borrow an eBook through their library than it would be to purchase it from Amazon or another corporate eBook seller, all too often leading to frustration for both patrons and librarians (Enis, 2014).

Despite the popularity and convenience of eBooks, the digital divide in this area is a concern, and the lack of ease with which library users are able to download eBooks causes problems for those who aren't yet technically adept enough to deal efficiently with the typically overcomplicated, multi-step process of downloading eBooks from libraries.

Libraries and eBook Vendors: A Troubled Relationship

Public libraries and sellers of eBooks got off to a rocky start, and things have not improved much in the years since. Between 2010 and 2011, when eBooks were becoming mainstream and new eReader devices seemed to be popping up all over, many book publishers were hesitant, if not outright hostile, about working with public libraries on eBook lending practices. Publishers, operating (understandably) as money-making corporations, insisted that customers wouldn't buy what they could just as easily access for free (Enis, 2014). Since then, through market analysis and testing efforts, these fears have been eased, and publishers have become more willing to see public libraries as allies rather than rivals.

A prevailing issue with eBooks is the ease—or, more precisely, the lack thereof—in which patrons may browse in-house collections versus digital collections in a public library's catalog. While this is beginning to change, the process of searching for an item on a public library's online catalog very often involves conducting two separate searches. This choppy service model frequently leads to confusion and frustration among patrons and complaints to vendors from librarians. Fortunately, this has begun to change in the past few years. Many libraries are beginning to offer seamless searching, which allows library users to find both print and digital sources together, making searching a library's catalog as simple as possible for all parties (LaRue, 2012).

Of course, print books and eBooks exist in completely different formats and will inevitably come with different issues. For example, print books are at risk of theft or damage, whereas eBooks are not. The good must sometimes be taken with the bad. Nevertheless, convenience to patrons is an important issue that has not been fully addressed or resolved by eBook vendors. Until eBooks can be borrowed from a public library with at least similar ease with which they can be purchased, the air of suppression caused by the digital divide will play a part in determining who is able to use these services and who is not.

CONCLUSION AND FURTHER THINKING

Although the digital age has been evolving for a good amount of time now, librarians and patrons alike are still learning to navigate this new and constantly changing world. While some might pine for the old days of card catalogs and printed pages, that simply isn't the world of public libraries anymore.

New media and digital offerings have opened up new expectations of public libraries, as well as new systems that excite and invigorate librarians. Offering a variety of choices is a substantial element of librarianship as a service profession. Still, as changes continue, it is important to remain alert to the profession's basic tenets of fairness, equity, and intellectual freedom, and to be on guard for any forms of suppression.

As long as the digital age's new contributions to librarianship are navigated through the lens of intellectual freedom and the Library Bill of Rights, it will be possible to maintain professional standards while opening up new worlds for public library patrons.

TIPS AND TRAPS: LENDING PRACTICES AND MEDIA MATERIALS

Tips

- According to the ALA and the OIF, minors have the same First Amendment rights as adults, and to deny minors this right is unlawful, as librarians do not have *in loco parentis* status over other people's children.
- The MPAA and the ESRB are private organizations, and their findings regarding age-appropriateness of movies and video games have no legal bearing on public libraries.
- While labels such as Young Adult, Mystery, or Rap Music are fine to use to help guide patrons to the items they desire, using arbitrary third-party ratings systems is not legally allowed in public libraries.

Traps

- In instances of issuing juvenile-only cards, consider the importance of having parents truly understand the parameters of the law and the library in regard to the protection of their children.

- If a library applies movie or video game ratings to borrowing privileges of minors, its staff must be prepared to explain the legalities of this decision.
- When creating catalog records, remember to avoid listing MPAA or ESRB ratings.

WHAT WOULD YOU DO?

Andrew was the director of a mid-sized public library with a policy that patrons under the age of 12 had to be accompanied by an adult, for their safety. Minors over the age of 12 had free reign of the library and, because the library did not make use of juvenile-only cards, were free to check out whatever items they chose. Andrew's philosophy, which he felt strongly about, was that minors' parents could make decisions about what their kids could and could not check out by simply joining them on their trips to the library and monitoring their borrowing habits. This was what he told Michael, the irate father of 15-year-old Lisa, after Michael found library-issued R-rated movies in Lisa's room. As far as Andrew was concerned, there was nothing to be upset about—Lisa was 15, so while she was not legally an adult, she was permitted by policy to check out library materials by herself. And if Michael didn't like that, then he perhaps should consider joining Lisa on her library excursions.

Michael shook his head at Andrew's idealistic belief of how easy parenting was. He was a widowed single father of two teenagers, he told Andrew. Of course, he did his best to monitor what his kids were up to, but how could he keep an eye on them every minute of the day while working full time and attending to the demands of his home life? Andrew held his ground, citing the First Amendment and the Library Bill of Rights. "Spare me the legalese," said Michael. "Anyone who would lend a teenage girl these movies obviously knows nothing about raising children."

Within a month, the issue was on the agenda for the library's board of trustees meeting. Many of the trustees cited the safety and well-being of children as trumping policy as it stood. If kids can't get into R-rated movies at the local movie theater, some reasoned, why should they be allowed to borrow them at their public library? Juvenile-only cards were brought up, discussed, and eventually voted in. Parents, when applying for library cards for their children as well as retroactively, were given a choice of what movie and video game ratings were acceptable.

Andrew, though disheartened, understood that the community had spoken, and he went along with the new policy in order to salvage his library's reputation. The catalog records for each movie and game were altered to add their rating ESRB or MPAA ratings. There were a few grumbles from the library staff and their younger patrons, but it blew over quickly, and Andrew soon found himself better liked by many of the adult patrons, who now displayed respect and kindness over his willingness to compromise. Andrew told himself he had been too strident, but now he was serving the community in a way that seemed to benefit just about everyone. At the end of the day, what could possibly be the harm in that?

QUESTIONS TO CONSIDER

- Do you support the issuance of juvenile-only cards, or do you feel that it defies the First Amendment? Why?

- Do you believe that public libraries should allow children to borrow violent or sexually graphic video games without their parents' knowledge? Why or why not?

- Do you believe that it is appropriate for public libraries to collect video games with ESRB ratings of M or above? If so, do you believe that library users of all ages should be permitted to check them out? Why or why not?

- How do you feel about the 2015 Harris Poll results indicating that the majority of Americans believe librarians should restrict access in many cases? Do they change your mind about the role of librarians, or do they strengthen your current beliefs?

REFERENCES

American Library Association. (2004, June 30). Access for children and young people to videotapes and other nonprint formats. Retrieved from http://www.ala.org/Template .cfm?Section=interpretations&Template=/ContentManagement/ContentDisplay .cfm&ContentID=31870

American Library Association. (2006, July 26). The Freedom to Read Statement. Retrieved from http://www.ala.org/advocacy/intfreedom/statementspols/freedomreadstatement

American Library Association. (2007, May 29). Questions and answers on labeling and rating systems. American Library Association. Retrieved from http://www.ala.org/ advocacy/intfreedom/librarybill/interpretations/qa-labeling

American Library Association Office for Intellectual Freedom (2015). *Intellectual freedom manual*. Chicago: ALA Editions, an imprint of the American Library Association.

Caldwell-Stone, D. (2004). Movie ratings are private, not public policy. *ILA Reporter*, *22*(2), 10–13.

Caldwell-Stone, D. (2015). The law regarding rating systems. In American Library Association Office for Intellectual Freedom, *Intellectual freedom manual*. Chicago: ALA Editions, an imprint of the American Library Association.

Collection dilemmas: Frequently missing items. (2012, March 21). Retrieved from http://cdstacked.blogspot.com/2012/03/collection-dilemmas-frequently-missing.html

Cook Library urges DVD policy for kids. (2008). *ILA Reporter, 26*(1), 25.

Danforth, L. (2010). The great (M-rated) debate. *Library Journal, 135*(17), 56.

Dean, S. (2012). Sweet movie. In V. Nye & K. Barko (eds.), *True stories of censorship battles in America's libraries* (pp. 91–96). Chicago: American Library Association.

Enis, M. (2014). Technology: Vendors talk e-book future. *Library Journal, 139*(14), 18.

Enis, M., & Schwartz, M. (2012). Freegal Android Apple apps simplify MP3 downloads. *Library Journal, 137*(12), 16.

Epstein, E. (2001, May 15). U.S. libraries checking out book theft: Most-stolen list will help curb crime. Retrieved from http://www.sfgate.com/news/article/U-S-libraries-checking-out-book-theft-2921164.php

From the Bench. (2011). *Newsletter on Intellectual Freedom, 60*(5), 178–202.

Harris Poll. (2015, July 8). Adults are more likely to believe there are books that should be banned than movies, television shows, or video games. Retrieved from http://www.theharrispoll.com/health-and-life/Censorship_2015.html

Kniffel, L. (1999, September). Mouths wide open. *American Libraries, 30*(8), 40.

Kutner, L., & Olsen, C. K (2008). *Grand theft childhood: The surprising truth about violent video games.* New York: Simon & Schuster.

LaRue, J. (2012). The last one standing. *Public Libraries, 51*(1), 28–32.

Morgan, C. D. (2010). Challenges and issues today. In American Library Association Office for Intellectual Freedom, *Intellectual freedom manual* [Foreword]. Chicago: American Library Association.

Narciso, D. (2011, December 12). Libraries differ on anti-theft measures. *The Columbus Dispatch.* Retrieved from http://www.dispatch.com/content/stories/local/2011/12/12/libraries-differ-on-anti-theft-measures.html

Nice, M. (2006, November). Multnomah County Library collection shrinkage: A baseline report. Retrieved from https://multco.us/file/26325/download

Nojonen, M. (2012). Reasonable accommodation: Why our library created voluntary kids cards. In V. Nye & K. Barko (eds.), *True stories of censorship battles in America's libraries* (pp. 64–68). Chicago: American Library Association.

Pattee, A. (2008). Street fight. *School Library Journal, 54*(7), 26–30.

Pinnell-Stephens, J. (2012). *Protecting intellectual freedom in your public library.* Chicago: American Library Association.

Procaro, J. P., & Galloway, B. (2011). First Amendment rights. *School Library Journal, 57*(1), 22–23.

TheRedditPaperClip. (2014, November 10). Have any of you had problems with theft at your library? *r/libraries.* Reddit. Retrieved from https://www.reddit.com/r/Libraries/comments/2lv754/have_any_of_you_had_problems_with_theft_at_your

Reid, C. (2000). Publishers, writers warn against censors. *Publishers Weekly, 247*(49), 10.

Schmidt, C. J. (2000). Sex-and-violence ratings: What's in them for libraries? *American Libraries, 31*(4), 44.

Study finds film ratings are more lenient. (2004). *Newsletter on Intellectual Freedom, 53*(5), 174–219.

Urban Libraries Council. (2016). Managing DVD access and theft. Retrieved from http://www.urbanlibraries.org/managing-dvd-access-and-theft-innovation-843.php?page_id=169

Chapter 5

PREVENTING AND PREPARING FOR CHALLENGES: A STRONG COLLECTION DEVELOPMENT POLICY, STAFF TRAINING, AND PROFESSIONAL RESOURCES

AN OUNCE OF PREVENTION

Only the most fortunate of librarians have never heard so much as a grumble of disapproval about the materials in their collections. Handling these comments, as well as dealing with more formal types of challenges, is one of public librarians' professional responsibilities, albeit an uncomfortable one. Feeling anxious and wishing to deliver that perfect zinger of a comeback is understandable, but it is important to remember that meeting anger with anger, or frustration with frustration, will only escalate the situation in the long run and heighten the odds of a complaint developing into a formal challenge. It is also counterintuitive to attempt to provide an instant solution in order to placate the complaining party's concern and supposedly put the issue to bed once and for all. Good, kind, and respectful library service in times of distress falls in between these extremes—and, as is so often seen in other areas of life, prevention is the key component.

Nothing can keep librarians better prepared to prevent or handle a challenge than ample preparation. Nobody relishes the idea of a community challenge, but prevention—or hoping for the best while preparing for the worst—is time and effort well spent. Should a challenge occur, having a strong, well-researched, and clearly written collection development policy is a preventative measure toward that challenge getting out of control (Meraz, 2014).

Preparation and prevention involve more than writing a strong policy—although doing so is, of course, a vital first step. It is also wise for libraries to develop and maintain clear systems for handling complaints, as this empowers employees and maintains consistency across departments and among individuals. Regular training for not only library staff, but for everyone involved with the library, is valuable as well. This includes governmental authorities such as boards of trustees, foundation members, and city councils. It is also helpful to keep in regular contact with other community agencies and partners, such as educational, political, and civic groups, because doing so helps keep alliances strong and expectations of a public library's role in its surrounding community accurate. Appearing in local media sources to speak about intellectual freedom issues is useful as well, as is maintaining familiarity with the wording and intent of both the Library Bill of Rights and the Freedom to Read Statement. Be ready to listen respectfully and speak confidently with all sorts of community members, as an expression of concern can potentially pop up in just about any conversation.

A strong knowledge base paired with solid communication skills and a well-written policy allows community members to understand the professional parameters of librarianship and the legalities behind library policies, and, therefore, prevents challenges.

ELEMENTS OF THE COLLECTION DEVELOPMENT POLICY

The time it takes to write and regularly revise a public library's collection development policy is ultimately time well spent, as a well-written policy can tamp down a potential challenge right at the start. This is not to suggest that policies in and of themselves can keep challenges from cropping up, but they do provide an opportunity to learn and practice the preferred responsive stance in advance and to become knowledgeable about the legal issues and ethics that lie beneath any such policy.

Why the Policy Is in Place

A comprehensive, well-written collection development policy explains the purpose and objectives of its own existence or reason to be, which, in a public library setting, will typically fall along the lines of providing freedom of choice among a wide variety of materials within the parameters of librarianship's professional and legal guidelines (American Library Association [ALA], 2013c). In this area, it is helpful to refer to the library's mission statement and the Library Bill of Rights, which should be included in appendices in the case of a printed policy or by link in the case of a policy posted online.

Also included should be a brief overview of intellectual freedom basics and an explanation of the public library's societal role of supporting the free exchange of information and ideas.

SAMPLE WORDING OF WHY THE POLICY IS IN PLACE AND INTELLECTUAL FREEDOM STATEMENT

The Anytown Public Library (APL) supports its mission of providing the Anytown community with a diverse and inclusive range of materials in various formats for both educational and entertainment needs of residents. APL proactively collects materials that reflect a range of opinions and interests in order to meet public libraries' societal role as places where the open discourse of ideas is encouraged and supported by the First Amendment. APL is committed to providing equal access for all library users and quality service to all who make use of APL's services.

APL supports the American Library Association's Library Bill of Rights, Freedom to Read Statement, and Freedom to View Statement. APL does not segregate or restrict access to any materials, regardless of its intended audience or age group. APL does not differentiate between various segments of the population and defers the responsibility of minors' selections to parents and legal guardians. While APL is open to suggestions for purchase and requests to reconsider the appropriateness of materials, the staff of APL opposes any attempts to censor its collection.

APL does not label its materials beyond standard Library of Congress cataloging categories and does not include ratings of movies or games in its records.

Organizational Structure

This section should make it clear *who* in the library is responsible for what is collected. If different people collect in different areas (e.g., one person might be in charge of collecting DVDs, while another collects fiction, and another collects music), these collectors should be identified by title. If one person collects everything, that person should be identified, also by title. The result should be clarity about who in the organization is responsible for collection development activities in all subject areas (ALA, 2013b; ALA OIF, 2015).

SAMPLE WORDING OF ORGANIZATIONAL STRUCTURE STATEMENT

As a medium-sized public library, APL assigns its collection development responsibilities to the following positions, under the supervision of the library director

- Adult fiction: Adult Services Coordinating Librarian
- Adult nonfiction
  - Dewey areas 0–300: Senior Adult Librarian
  - Dewey areas 400–600: Adult Reference Librarian II
  - Dewey areas 700–999.999: Adult Reference Librarian I

- Adult movies and video games: Adult Reference Librarian II
- Adult audiobooks and music CDs: Adult Reference Librarian I
- Children's picture books: Children's Coordinating Librarian
- Children's fiction: Senior Children's Librarian
- Children's nonfiction:
  - Dewey areas 0–500: Children's Reference Librarian II
  - Dewey areas 600–999.999: Children's Librarian I
- Children's movies and video games: Children's Reference Librarian II
- Children's audiobooks and music CDs: Children's Librarian I
- Young Adult fiction and classics: Young Adult Reference Librarian II
- Young Adult audiobooks: Young Adult Reference Librarian I
- All other categories, including electronic resources, are the responsibility of the library director

Maintenance and weeding tasks are performed by those who collect in each area.

Just as library systems are constantly changing organizations in terms of employee ranks and titles, the collection development policy must be dynamic as well—meaning that whenever changes are made in terms of who collects what, the document must change as well. This keeps the policy fluid and also serves as a helpful way of making sure it is always up to date.

Explanation of Collection Criteria

The collection development policy should identify criteria for adding materials to the library's collection, along with a selection philosophy guiding the policy (ALA OIF, 2015).

SAMPLE WORDING OF COLLECTION DEVELOPMENT CRITERIA EXPLANATION

APL's collection development criteria are based on inclusivity and range of interest. To this end, APL collects materials based on popularity, interest to the community, quality, diversity, and appropriateness to the collection. APL makes use of popular review sources including *Booklist*, *Publisher's Weekly*, and *Kirkus*, as well as alternative review sources including the

Stonewall Book Awards and the American Library Association's Gay, Lesbian, Bisexual, and Transgender Round Table's recommendations, as well as small presses including Graywolf, Queerteen, New Directions, OR Books, Candlewick, and Just Us Books, among others.

APL strives to strike a balance between bestsellers, educational items, and lesser-known works that have received critical acclaim. In media collections, APL collects a range of blockbuster movies, independent films, and foreign films.

Donated materials are held to the same criteria that determine the purchase of new items. All items not added to the collection will be placed for sale by the Friends of the Anytown Public Library Bookstore, and all proceeds from the sale of these items will go into APL's general fund. APL regrets that it cannot guarantee that donated items will be added and that the library cannot commit to contacting the donor should the item be weeded or otherwise removed from the collection.

To the greatest extent possible, the collection development policy should address the criteria and guidelines that librarians use in examining the subject matter of materials, which may include measures such as appropriateness, interest to the community, and quality (ALA OIF, 2015). This may be done by explaining how librarians use review sources, suggestions for purchase, and bestseller lists in their collection development activities. This allows community members to understand how librarians go about making selection decisions.

An explanation of how the library handles donations belongs in this section as well. Donated materials should always be held to the same requirements as those purchased (ALA OIF, 2015).

Special Collections

If a public library houses any specialized collections, such as a local history collection, a photo archive, donated items of interest, or other unique resources, note should be made of this. If the library accepts donations to add to the special collection, information should be offered about how to donate and what the criteria are for adding donated items (Disher, 2007).

SAMPLE WORDING OF SPECIAL COLLECTIONS

APL offers a collection of books, newspapers, articles, photographs, and physical objects relating to the history of the Anytown area. These items are housed in the local history room and cannot be checked out, although photocopies may be made of print sources with the assistance of a librarian.

APL accepts donations of local history objects, but regrets that not all donations will necessarily be added to the collection. Please contact the Local History Librarian if you are interested in donating to the collection.

APL keeps records of who has donated items to the local history collection and will return any items that are deselected or requested to be given back. Please keep us informed of any contact information changes so this information can remain current.

How to Make Requests

Should a patron wish to request that a specific item be purchased, the process for doing so may be stated here (ALA OIF, 2015), along with an explanation that all requests will be considered in light of the collection development policy, and that while each request will be given full consideration, no guarantees can be made that all requests will be purchased.

SAMPLE WORDING OF HOW TO MAKE REQUESTS

APL accepts suggestions for purchase, and attempts to provide as many requested titles as possible in order to meet community desires. Requests for purchase forms are available at all APL service desks, as well as on the APL website.

APL strongly encourages Anytown residents to make their desires known through the use of this form, or by speaking directly with the library staff. While APL takes every request for purchase seriously, it regrets that it cannot purchase every request. The same criteria that determine the purchase of new items applies to requested items. APL staff will consult a wide variety of review sources in determining which requests to purchase.

Controversial Materials

Including a section on controversial materials can be very helpful in anticipating and preventing challenges. A statement addressing the fact that materials reflecting a range of viewpoints is necessary for a comprehensive collection serving the community in all its areas is certainly warranted in this section, as is a declaration about the tenets of intellectual freedom and the First Amendment and the Library Bill of rights (ALA, 2013b; ALA OIF, 2015), plus an assertion of the library's commitment to inclusiveness. Statements like these make it crystal clear that the library holds itself responsible to work within its professional and legal parameters, and that its policies are based on standards of legality and professional excellence, not merely whims or individually held opinions.

SAMPLE WORDING OF CONTROVERSIAL MATERIALS STATEMENT

APL believes that public libraries are responsible for creating comprehensive collections through the collection of materials that reflect a range of opinions, viewpoints, and interests. Therefore, library users may occasionally find materials that they find controversial or contentious on the shelves. The Library Bill of Rights states that library materials should not be withheld from collections due to disapproval, and that free expression of a variety of ideas should be represented in collections. APL strives to create balance in its collections in order to support intellectual freedom and to facilitate the free exchange of ideas, a central theme of democracy.

APL strives to achieve inclusiveness in all areas of its collection. Therefore, materials can reasonably be expected to reflect a wide range of political, religious, social, and sexual stances. Doing so allows APL to serve all segments of its community equally. APL selectors do not necessarily endorse the ideas in every item in the collection, nor is it expected that library users will endorse or agree with every idea contained in every item. APL strives for balance and diversity above all.

Collection Maintenance and Weeding

A short section on weeding is recommended, as community members sometimes become concerned or upset if they can't locate an item that had been previously held in their public library. This section should explain the criteria used in weeding, such as wear and tear, being outdated, and being duplicated by either a newer edition or lack of circulation. This part of the policy should also explain what happens to items once they are weeded and deleted from the catalog—for example, they may be sold, thrown away, recycled, or donated to other libraries or agencies (Disher, 2007).

SAMPLE WORDING OF COLLECTION MAINTENANCE AND WEEDING STATEMENT

APL maintains its collection regularly and occasionally deletes items from its collection due to circumstances such as wear and tear, lack of current relevance or accuracy, and low circulation rates. Whenever possible, APL strives to update items with newer editions or newer items with similar themes.

Items deselected from APL's collection are sold at the Friends of the Anytown Public Library Bookstore whenever possible. Items that are in such poor condition that they cannot be repaired are recycled whenever possible and discarded if recycling is not an option. Items that have gone unsold in the bookstore for more than two years are donated to the Anytown State Prison and/or the Anytown Juvenile Detention Center.

Handling of Complaints and Challenges

A quality collection development policy must also address how the library handles community challenges. Ideally, the policy should include a statement of commitment to respond to challenges with the utmost courtesy and consideration, making it clear that any and all feedback is welcomed (ALA OIF, 2015) but also reiterate the principles of intellectual freedom, the First Amendment, and the Library Bill of Rights, in order to establish that any reconsideration efforts will be undertaken under that lens (ALA, 2013b). The correct course of action should be provided on how to proceed if a discussion with a librarian or manager fails to satisfy a complainant's concerns. For most library systems, this will include providing the complainant with a copy of the selection policy and a verbal or written explanation of the library's selection procedures, as well as a Request for Reconsideration Form for the complainant to fill out if so desired. A copy of this form should be included in this section (ALA OIF, 2015).

SAMPLE WORDING OF HOW THE LIBRARY HANDLES COMPLAINTS AND CHALLENGES

APL welcomes any feedback regarding its collection. Library users are encouraged to speak with library staff about material selection, intellectual freedom, the Library Bill of Rights, and complaints about certain materials. APL is committed to handling complaints and challenges with courtesy and professionalism.

Library users who have strong objections to certain items are invited to fill out a Request for Reconsideration Form. This form will be accompanied by a copy of APL's collection development policy, the Library Bill of Rights, the Freedom to Read Statement, and the Freedom to View Statement. Please be as objective and detailed as possible about how the item in question fails to meet APL's collection development criteria.

Please be advised that filling out a Request for Reconsideration Form will not result in the immediate removal of the item in question but rather will prompt a process of review and reflection in which the complainant will be invited to share more feedback in light of the collection development policy, the Library Bill of Rights, the First Amendment, and the tenets of intellectual freedom. APL does not remove items from its collection simply because an objection has been raised. All complaints and challenges will be handled with the utmost courtesy and consideration, using this policy as a guide.

The Importance of Regular Review and Revision

The work isn't done once a collection development policy is written. Regular review and revisions keep the policy dynamic and fresh and give everyone involved an opportunity to stay familiar with the reasons for creating a fair, balanced collection. Revision is also a chance to ask questions and clarify anything that may seem muddled (Selby, 2012). The IFC, in its guidelines regarding policies, recommends that any policy be reviewed at regular intervals by the governing body of the library as well as its legal counsel (ALA OIF, 2015).

COLLECTION DEVELOPMENT POLICY CHECKLIST

- Purpose of the Policy
  - Why this policy is in place.
  - What the community should know about the library's mission and the guidelines of public librarianship.
- Organizational Structure of the Library
  - Who, by title, is responsible for ordering what.
  - Revise this section whenever organizational changes are made.
- Collection Criteria
  - Explanation of guidelines and criteria selectors use when deciding what to purchase.
  - How donations are handled.
- Making Requests
  - How to go about making requests for purchase.
  - Explanation that not all requests are able to be honored.

- Controversial Materials
  - Explanation of the importance of representing varying viewpoints.
  - Statement of commitment to intellectual freedom and the Library Bill of Rights.
- Complaints and Challenges
  - All complaints and challenges will be met with respect and professionalism.
  - Complaints and challenges will be reviewed in light of librarianship's professional guidelines.
  - Information about how to move from complaint to formal challenge.
  - Copy of the Request for Reconsideration Form.

THE REQUEST FOR RECONSIDERATION FORM

While collection development policies must be clear and strongly written, the same holds true for the forms that accompany it—especially the Request for Reconsideration Form, sometimes called a Complaint Form or Challenge Form.

In most library systems, a complaint, which may or may not end in a formal challenge, is put into motion when a patron fills out the Request for Reconsideration Form and hands it over to a member of the library staff. Doing so indicates that the complainant finds the material disturbing in some way, wishes to have it reviewed, and hopes for action to be taken regarding its presence in the library.

The purpose of the form is to collect information about the complainant's concerns regarding the material in question and to formally move into action on reviewing the material (LaRue, 2007). As the form is received, it is important to remember to be gracious and thankful—after all, complainants are being actively involved and engaged with their library system (LaRue, 2007; Meraz, 2014). It is possible that complainants may be misguided when filling out the form, but they also very well may not be. This is a time to be polite and calm and to let complainants know that their requests will be handled with the utmost consideration (ALA OIF, 2015).

When giving the form to a complainant, it is advisable to also provide a copy of the library's collection development policy, and, if it feels appropriate, to offer a short explanation, in print or in words, of the library's selection procedures (ALA OIF, 2015). This allows the complainant to have all the information needed to fill out the form in an informed manner.

The wording of the Request for Reconsideration Form ideally consists of neutral language and objective questions, and the questions should direct the complainant to explain how the material in question fails to meet the library's collection development policy, the First Amendment, and the Library Bill of Rights (ALA OIF, 2010). This makes it clear to the complainant that simply disliking the item is a different matter than objecting to it on the grounds that it does not fit within the library's collection.

Depending on the complainant's tone and mood, the time at which the form is handed over may or may not be a good time to initiate a conversation. At any rate, both the tone of the employee providing the form and the language contained within it should encourage the complainant to also use objective, unemotional language. This establishes that filling out the form is a formal procedure and will be taken seriously (Preer, 2014).

SAMPLE WORDING OF THE REQUEST FOR RECONSIDERATION FORM

Anytown Public Library supports intellectual freedom and strives to provide an inclusive, diverse collection representing a wide range of opinions, viewpoints, and beliefs. It is the expectation of APL that any complaints and challenges refer directly to the collection development policy, the Library Bill of Rights, and either the Freedom to Read Statement or the Freedom to View Statement, all of which are included with this form for your convenience. APL recommends that these be read thoroughly before this form is filled out, as complaints and challenges will be assessed in light of the tenets presented in these documents. Please note that this form may become part of the public record.

Please note that anonymously submitted Request for Reconsideration Forms, phone calls, or e-mails will not generate a response from APL.

Name _____

Address _____

City _____ State _____ Zip Code _____

Phone _____

E-mail _____

I am filling this out as _____ an individual; _____ as part of an organized group

Name of group, if applicable _____

Contact information of group, if applicable _____

Type of material in question:

Book ___ Movie ___ Video game ___ Magazine ___ Newspaper ___ Library event ___ Music CD ___ Downloadable eBook ___ Downloadable audiobook ___ Downloadable music ___ Other (please specify) ___

In which area was the item or event located?

Adult _____ Young Adult _____ Children's _____

Name of material _____

Author, editor, or producer _____

Have you examined this item or event in its entirety? Yes _____ No _____

What are your concerns about this item or event? _____

In what way(s) do you feel this item or event violates APL's collection development policy? _____

In what way(s) do you feel this item or event violates the Library Bill of Rights? _____

In what way(s) do you feel this item or event violates either the Freedom to Read Statement or the Freedom to View Statement? _____

Can you recommend any items or events that would provide a counterbalance to your objections to this item or event? _____

Please understand that all Requests for Reconsideration will be treated with the utmost respect and courtesy. You will be contacted by a library official within one week of submitting this form to discuss your concerns in greater detail.

Statement on Intellectual Freedom

It is recommended that a statement on basic intellectual freedom tenets be included at the top of the Request for Reconsideration Form in order to set a tone of objectivity and to remind complainants that their concerns will be seriously considered within the parameters of the library's guiding principles (LaRue, 2007). This statement can be educational to complainants as well, as it can help guide their answers and avoid having to re-clarify any statements.

Contact Information

The Request for Reconsideration Form should identify who the complainant is and how she wishes to be contacted. It is not advisable to allow anonymous forms, as this only diminishes the seriousness of the procedure and does not allow for any quality follow-up (Preer, 2004). It should also be noted that no response will be provided for rumors, anonymous phone calls or e-mails, or for voiced complaints with no formal written follow-up (ALA, 2013d). Asking if the complainant is filing the form as a single party or part of an organization is recommended as well, as this allows the library staff to know the nature of the complainant or complainants. What begins as an individual filling out a form can often blossom into a public debate with a pressure group—so the more the library staff knows about the group, the better prepared they will be (Evans & Saponaro, 2005; Evans & Saponaro, 2012). Additionally, if the form is being filled out on behalf of an organization, it should include instructions to provide that organization's contact information, so they may be reached for questions and clarification (ALA, 2013d; LaRue, 2007).

Type of Material in Question

This next portion of the form asks, usually in the style of a questionnaire in which the complainant checks off all elements that apply, if the material to which the complainant objects is a book, magazine, DVD, or library program and whether it is an adult, teen, or children's resource (ALA, 2013d; ALA OIF, 2015). On an individual library level, of course, these questions should be based on the types of materials and departments the library offers.

Objections to the Material

From here out, questions should focus heavily on policy and not on political, religious, or other personal viewpoints. Questions such as "Have you examined this material as a whole, and if not, what specific parts have you examined?" and "What specifically about this material do you find offensive in regard to the library's collection development policy?" and "What do you feel is the main theme of this material?" steer complainants toward objectivity in their answers, and reiterate the importance of examining the material in its full context. Other recommended inquiries include asking if complainants are aware of any reviews of the material, if they would recommend any similarly themed materials to counterbalance their objections to the one in question, and if they find anything positive in the material (ALA, 2013d; LaRue, 2007).

The tone of the Request for Reconsideration Form, while respectful and genuinely curious, should focus heavily on policies and intellectual freedom tenets, not on the complainant's personal objections or beliefs. The overriding question is not why the complainant is offended by the item, but in what ways it fails to meet the criteria of the library's collection development policy, the tenets of the Library Bill of Rights, or the standards of the First Amendment.

Of course, keeping the language of the form objective and impersonal won't necessarily prevent a complainant from answering the questions in religious or political terms. People hold a wide variety of belief systems, and they often spill over into their beliefs about what types of materials public libraries should offer. Therefore, if a complainant's answers indicate an alliance with a certain political or religious group, it may be a good idea to study up a bit about that group in order to ensure respectful, tactful communication in future communications.

RESPONSIBILITY GOES BOTH WAYS

None of what is written earlier is meant to imply that patrons should refrain from following through on challenges. The goal is not to convince patrons that their concerns are faulty but simply to provide an explanation of both the individual library's policy and the professional and legal guidelines that shape it.

In the end, when a book or other item is formally challenged, it becomes the responsibility of the complainant to understand the library's collection development policy and the Library Bill of Rights. The burden is on the challenger—not the challenged—to prove that the item in question violates the parameters of at least one of these policies (Preer, 2014). The patron may, in fact, be completely correct that the item actually does violate these parameters—and, in that case, it becomes the library's responsibility to correct the problem—but unless that happens, the item must not be removed or relocated. The guiding issue is not that someone is offended, but how the offending item fails to fall under the protection of specifically stated policies. A challenge also does not necessarily require a meeting with the board of trustees or even library management personnel. Often, an assigned librarian can smooth out the issue with the offended party in a respectful way that satisfies everyone. For example, if a parent files a complaint about a children's book, a meeting between just the parent and a children's librarian might be more appropriate than a large meeting with the director and members of the board. Often, the more people and opinions there are in a room, the more tensions flare up and arguments escalate. Keeping the conversation simple, straightforward, and informational can yield positive results and often leaves both parties content with the outcome (Preer, 2014).

CHALLENGES AND RESPONSIBILITIES

In the case of a challenge to a library item, the burden of proof lies with the challenger, not with the library being challenged. Simply not liking or approving of an item in the collection is not reason to remove it. The challenger must be given every opportunity to understand that the item will be examined under the lens of the collection development policy, the Library Bill of Rights, the First Amendment, and either the Freedom to Read Statement or the Freedom to View Statement. This reality must be made clear both on the Request for Reconsideration Form and in person when library staff members speak to patrons about their concerns. There may be times when the challenged item truly does not meet the parameters of the collection development policy and the library must act accordingly when this happens. On the other hand, complaints are sometimes based simply on the challenger's belief system, opinions, or ideas. In cases like these, when the item does indeed meet the stated criteria, there is no objective reason to remove it from the collection, hide it behind barriers, or apply a label to it. Challenges may feel intimidating, but remember—the burden of proof is on the complainant.

TRAINING AND EMPOWERING STAFF

In a public library setting, regular training on the collection development policy for all employees is essential, as is empowering staff members to speak with complainants in a respectful and confident manner before simply handing over a Request for Reconsideration Form or calling a supervisor (unless this is clearly what the complainant wants). If the management of a public library can't or won't trust its front-line employees to speak with patrons about difficult issues, then there is really no point in training them at all. While facing an angry, disappointed, or hostile patron and having a difficult conversation in a calm manner is probably nobody's idea of a pleasant time, handling confrontation in a professional manner is part of the job. Wishing not to have to deal with confrontation is normal and human, but when front-line employees are supported and given the freedom to use their voices for the overall good of the profession, an important service is being done to both the employees of the library and the public they serve (Pinnell-Stephens, 2012).

It has been reported that up to 90 percent of challenges that begin at the reference desk never go any further than there, due to librarians' and other library employees' respectful communication skills and understanding of their collection development policies, as well as how to explain these in the form of a conversation, rather than an argument or debate (Pinnell-Stephens, 2012). With quality ongoing training and support, front-line librarians and other library employees can do a great deal to quell patrons' concerns and help them manage their upset feelings productively. While there will certainly be times when it's advisable to call a supervisor or give the patron a Request for Reconsideration Form, these actions do not necessarily need to be the first things library employees pull from their bag of tricks.

When patrons are concerned or upset about a library item, they tend to speak first to whoever is present at a service desk. This could be a librarian, a library assistant, a clerk, or anyone else involved with the library. Unless a patron begins the conversation by insisting that a supervisor be contacted right away, doing so will likely only add to that patron's frustration. The same goes for simply handing over a Request for Reconsideration Form. While both contacting a supervisor and giving a patron a form may end up being necessary actions, both can appear uncaring and even outright rude to patrons who simply want someone to listen to them explain why they are upset and empathize with their situation (Evans & Saponaro, 2005).

Being familiar with the library's policy is necessary for all employees, as is training on communication skills, diffusing high-conflict situations, and active listening. Some libraries develop their own staff training programs, and others use outside trainers, either in person or online. Either way, some common helpful elements of staff training include group role-playing of difficult patron interactions, going over agreed-upon processes of communication methods and talking points to employ when faced with angry patrons. Even having written statements posted at service desks with such phrases as "Thank you for bringing this to my attention" and "Can you tell me a bit more about your concern?" can help employees feel more comfortable and supported in difficult interactions (Disher, 2007).

A quality staff training program serves to help front-line library employees gain the competence and confidence to maintain sound customer service skills even when confronted by irate patrons. It should also address intellectual freedom issues and help employees understand how these issues influence their everyday work as public library staff members. Unfortunately, this is an area in which many library support staff feel that they need more training and support from their management (Osa, 2002). The more library employees understand about intellectual freedom, and the more supported they feel by their library's management, the easier it will be for them to engage in constructive conversations with library users about their collection development policy and the tenets that shape it (Pearsall, 2014).

It is very helpful for library directors and other members of the management team to attend training with their employees. Although this may seem obvious, employees are often sent to training sessions or to view webinars at their desks, while the management team stays behind and doesn't take part. Participating in the training allows employees to discuss their concerns with their higher-ups and goes a long way toward establishing a sense of teamwork and cooperation (Pearsall, 2014).

ELEMENTS OF A QUALITY STAFF TRAINING PROGRAM FOR HANDLING COMPLAINTS

- The collection development policy guides staff training—all employees should be made familiar with the details of the policy first and foremost.
- Build competence and trust by letting your staff know with your words and actions that you are there for them, but that you also trust their expertise— avoid the extremes of micromanaging or being overly absent.
- Emphasize active listening skills and methods of diffusing tense situations such as paraphrasing the complainant's concern, avoiding defensiveness, and remembering not to take the complaint personally (for more in-depth information on active listening, see Chapter 9).
- What begins as a complaint might escalate into a situation in which some- one feels threatened—if this happens, remember that the safety of yourself and your employees is essential, and either step in or call for help from law enforcement if necessary.
- Repeat, repeat, repeat—one training session is good, a series is better, and ongoing training is best.

There may be times when the concepts taught in training or written in the collection development policy will clash with an employee's personal beliefs. The key issue here is that while self-censorship is never an acceptable method of handling discomfort, employees must be supported and valued as long as they are able to hold their personal feelings at bay in deference to the defense of free access (Pearsall, 2014). Make no mistake—this can be a hard thing to do. It can be uncomfortable for library staff members to defend books or other items they don't personally approve of, but ultimately this discomfort can help in understanding and empathizing with patrons who voice their complaints about library collections. It seems fair to say that most librarians, in the process of their collection development tasks, will purchase books by authors whose politics or ideas they don't agree with or that contain content they find distasteful. If personal feelings cannot be set aside at these times, it will prove difficult indeed to engage in collection development fairly and objectively in the long run.

The bottom line when it comes to training and empowering staff to handle complaints is to maintain an attitude of respect toward complainants, who certainly have every right to voice their concerns about the collection at their public library. This doesn't mean that the library will forfeit or lose the challenge—it simply means that customer service skills and professionalism must be maintained even under great pressure.

Educating Other Stakeholders

Other than front-line library staff such as reference librarians, who should receive training on collection development policies and procedures? The answer will vary from library to library, but it is usually agreed that higher-ups such as library board members, Friends of the Library volunteers, and foundation members should receive regularly scheduled educational opportunities about the policies of the system they have chosen to support. At the absolute least, trustees should certainly be expected to review and approve any policy (ALA OIF, 2015), but, beyond that, it is advisable to offer ongoing training to these laypeople who care enough to use their valuable time to support their library, but who rarely have received any formal training on the professional guidelines and legalities of librarianship (ALA, 2013a). Trustees and other groups involved in the running of the library need to understand from the get-go that they might sometimes have to put their own discomforts aside during a challenge in order to support the organization they have chosen to represent (Preer, 2014). In-depth training involving vignettes and role-playing activities can be valuable training exercises for these groups (Evans & Saponaro, 2012).

Board members may elect to write their own intellectual freedom statements, or they might wish to refer to the First Amendment, the Freedom to Read Statement, and the Library Bill of Rights as their formally accepted guidelines on the issue. They may also wish to assist librarians in helping to spread the word about intellectual freedom to city council members and other elected officials, as well as community organizations and potential allies, as this is a wise way of gaining experience with discussing intellectual freedom before a challenge occurs, thus making it easier to speak on the issue while under pressure (Preer, 2014).

Because laypersons make up the trustees on public library boards, it can be very helpful for them to undergo specific training on their particular library's policies, and they must understand that there may be times in which their personal feelings will have to be set aside in order to implement those policies. A thorough understanding of intellectual freedom can reasonably be expected to be a requirement of library board members. The responsibility of understanding that policy trumps personal feelings falls to the trustees as well as the library staff and is most effective when training on the issue is ongoing and dynamic in nature. Involving trustees with the initial writing and regularly scheduled rewriting of the collection development policy, as well as similar policies of their own, can go a long way toward developing mutual understanding and support of intellectual freedom issues. Making use of surveys and face-to-face discussions with community members about intellectual freedom issues can be helpful as well. Simply put, the more the community is involved in the development of library policy, the lower the risk of difficult challenges cropping up (Preer, 2014).

KEEP YOUR ALLIES CLOSE AND CONNECTED

The more a community is involved with its public library's collection development policy, the greater the chances are of that community coming to the aid of its library when a challenge occurs. Involving trustees, volunteers, Friends of the Library groups, government officials, patrons, and other allies in the process of creating the collection development policy is a form of insurance against challenges. Creating a policy cannot be done well without having discussions about intellectual freedom. The more your community understands the tenets of intellectual freedom, the more support you will have if a challenge is issued.

The more a community's members and representatives know about their public library's intellectual freedom stance and collection development policy, the better off that library will be if a challenge should occur. It's never too soon to educate the public and other allies on this topic, but the longer it is put off, the more likely it is that it will eventually become too late.

PROFESSIONAL RESOURCES

Policy writing and staff training may seem like daunting tasks, but plenty of professional resources exist to make the process simpler.

The ALA and Office for Intellectual Freedom (OIF) offer a Web page called Essential Preparation, which offers a wealth of information on dealing with complaints. Information is provided about the common motives of censors and how to address them sensitively and responsibly. There is even a workbook to use in writing a collection development policy (ALA, 2013c).

The ALA also offers helpful checklists to use when speaking with library board members, Friends of the Library groups, elected officials and their employees, and local media, as well as allies and citizen groups who could potentially become allies (ALA, 2013d).

The latest edition of the OIF's *Intellectual Freedom Manual* provides policy checklists for both general collection development and for the reconsideration of challenged materials (ALA OIF, 2015).

CONCLUSION AND FURTHER THINKING

When it comes to community challenges, prevention is the key. Writing a strong collection development policy and regularly revisiting and revising it may be time-consuming, but should a challenge come along, it will have been time well spent.

Policy writing is as much a science as it is an art. Using checklists and other professional resources makes the task simpler. A little research goes a long way when it comes to writing a quality collection development policy.

Public library patrons have every right to express their concerns about items they find objectionable. There is no sense in arguing, becoming defensive, or pulling the item in question from the shelf without a formal review process. Oftentimes, a concern is simply that—a concern that goes no further. Part of a librarian's responsibility is to listen actively and with attention. Politeness and understanding often tamp down a complaint and ultimately avoid the occurrence of a formal challenge.

That being said, challenges do happen. Being prepared, having a strong policy, a well-trained staff, and supportive trustees and other allies is excellent prevention for a challenge getting out of control.

Staff training is essential in preventing challenges. Employees of all ranks who feel empowered and trusted through ongoing, quality training will feel more at ease speaking with upset patrons, and they can often stop a challenge right there at the source. While help should be available in the case of a very upset patron, confidence in your employees is also of the essence.

TIPS AND TRAPS: PREVENTING CHALLENGES THROUGH KNOWLEDGE AND POLICY

Tips

- Education of library employees and stakeholders on the collection development policy must be dynamic and ongoing—the more empowered your employees feel, the better off everyone will be in the case of a complaint.
- If you are a supervisor or manager, don't just send your employees to a training session—go with them to provide your support and solidarity.
- Use the checklists provided by the ALA to help with policy writing—there is no need to reinvent the wheel.

Traps

- Writing a strong policy is only the first step in an ongoing process—if you get too busy to revisit and revise the policy with your staff, your team is likely become less familiar with it as time goes by.

- Your patrons have every right to voice their concerns about items in the collection and to be listened to with respect, but removing an item from the collection without any formal proceedings is a form of censoring it—remember to follow the proper channels.

- Don't forget to involve trustees, volunteers, Friends of the Library groups, and members of your local governing body in the creation of your policies—they are part of your team, and the more they're involved, the more allies you have.

WHAT WOULD YOU DO?

As the director of a small public library, Adam was very proud of the collection development policy he wrote. When he took the job, he found an old, outdated policy manual that nobody seemed to pay much attention to. Noting this, Adam made it his first task to write a new policy highlighting intellectual freedom, the Library Bill of Rights, and the First Amendment. He also put together a Request for Reconsideration Form and placed copies of it at all the service desks in the library.

When Adam was finished with his project, he sent a group e-mail to all the library employees and trustees, asking them to read and memorize it, and he put a printed copy in the employee conference room, in a binder with the other library policies.

A few months later, one of Adam's reference librarians, Shelly, came to his office very upset. A patron had complained about a book in the children's section of the library, saying it was obscene and completely inappropriate for a public library. The patron was waiting in the children's room to speak to the director.

"Why didn't you talk about our policy with him first?" Adam asked. Shelly looked confused. "What policy?" Adam rolled his eyes in frustration. Didn't anyone around here bother to read their e-mails? "The policy I sent out months ago," he told Shelly. "Didn't you read it?"

Shelly remembered the e-mail but not very many details about it. She had read it in a hurry when it first came out, but that was the last she'd heard about it. Adam went to the conference room to get Shelly the policy manual and instructed her to read it while he spoke with the patron. Looking through the policy, Shelly realized that she could have handled the irate patron in a better manner, but she felt unsupported by Adam. If it was so important to him, why didn't he make it clear to everyone that they should familiarize themselves with it to the point of near-memorization?

In her next performance review, Shelly got dinged for not knowing the collection development policy well enough. She protested, saying she certainly wasn't the only one who didn't know it was meant to be as important to everyone else at the library as it was to Adam. "It wasn't even discussed at a staff meeting or anything," she said. "One little e-mail doesn't change the way we've done things here for years."

Adam was still frustrated with Shelly, but he had to admit that her words rang true. Perhaps he had been so busy with his new position that he forgot that policy writing is just one step in getting his staff up to speed. After their meeting ended, he took a deep breath and began to think about how to work with his employees in a more supportive way.

QUESTIONS TO CONSIDER

- As a library patron, have you ever found an item in your public library that you found objectionable or that you felt didn't belong in the collection? If so, did you do anything about it? Why or why not?

- What are a few communication-based alternatives to immediately calling a supervisor or handing over a Request for Reconsideration Form to a patron who objects to an item in the collection?

- As a supervisor, if you saw an employee being berated by a patron and felt concerned for her safety, how would you intervene?

- As a librarian, if a trustee, volunteer, or government official expressed confusion about the collection development policy, what steps would you take to help clarify it?

- What professional resources would you turn to if you were tasked with writing or revising your library's collection development policy or Request for Reconsideration Form?

REFERENCES

American Library Association. (2013a, March 26). Checklist & ideas for library staff working with community leaders. Retrieved from http://www.ala.org/bbooks/challengedmaterials/preparation/checklist

American Library Association. (2013b, March 26). Dealing with concerns about library resources. Retrieved from http://www.ala.org/bbooks/challengedmaterials/preparation/dealing-concerns

American Library Association. (2013c, March 26). Essential preparation. Retrieved from http://www.ala.org/bbooks/challengedmaterials/preparation

American Library Association. (2013d, March 26). Sample request for reconsideration of library resources. Retrieved from http://www.ala.org/bbooks/challengedmaterials/support/samplereconsideration

American Library Association Office for Intellectual Freedom. (2010). *Intellectual freedom manual*. Chicago: American Library Association.

American Library Association Office for Intellectual Freedom. (2015). *Intellectual freedom manual*. Chicago: ALA Editions, an imprint of the American Library Association.

Disher, W. (2007). *Crash course in collection development*. Westport, CT: Libraries Unlimited.

Evans, G. E., & Saponaro, M. Z. (2005). *Developing library and information center collections*. Westport, CT: Libraries Unlimited.

Evans, G. E., & Saponaro, M. Z. (2012). *Collection management basics*. Santa Barbara, CA: Libraries Unlimited.

LaRue, J. (2007). *The new inquisition: Understanding and managing intellectual freedom challenges.* Westport, CT: Libraries Unlimited.

Meraz, G. (2014). BANNED BOOKS: "We believe in an educated citizenry." *Texas Library Journal, 90*(3), 100–102.

Osa, J. O. (2002). The difficult patron situation: A competency-based training to empower frontline staff. *Reference Librarian,* (75/76), 263–276.

Pearsall, D. (2014). An interview with an intellectual freedom training whiz: King County Library System's Catherine Lord. *Alki, 30*(3), 6–7.

Pinnell-Stephens, J. (2012). *Protecting intellectual freedom in your public library.* Chicago: American Library Association.

Preer, J. (2014). Prepare to be challenged! *Library Trends, 62*(4), 759–770.

Selby, C. (2012). Honesty is the best policy: Collection development policy revisions in an era of change. *AALL Spectrum, 16*(4), 6–7.

Chapter 6

GETTING TO KNOW YOUR COMMUNITY: FACTS, FIGURES, AND ASSUMPTIONS

COMMUNITY NEEDS ASSESSMENTS AND PUBLIC LIBRARIES

Back in the early days of American public libraries, obtaining information about libraries' surrounding communities was simple—perhaps overly so, at least by today's standards. In 1904, the American Library Association (ALA) characterized communities as the librarians and book-buyers living within a certain geographic area, and it published a booklist known as the *ALA Catalog* as a guide for collection development activities, regardless of the uniqueness of communities (Huynh, 2004). This may sound elitist to modern sensibilities, but at the time, librarians were considered the voice of their communities, and they were tasked with deciding what was best for their public, with help and guidance from the ALA. Reaching out to the community and asking members what they would like was not considered particularly appropriate, and censorship concerns rarely surfaced.

Times have changed indeed. These days, one would be hard-pressed to find a public library system that has not undergone some form of community assessment. After all, how better to know and best serve a community than to actively seek out information about the wants and needs of its members? A quality community assessment provides valuable information on how to meet the needs of as many community members as possible, while still reaching out to those who could make better use of its services with a few tweaks and changes. Everything from service hours to space issues to collection budgets can be determined in part by community assessment results (Evans & Soponaro, 2000).

This chapter does not purport to teach the reader all the details and nuances of conducting a community assessment, as many resources to deal with this topic can be found with a simple Web search. Rather, it is meant to serve as an overview of assessment procedures in light of the importance of supporting and servicing a community in its entirety, while keeping alert to censorship and intellectual freedom concerns.

People and Communities: The Simple and the Complex

A community, put simply, is a group of people living, learning, working, or playing within a common geographic area (Disher, 2007). Geography itself can determine quite a lot. For example, a community in which the majority of people or families own a home and where the median price of a single-family house is $500,000 is bound to have more wealthy folks than a community largely made up of renters and with a median house price of $150,000. Looking at communities this way helps to make things simple, and yet it may cloud judgment if one comes to believe that *more* or *most* equals *all* and goes about running a library with this mind-set. While it's certainly true that more well-off people live in rich areas, and more struggling people live in poor areas, it is important to keep in mind that every majority has its mirror minority—or more likely, a group of subcommunities and individuals who do not fit cleanly into the overall snapshot of the community.

When conducting a community assessment, one must, of course, become familiar with the majority, as they will be the ones making the most of the public library's services, but it is imperative to remember to equally acknowledge the various sub-demographics. It has been said by many a library school instructor that the perfect library is one with nothing on the shelves—a library with the right book for every patron and the right patron for every book. As unlikely as this romanticized scenario is to occur at all, except perhaps in the tiniest of libraries serving the tiniest of communities, it most surely can never stand a chance of even coming close to happening without a range of materials designed for a range of individuals—standard and not-so-standard, majority and minority, average and distinctive individuals whose common interests and wonderful quirks make up a true community. To disregard less-represented groups and subcommunities is to do a disservice to the community, as collections and programs will reflect the needs of the majority. If librarians go about their collection development activities with predominantly the needs of the majority in mind, self-censorship is very likely to come into play, resulting in a skewed, censorious collection.

Public libraries conduct community assessments for a variety of reasons. The most common, certainly, is to get a grasp on the wants and needs of the library's surrounding population in order to provide services that will best meet those desires. Often, these assessments are created and conducted by the library staff, although outsourcing the task to hired consultants has become quite common in recent years (Kyrillidou, 2005). Even when libraries conduct their own assessments, there are many professional tools and certifications that may be utilized. The ALA recently launched the Libraries Transforming Communities initiative in order to provide libraries with new assessment materials and protocols and to strengthen libraries' understanding and engagement with the communities they serve (ALA, 2013). The steps and actions involved in the Libraries Transforming Communities initiative can serve as valuable tools for do-it-yourself library assessments.

BACK TO BASICS: THE COLLECTION DEVELOPMENT POLICY

Starting off with a clearly written, up-to-date collection development policy goes a long way toward using community assessment results wisely and fairly. When libraries of any size rely on staff to order materials without the benefit of a shared framework and common set of goals, the odds of bias and confusion inevitably become much greater. A collection development policy ideally should also be a public document—after all, it was generated by the data provided by the public—in order to help the community understand assessment results and library goals. The collection development policy must also be dynamic. As communities change, policies need to change along with them (Disher, 2007).

Transparency is the key to a quality, solid collection development policy. Should a situation arise in which library staff are at all worried about having to show their collection development policy to any member of the community, it's a clear sign that the policy is in need of attention. It may be outdated, unclear, or slanted. The wants, needs, and desires of a community member who represents the majority demographic will ideally be represented in the policy with as much significance as those of members of subcommunities or outliers who for whatever reason do not fit into the mainstream, and the reasons for this should be clear as well—to strive for balance in collections and to reach out to all segments of the community, both majority and minority.

Types of Data Involved in an Assessment

While data is often perceived as hard-and-fast numbers or facts, true data comes in many varieties, from statistics to anecdotes noted in conversations or while wandering through the community (Disher, 2007). As important as it is to look at census figures, circulation statistics, and program attendance numbers, it is equally valuable to remain alert to both long-standing norms and new changes within a library's service population.

Wants, Needs, and Demands

Needs are situations that provide solutions to problems (Evans & Saponaro, 2012). For example, if a significant amount of community members share that they are out of work and don't understand how to write a resume or apply for jobs in an online environment, then these services would be classified as a need.

Wants are things that community members are prepared to spend time, money, or effort to obtain (Evans & Soporano, 2012). While a weekly children's story-time may not be something a person absolutely needs, it could be something that person would be willing to stand in line for or cancel other plans for, thus making it a want.

Lastly, demands are things that community members are willing to fight for (Evans & Soporano, 2012). A quality LGBT (lesbian, gay, bisexual, and transgender) collection or increased hours in order for high school students to be able to complete their homework could be classified as demands, if community members felt strongly enough about these things to engage in actions such as writing letters or holding protests.

Program Attendance Statistics

Developing programs people enjoy and come back to is part of what public librarians do. There are a few pitfalls in this area, though, to be alert to. Creating impressive-sounding programs and events and generating abundant attendance statistics may look good in the short term, but it is also important to fit these programs into a wider service plan and the library's mission (Pakaln, 2014). For example, if the results of an assessment reveal that teens are not using the library as often as other public services such as parks and community centers, it might make sense to reach out to this demographic in order to find out what they would like from their library (and is not being offered elsewhere in the community) and then create programs to meet this need based on their answers and comments. This is scientific and measurable, making it a well-thought-out plan with outcomes tied into the library's greater mission. On the other hand, noting that there aren't as many teens at the library as there used to be and creating board game nights in an effort to bring them back, well-intentioned though this plan may be, is more of a shot in the dark than a scientific plan based on assessment results.

Census and Other Survey Information

Survey and census information allows it to be known approximately how many people live (although not necessarily how many work or play) in a service area, how many are children, teens, adults, or seniors, and what the gender breakdowns and language preferences are (Disher, 2007).

Socioeconomic factors such as salary averages, house prices, family sizes, and languages spoken in the home can reveal a great deal about the members of libraries' communities as well, as can information about average education levels of adults, as these facts will help determine such things as standard reading levels of adults, and whether collections of materials in other languages are warranted. These statistics allow for a greater understanding of the overriding socioeconomic norms of the community (Disher, 2007).

Of course, when analyzing survey data, it is important to remain alert to the fact that these socioeconomic factors apply only to those in the majority of the community. A largely blue-collar town in which 75 percent of residents have no formal education beyond high school still has a quarter of its adult population with other educational statistics—both lower and higher, most likely. Looking at this data as well as that reflecting the majority's status is bound to reveal some unexpected surprises.

Analytics and Geographic Information Systems

The digital age has brought about new technologies that can be used to collect information about communities. For example, many public libraries have begun to use geographic information systems (GIS)-derived data to map out where their card-holders live within the greater community, analyzing neighborhood by neighborhood who uses the library and who doesn't, and where greater efforts to promote library services may be needed (LaRue, 2007).

Library-specific analytics software such as Gale's Analytics on Demand combines community data with circulation data, generating an overall picture of who is and isn't using the library. This helps with both bolstering services to existing patrons and reaching potential new patrons (Enis, 2014).

Circulation Statistics

Circulation data, being raw and simple in nature, can reveal important facts about the people in a community who already make use of their public library, and how. It cannot, however, reveal anything about those in the community who do not make use of the library, or why (Disher, 2007). Also, circulation statistics do not account for those who spend time at the library, but do not check out materials. A library may have several regular patrons who come for a variety of reasons other than to check out materials—for example, some may stop in to browse the newspaper, use the library's online databases, ask reference questions, or use public computers.

Anecdotal Data

Anecdotal data is not measurable, which makes it difficult to cite with confidence in assessment results, but its importance cannot be understated. Gained through observations and conversations, anecdotal data may serve as a clue as to what is missing in public library services (Disher, 2007). This type of information can come from both library users and nonusers. For example, a librarian may notice during day-to-day interactions that a pattern of patron complaints about reduced service hours has emerged, or perhaps that patrons are expressing gratitude about a beefed-up collection of audiobooks. This casual, informal data may not make it into a formalized assessment under normal circumstances, but it is important all the same.

Of course, it is not just active library users from whom anecdotal data may be gained. Reaching out to nonusers to ask them why they don't use their public library's services can provide a wealth of insightful information about how to better serve communities. This can be accomplished by such actions as sending surveys or questionnaires to nonusers, inviting them to be interviewed or to participate in focus groups in order to gain reportable data, and by engaging in observations and conversations while out and about in the community.

There is nothing scientific about anecdotal data, but it has an important place in the big picture of assessment. Gaining information can be done with something as simple as a suggestion box, as off-the-cuff as a casual conversation, or as difficult as a longitudinal study. In the end, it's all data, and it's all useful.

What's Censorship Got to Do with It?

Analyzing assessment results in order to better meet the public's wants, needs, and demands through collections, programs, and other means would be simple enough—if communities were simple enough. The desire to serve communities and the need to avoid censorship intersect in often-unexpected ways. For example, assessment questions about what the library is lacking, even what the library might seem to be avoiding, can reveal some surprising answers, especially from those who see their public library as a less-than-welcoming place. This type of feedback is invaluable when it comes to enhancing collections and working toward inclusivity.

Conversely, an assessment could reveal that some members of the community support or even encourage censorship, perhaps innocuously and perhaps in a discriminatory manner. Answers may come in suggesting that the library purchase fewer materials on certain subjects due to distaste or dislike of the subject matter. Dealing with pro-censorship feedback is tricky for any librarian—how can the public ethically be given what it wants when what it wants is censorship? One resolution might be to spend more time in conversation about intellectual freedom and the role of public libraries with community groups, partners, and the public at large. Another might be to strengthen the collection development policy to reflect a strong stance against censorship. Still another could be to consistently educate the entire staff on how to discuss censorship concerns with patrons as these concerns arise. Whatever approach is taken, communication and education must be front-and-center if the library intends to maintain its position as a place of democracy.

Public librarians, by and large, want to serve and please their communities—and this is a good thing. At the same time, education about anti-censorship efforts and intellectual freedom tenets is often part of the process. Discovering that many community members support censorious activities can be quite disheartening, but it is also a chance to open a dialogue and keep it going. The goal is to educate and discuss, not necessarily to convince people to change their convictions. Just as therapists are held to confidentiality agreements and teachers are held to act *in loco parentis*, librarians have professional responsibilities that extend beyond pleasing all people at all times. The promotion of intellectual freedom is part of the package of being a librarian.

BECOMING FAMILIAR WITH OTHER COMMUNITY SERVICES

When conducting a community assessment, it can be helpful to gather data from other community agencies and organizations. Knowing what other services are available to the community helps in planning and implementing services. Also, having a good amount of community information at hand helps with providing referrals to patrons finding themselves in need of services such as counseling, domestic violence help, homeless assistance, English as a second language education, and the like.

Another reason to become familiar with community resources is to avoid duplication of services. For example, while the idea of forming a book discussion group specifically for seniors might be exciting, this plan may need to be revisited if it is learned that the local senior center already offers book clubs. Perhaps, in a case like this, the library's time and effort would be better spent forming a partnership with the senior center.

DO-IT-YOURSELF VERSUS HIRING A CONSULTANT

Librarians are adept at knowing their communities, or at least those members of the community who visit the library and make use of its services. Knowing the community is part of the job, and it may be argued that those who know the community in this manner are better suited to conduct community assessments than outside consultants. Issues can easily crop up whether libraries do their own assessments or hire outside consultants to do the job for them. Being alert to these potential pitfalls is the best defense against falling victim to them.

When libraries conduct their own community assessments with the efforts of staff, volunteers, and community members, there is an automatic, inherent risk that conclusions will be made based on biases, knowingly or unknowingly. While the do-it-yourself approach saves money, conducting an assessment in-house takes a great deal of time, and may create issues with scheduling and service (Evans & Saponaro, 2000).

Hiring an outside consultant to conduct a community assessment may seem like a wise way to avoid these issues. While doing so helps ensure objectivity, it will likely take an outside party longer to understand the nuances of a community than it would for those who live and/or work there. Furthermore, it has been found that library employees tend to be more excited about the results of an assessment and more willing to make changes and implement new policies if they were involved in the research stage of the plan (Evans & Saponaro, 2000).

There is no right or wrong answer when it comes to deciding to do an assessment in-house or through hiring a consultant. Whichever method is utilized, however, it is essential to remain aware of the pros and cons of the chosen method. The more this can be accomplished, the more accurate and useful the assessment results will be.

THE PROS AND CONS OF OUTSOURCING

Pros:

- Allows library employees time to focus on their usual tasks and schedules.
- Aids in objectivity.
- Helps eliminate bias.

Cons:

- Takes longer for a consultant to grasp the nuances of the community.
- Monetary concerns—how much will the consultant be paid?
- Library employees tend to be more enthusiastic about initiating changes when they've been involved in gathering community information.

Remaining Objective

When library systems elect to conduct their own community assessments, they must be alert to their own biases. If there is any chance of fishing for information that serves a preexisting agenda, the results will almost certainly be skewed. The agenda may seem to be perfectly reasonable and even honorable, such as proving the library's worth to the community it serves, but knowing the intended answer before asking the questions is likely to create a self-fulfilling prophecy.

Staying neutral and unbiased is very difficult when budgets and reputations are at stake. The digital age brought about many changes in terms of how the public views public libraries. More than ever, libraries are expected to prove their worth as they compete with police and fire services, public schools, and other necessary services for public funding and support—and a community assessment is often the first step in accomplishing this (Kyrillidou, 2005).

Unlike corporations or private libraries, public libraries cannot go about proving their value through profit revenue or sales statistics. They tend to rely more on circulation statistics, program attendance, new memberships, and the like (Kyrillidou, 2005). However, there is an inherent danger in conducting a community assessment with the end goal of proving the library's worth. Assessment, when done purely and without prejudice, is an action that aims to obtain information through objective means, not to fit information subjectively into a preexisting framework. The intent of true assessment is to measure, not to prove a point—no matter how valuable that point may be.

Still, knowing how stakeholders and taxpayers can breathe down libraries' necks, how objective can librarians truly be about the communities they serve? Furthermore, how can they best serve all members of their communities when they know that what their stakeholders want to see is impressive numbers? It may help to keep in mind that, when done properly, community assessments open librarians' eyes to demographics and individuals they were previously unaware or under-aware of, and they help bring the concerns of these individuals and demographics into service plans and policies (McCleer, 2013). Knowing the community, and staying open to the possibility of being surprised by the community, ultimately helps the profession serve the greatest number of people in the most beneficial way possible. With this goal in mind, it's hard to go wrong when beginning with objective, strong assessments.

WELCOME TO WALMART PUBLIC LIBRARY

Public libraries typically rely on money generated from public funds like taxes to cover their expenses, but other funding sources are available as well. Especially in times of budget cuts, libraries tend to explore alternative sources of funding in order to develop new programs and services that can't be covered by their usual budget. When this happens, the library is often expected to conduct an assessment on the demographic the program will serve. This, of course, is wise, as it is important to know any subcommunities' wants, needs, and demands in order to best serve them. However, when assessments and money are intertwined, issues can arise—most notably a lack of objectivity and inclusiveness.

In the mid-2000s, the well-known retail corporation Walmart donated $1.6 million to libraries throughout northwest Arkansas in order to be of service to libraries suffering from lack of public funding. The much-needed money gave public libraries opportunities to expand on their children's services during the height of the recession. The city of Fayetteville received $300,000 and soon opened the new Walmart Story Time Room at its Blair Library. The Bentonville Public Library, which received $1 million, opened a new public library location, home to the Walmart Meeting Room for community events. The Benson Public Library, which received $300,000, built a new wing which housed the Walmart Children's Library (Oatman, 2005).

While the money Walmart donated was certainly well-intended and well-used, the naming of rooms after Walmart didn't sit well with everybody involved, and the obvious marketing Walmart received by having community rooms and services named after it added to the distaste (Oatman, 2005). The fact that Walmart has been known to refuse to carry certain books in their stores due to the corporation's disapproval of the material or artwork didn't help matters (Books: Bentonville, Arkansas, 2005).

Private money comes with expectations, be it the inclusion of a logo or name on a building, or a public endorsement of the corporation. Even when a community assessment isn't a condition of receiving private money, the discrepancy between public libraries and private corporations is enough to make library directors and trustees, not to mention community members, uneasy. What one person views as charitable philanthropy may be seen by someone else as inappropriate advertising in public places.

In the case of Walmart and other private donors, it may be tempting to think one must report back that the community appreciates the donor's contribution, and it might even be seen as appreciative to report that the donor's philosophy is appreciated by those receiving its benefits (Agosto, 2008). The simple act of naming a room after a corporation might be seen as an endorsement of that corporation's practices, and it might also imply that those who make use of the room are accepting of corporate sponsorships and comfortable with the corporation in question. This is, in fact, exactly what may happen—those who disapprove of Walmart may be compelled to avoid a public institution that bears its name, thus creating a self-fulfilling prophecy in which those who don't support Walmart don't visit the library as often as those who support it do.

If this phenomenon is to be avoided, it is essential to remain alert and careful to conduct assessments and accept the findings without holding too tight to preexisting theories or hypotheses about what would be beneficial to discover. While receiving alternative funding can be a huge benefit to libraries (especially those who would like to work with the funder again in the future), honesty about the community's expectations is of the utmost importance.

Understanding What the Community Expects

Community assessments help in understanding how community members tend to view the role of public libraries in their lives. Even while holding tight to the goal of staying objective and open, it's not uncommon to be surprised—positively or negatively—to learn what communities expect from their libraries.

For example, while it can be useful to learn that there is an expectation that a public library will provide a summer reading program for children while they're out of school, it might be unsettling to learn that some parents view the library as a safe place to leave their young children unsupervised. Similarly, while some members of the public may understand that libraries strive to provide materials reflecting various points of view, others might believe that they are required to provide materials reflecting the political, religious, or other personal views of the majority, even at the expense of the minority, or that every item within a collection serves as an endorsement of the ideas within (LaRue, 2012).

Misconceptions such as these highlight the importance of communicating effectively with patrons about what their library can and can't reasonably offer in terms of service. There are expectations that can be met and others that cannot. Knowing where the misconceptions lie can go a long way toward generating greater understanding of a public library's role within its community.

REACHING OUT TO SMALLER DEMOGRAPHICS

A community assessment does not necessarily have to involve an entire community. Many public libraries are beginning to identify and evaluate smaller demographics within the larger community in order to be sure that subcommunities are made to feel welcome and represented in the library, and that their information and entertainment needs are being met as well as possible. Conducting these smaller assessments reiterates the importance of remembering that it is not only the majority demographics in assessments that need improved services but also those less-represented and yet still vital members of their communities.

EXAMPLES OF EXCELLENCE IN SERVING SUBCOMMUNITIES: MILITARY MEMBERS AND FAMILIES

Cumberland County Public Library and Information Center (CCPL&IC), located in North Carolina, serves a geographic area which includes Fort Bragg, home to over 60,000 members of the military and their families. Despite the often-transient nature of military deployment, the management at CCPL&IC wanted to learn as much as possible about the subcommunity of active-duty military and those who share their lives, especially in this era of prolonged active deployment (Taft & Olney, 2014).

In 2013, CCPL&IC received a grant from North Carolina State Library's Library Services and Technology Act (LSTA) in order to fund the assessment (Taft & Olney, 2014). Throughout the assessment planning and execution processes, the contractors followed the protocols of the ALA's Libraries Transforming Communities initiative, which was launched in order to strengthen libraries' roles as community cornerstones and agents of community transformation (ALA, 2013).

Local service groups involved with serving the military population were brought into the assessment process, and a library staff member partnered with a group representing the needs of the military community. A great deal of information was collected through the use of interviews and focus groups with military members, their families, veterans, retired service members, and employees working at agencies supporting military members and their families (Taft & Olney, 2014).

The results of this assessment allowed CCPL&IC staff members to understand what types of programs and services would best serve the Fort Bragg community. As a result, new programs, marketing strategies, and partnerships with local agencies serving the military community were launched. The most telling and useful information the library received was related to the emotional strain of multiple deployments, in which service members may go through up to five deployments. Each time, if the service member has a spouse and/or children, the family unit must deal with the stressors of preparing for their family member to leave, followed by the family member being away for some time, and then the process of reintegration. The more often a service member deploys and reintegrates, the more cumulative stress the family unit bears. This group was found to be deeply concerned for the well-being of their spouses and/or children and wanted to see more family support and children's programming from their public library. Assistance with career changes and continuing education were also noted as important for those transitioning, or planning to transition, from military life into civilian society. This was a need especially suited to the public library, as conducting research about leaving the military while on the base may make service members feel uncomfortable and perhaps even unsafe (Taft & Olney, 2014).

Conducting this subcommunity assessment allowed CCPL&IC staff to connect with their patrons and potential future patrons at Fort Bragg in a respectful and practical manner and also allowed them to serve this group in the most comprehensive and supportive way possible. After the assessment, new programs taken into consideration at CCPL&IC included a military book club, several targeted children's programs, exhibits, and beefed-up job-search resources. These programs are intended to focus on not just providing service to military members and families but on bridging the gap between service members and their allies with the greater community, thus providing a heightened sense of community cohesiveness (Taft & Olney, 2014).

EXAMPLES OF EXCELLENCE IN SERVING SUBCOMMUNITIES: DEVELOPMENTALLY DISABLED PATRONS

Researchers in Colorado used Adams County as a sample population to determine the needs of developmentally disabled adults in public libraries in order to help librarians serve this demographic more proficiently. Through the use of two surveys, the researchers found that developmentally disabled adults are frequent users of public libraries, especially for recreational purposes and to check out books. Use of computers and knowledge of nonprint collections such as music and movies was less frequent (Holmes, 2008).

Conclusions based on the findings of the study revealed that it shouldn't necessarily be assumed that developmentally disabled adults prefer children's books, although many in the demographic do enjoy the sensory aspect of these books. Nonfiction books, particularly in the subject areas of animals, history, and sports are frequently enjoyed by developmentally disabled adults, and therefore it is useful to have a wide selection of these in the collection.

Audiobooks and large print books are often enjoyed by those who are unable to read or have difficulty reading. Finally, a wide collection of Hi/Lo books, which have high levels of content but are suitable for those who read at a lower level, are recommended for this demographic. It was also found that librarians and other library staff members often experience discomfort communicating with their developmentally disabled adult patrons and could benefit from training and continuing education on sensitivity to the needs of this demographic. Because developmentally disabled adults often come to libraries in groups with staff members from group homes or agencies, librarians are encouraged to proactively build relationships with the staff members and clients in order to learn how the library can best serve their needs (Holmes, 2008).

CHANGE IS THE ONLY CONSTANT

Communities, even those famous for their majority residents' social views, are changing all the time. They are dynamic and multifaceted. This is why it is so important to perform follow-up assessments throughout the lifespan of a public library.

It's simple, and very often accurate, to view San Francisco as liberal, Detroit as troubled, Santa Fe as artsy, Birmingham as conservative, and Austin as quirky. One might make similar judgments about smaller communities where people live, work, and play—and these assumptions may be true, for the most part. But, even when librarians believe they have a grasp on what makes their service areas tick, communities change every day. People move in and out. They take jobs, leave jobs, get married, get divorced, and simply come and go as their lives move along. Ongoing data collection and analysis and longitudinal studies can help in understanding how communities shift and change through time.

The Importance of Inclusivity

It makes sense, to a certain degree, to cater to the needs of the majority within a community, and to be visible, welcoming, and accommodating to the needs of those who are likely to make the most use of the public library. The same also goes for those most likely to give back to the community by making donations, becoming library volunteers, serving on library boards, Friends of the Library groups, and committees.

All this being so, a quality assessment reaches out not only to those who do use the library or are likely to do so, but to those who don't, or who don't use it very often. A well-rounded assessment reaches out to these people and asks the tough questions. What about the library seems unwelcoming, unpleasant, or inconvenient? Perhaps it's difficult to get to the library from certain neighborhoods or by using public transportation. Maybe the collection isn't particularly geared toward the interests of some community members. It could be that the hours of operation are inconvenient, or perhaps a feeling of unfriendliness is sensed by certain folks. These answers might be difficult to hear and process, but they are crucially important if the library truly wishes to serve the entirety of its community.

During an assessment, it makes sense to add a survey to the library's website or to have written surveys at the service desks—but, again, this only reaches out to current library users. Mailing surveys randomly to all or a significant percentage of addresses and dropping them off at local businesses and organizations helps reach those who otherwise might not know of the assessment or even have the library on their radar. Partnering with nonprofit agencies, workforce development groups, and social service agencies helps get the word out as well, and, as a bonus, could potentially be a way of reaching nontraditional future library patrons. Interviews and focus groups with both employees and clients of these agencies would surely result in a wealth of information.

As was previously mentioned, circulation statistics are often front-and-center in the results of a community assessment, and they are, of course, very important. But it is wise to keep a few points in mind when analyzing this data. The most obvious is that not all members of a community have an active library account. Circulation statistics only account for people who check materials out from the library, and they provide no information at all about those who don't. Circulation statistics also don't account for use of reference books or for other materials used in-house but not checked out (Disher, 2007). Materials seen as potentially controversial or overly personal would certainly fall into this category, and it's no challenge to imagine several hypothetical situations to illustrate this. An abused wife contemplating leaving her spouse might very well sit in the library and read about safety plans, restraining orders, and child custody, but she would be unlikely to check out books in these areas and take them home. Or consider a young woman recently diagnosed with a serious mental health disorder, or a man struggling with how to tell his family he is in the beginning stages of Alzheimer's disease. This is where libraries help people without anyone knowing it—by having the information right there, free and ready, with no judgment and no prying eyes.

WHAT IS THE VALUE OF PUBLIC LIBRARIES?

In the ongoing digital age, public libraries are often called upon to prove their own worth. Within municipalities, this is most often achieved by conducting a community needs assessment and then striving to meet the needs, wants, and demands of the community based upon the results. While doing so is certainly helpful to individual communities, there is a larger issue at play—the overall perception Americans hold regarding not only their own communities' public libraries but of public libraries in general.

In 2012, two library science researchers drew upon information from a similar study done in Finland to conduct an extensive study aiming to determine the impact of public libraries on various areas of Americans' lives. Their hope was to show that public libraries remain not only relevant but also indispensable in modern society, where so many are quick to dismiss their role as either passé or easily replaceable by the Internet.

The researchers delivered a questionnaire to over 1,000 Americans asking about demographics, library use, and perceptions of the benefits offered by public libraries. Questions were asked about public libraries' role in 22 areas of life, such as work, education, everyday activities, and leisure. These 22 areas were further broken down into smaller areas. In each area and sub-area, respondents indicated whether public libraries benefitted them never, seldom, sometimes, or often.

The findings of the study indicated that the majority of Americans view public libraries as beneficial to their lives, most notably in the areas of self-education and leisure reading. The top five areas of benefit were self-education during leisure time, reading fiction, reading nonfiction, interest in health, and interest in history or society.

Women and ethnic minorities were found to be more likely to be library users. Younger respondents (aged 25–34), as well as those with higher education levels than the median were found to be more likely to report benefitting from public libraries.

While a strong amount of diversity was noted in the findings of the study, it was also reported that certain demographic groups could benefit from augmented services and outreach efforts, particularly those with lower levels of education and/or income than the median. The researchers stressed the importance of public libraries' presence in lower-income neighborhoods, and suggested increasing funding and outreach as well as engaging in targeted marketing planning for lower-income potential library patrons (Sin & Vakkari, 2015).

Seniors also reported fewer benefits of public libraries in their lives. Considering that nearly 70 percent of public library programming is geared toward children and young adults (Institute of Museum and Library Services, 2014), this is not particularly surprising news. As longevity increases and baby boomers reach retirement age, it was recommended that libraries reach out to the older adult demographic to help close this gap.

In addition to finding conclusive research data, this study highlights the importance of providing services aimed at not just the majority but to those demographics that could benefit the most from increased services. The researchers make strongly supported suggestions for closing the gap between public library users and potential future users (Sin & Vakkari, 2015).

CONCLUSION AND FURTHER THINKING

Community assessments are important tools librarians can use to understand and serve their communities as best as possible. While going about this important work, it can help to keep some important points in mind in order for assessment results to serve as true snapshots of community demographics.

Before, during, and after the assessment phase, simply remembering that every majority has its mirror minority allows librarians to become more aware of gradations, subcommunities, and smaller demographic groups. Blending hard-and-fast statistics with observations and conversational data results in a more accurate and nuanced picture of those served by a community's public library.

A clear and concise collection development policy containing assessment information is a good starting point. Making note of program statistics, circulation numbers, and census information provides strong data, while anecdotal data provides the human touch.

Partnering with other service agencies can help ease librarians' workloads, while encouraging them to learn more about the services available to their patrons outside of the library's walls.

Whether conducting an assessment in-house or by contracting with a consultant, objectivity and genuine curiosity about communities and subcommunities are key concepts in understanding public libraries' patrons.

TIPS AND TRAPS: ASSESSMENTS AND ASSUMPTIONS

Tips

- When reviewing community assessment results, keep in mind the wants, needs, and demands of the majority as well as smaller subcommunities.
- If a community is found to have significant subcommunities, smaller assessments regarding their needs are recommended in addition to an overall assessment.
- A blend of statistical data and anecdotal data makes assessment results personal as well as objective.

Traps

- Keep in mind that *most* does not equal *all*—no matter how vocal the majority is, the needs of less-prominent people in the community must be met as well if a community assessment is to be a success.
- Beware of personal bias if conducting an assessment in-house—it's okay for the findings to be surprising.
- Without a clearly-written and understood collection development policy, assessment results can't be applied objectively and accountably.

WHAT WOULD YOU DO?

Lynne used to enjoy spending time at her community's public library, before her life became so busy. At age 50, divorced, and with two kids in college, she worked full-time and had little time or energy to attend library events. She dropped in once in a while to check out a book or movie, and she always checked to see what programs were being offered, but none seemed to fit her interests or schedule.

The library offered a great deal of children's programs, from story-times to teen programs, but Lynn's kids were off at college. There was an adult book club and a few programs here and there, but they tended to be aimed at seniors and retirees. Lynne couldn't take time off during the day to attend the midday book club, and she wasn't interested in knitting or genealogy. She wished the library offered evening and weekend programs for busy adults. She'd like to attend an evening book club, she wanted to learn stress management techniques like meditation to help deal with her busy life, and she wanted to meet people with interests similar to her own.

One day, Lynne received a survey in the mail, which had been sent out to all library cardholders in her community. She read through the multiple-choice questions and answered them honestly. She knew her community had many young families and seniors, but she didn't belong in either category, and she wrote this on the survey. She checked off the times and types of programs that were of interest to her and mailed the survey back, hoping that her feedback would make a difference.

A few months later, Lynne stopped by the library to pick up a book she had on hold. She chatted for a few minutes with the librarian on duty, and asked if any changes had been made based on the survey results. "Oh, yes," the librarian answered. "We're adding another weekly after-school program for teens and a book club at the senior center."

Lynne understood that she was just one person out of many in her town, and she couldn't expect the library to cater to her needs if they weren't representative of most survey respondents, but she couldn't help feeling a bit disappointed. Meeting new people was hard for her, with her busy schedule and tight budget. It seemed like everyone else fit into categories that didn't apply to her.

What Lynne didn't know was that she was in no way an outlier. The library only surveyed those who had active library accounts—and that group was over-represented by young parents and seniors. Lynne was one of many people in her age group who worked full-time and had busy lives. The only odd thing about her was that she was a library cardholder. The library knew this when they looked at community data for their assessment, but they decided that the 27 percent of working adults without children at home weren't well represented by cardholders. Wanting to impress their city council in hopes of getting a larger budget in the next fiscal year, the library's management decided to focus their services on those who already made the most use of the library—young families and seniors.

Lynne continued her trips to the library, but realized that her hopes of finding programming aimed at her demographic were for naught. She looked forward to the day she could finally retire and join the daytime book club. Until then, she decided, there really wasn't much of a place for her at the library.

QUESTIONS TO CONSIDER

- If money were no object, would you feel it would be best to hire a consultant or conduct an assessment using library staff? Why?
- Have you checked recent census figures on the community where you live or work? Were you at all surprised by what you found?
- What subcommunities immediately come to mind when you think of your own community?
- What other services in your community come to mind as potential partners?
- What anecdotal data can you find in your own community that might be useful in a community assessment?
- What are your feelings on corporate sponsorships and public libraries? Does the money generated help negate any discomfort about the source?

REFERENCES

Agosto, D. (2008). Alternative funding for public libraries. In D. A. Nitecki & E. G. Abels (eds.), *Advances in librarianship. Volume 31, Influence of funding on advances in librarianship* (pp. 115–140). Bingley, UK: Emerald.

American Library Association. (2013, February 22). Libraries transforming communities. Retrieved from http://www.ala.org/transforminglibraries/libraries-transforming-communities

Books: Bentonville, Arkansas. (2005). *Newsletter on Intellectual Freedom, 54*(1), 31.

Disher, W. (2007). *Crash course in collection development*. Westport, CT: Libraries Unlimited.

Enis, M. (2014). Technology: Gale introduces analytics on demand. *Library Journal, 139*(8), 16.

Evans, G. E., & Saponaro, M. Z. (2000). *Developing library and information center collections*. Greenwood Village, CO: Libraries Unlimited.

Evans, G. E., & Saponaro, M. Z. (2012). *Collection management basics*. Santa Barbara, CA: Libraries Unlimited.

Holmes, J. L. (2008). Patrons with developmental disabilities: A needs assessment survey. *New Library World, 109*(11/12), 533–545.

Huynh, A. (2004). Background essay on collection development, evaluation, and management for public libraries. *Current Studies in Librarianship, 28*(1/2), 19–37.

Institute of Museum and Library Services (2014). Public libraries in the United States survey: Fiscal year 2011. Retrieved from https://www.imls.gov/assets/1/AssetManager/PLS2011.pdf

Kyrillidou, M. (2005, June 13). Library Assessment: Why Today and Not Tomorrow? Paper presented at Library Assessment Conference. Thessaloniki, Greece.

LaRue, J. (2007). *The new inquisition: Understanding and managing intellectual freedom challenges*. Westport, CT: Libraries Unlimited.

LaRue, J. (2012). Uncle Bobby's wedding. In V. Nye & K. Barko (eds.) *True stories of censorship battles in America's Libraries*. Chicago: American Library Association.

McCleer, A. (2013). Knowing communities: A review of community assessment literature. *Public Library Quarterly, 32*(3), 263–274.

Oatman, E. (2005). Wal-Mart gives libraries 1.6 million. *School Library Journal,* 5(19), 16.

Pakaln, A. (2014). Public libraries: How to save them. *Public Libraries,* 53(4), 7–9.

Sin, S., & Vakkari, P. (2015). Perceived outcomes on public libraries in the U.S. *Library & Information Science Research,* 37(3), 209–219.

Taft J., & Olney, C. (2014). Library services for the "new normal" of military families. *Public Libraries,* 53(6), 28–33.

Chapter 7

SELF-CENSORSHIP AND THE IMPORTANCE OF INCLUSIVENESS

SELF-CENSORSHIP AND AMERICAN LIBRARIES: A BRIEF OVERVIEW

Blatant instances of censorship, such as destroying or concealing books in order to keep them from being read, are common enough to be widely frowned-upon, if not despised. A quick glance at the First Amendment and the Library Bill of Rights should be enough to keep the profession of librarianship alert and responsive to these acts. It's easy for librarians to respond to obviously outlandish acts of censorship with an appropriate and professional tone, often with the support of the public. But just as censorship can be extreme and outrageous, so can it be stealthy and silent—and it can happen in the shadows of the good work librarians do every day in their collection development activities.

For as long as the United States has had libraries, self-censorship, in one form or another, has been taking place. Collections at the earliest American public libraries were built largely on the notion that books should promote certain religious and political stances for the betterment of the communities they served (Moellendick, 2009). Carnegie-funded libraries had the added burden of being expected to prove their worth, as many citizens felt that Carnegie's money could have been better spent elsewhere. This often led to an atmosphere in which librarians felt the need to take great care to ensure that their collections reflected what was considered at the time a politically appropriate atmosphere (Moellendick, 2009). Despite the American Library Association's (ALA's) adoption of the Library's Bill of Rights in 1939 and its reinforcement of those tenets in 1948 with the renamed Library Bill of Rights, self-censorship wasn't seen as much of a concern throughout the first half of the 20th century (Robbins, 2014).

Self-censorship as a deliberate rationalization for keeping books librarians disapprove of out of their collections began to be recognized in the late 1950s, just a few years after the Freedom to Read Statement (FTRS) was adopted by the ALA. In 1959, the sociologist Marjorie Fiske published *Book Selection and Censorship: A Study of School and Public Libraries in California*. Based on a study, which was soon commonly known as the Fiske Report, the book called into question the professionalism of librarians at school and public libraries throughout California after it was found that a substantial majority of public and school librarians in the study practiced self-censorship, even while vehemently claiming to be supporters of intellectual freedom (Fiske, 1959).

Despite the publication of *Book Selection and Censorship*, self-censorship continued to go largely unnoticed or unspoken of, and the Fiske Report began to be considered an out-of-fashion relic of the McCarthy-era United States or an example of how low women's professional status was during the 1950s—if not outright misogyny in action, as almost all of the librarians surveyed were female (Latham, 2014). More than 20 years passed before the publication of a 1983 *Library Journal* article by Celeste West, "The Secret Garden of Censorship: Ourselves," which challenged librarians to explore not only their own censorious activities but those of the hierarchies in which they worked, as well as those of major publishing houses. Small and independent presses were too often overlooked, West asserted, adding that a librarian's role must be to work toward the goal of inclusion, not exclusion. While publishers, by their nature, operated as corporations, librarians had a professional responsibility to go outside the mainstream in order to offer truly comprehensive collections to their communities (West, 1983).

West and Fiske's calls to action may have reached some librarians, but the issue of self-censorship continued to fall below the radar for quite some time to come. The school librarian Debra Lau Whelan (2009a) brought the issue to light with her *School Library Journal* article "A Dirty Little Secret." Taking note of the peculiar combination of new and exciting young adult (YA) novels with favorable reviews and the all-too-common lack of these novels in library collections, Whelan wrote about the results of a 2008 *School Library Journal* survey revealing that the majority of school librarians purposefully avoided purchasing books that might be considered controversial in order to avoid angry responses from parents—even when the books themselves were well-reviewed or widely recommended (Whelan, 2009b). While the survey focused on school librarians, who have the added burden of being *in loco parentis*, which may well make them more prone to self-censorship, it isn't much of a stretch to assume that this practice is common among public librarians as well. In her article, Whelan called upon her fellow librarians in both the school and public milieus to ditch the excuses and put an end to the actions of either keeping certain YA books out of the collection altogether or sequestering them in the adult section instead of displaying them in their proper place among other YA books and to seriously consider the ethical implications behind actions such as these.

Whelan's article resonated with others in the library world, and it accomplished a great deal in terms of both defining the practice of self-censorship and bringing its existence to light. No longer was the focus only on dealing with community challenges—now, new attention was being paid to the actions taken by collectors to prevent those challenges from occurring.

WHAT IS SELF-CENSORSHIP?

Self-censorship is notoriously difficult to define. Detractors often claim that self-censorship is just selection. There are subtle differences, though, that librarians must remain alert to if they want to avoid falling into the trap of self-censorship.

Self-Censorship Involves:

- Looking for a reason to say no
- Imagining potential controversies and allowing them to influence your choices
- Fearing that your selections will reflect poorly upon you as a person or cause your community to judge you
- Allowing your collection to reflect your own personal biases or preferences
- Making excuses or rationalizations for bypassing certain topics or themes during your selection work

True Selection Involves:

- Looking for a reason to say yes
- Caring enough about your collection and your community to build a wide-ranging collection
- Keeping the collection inclusive and diverse during both collection and weeding tasks
- Keeping alert to your own personal biases or preferences, and actively refusing to allow them to interfere with your selections
- Being professionally accountable to all segments of your library's community

RECOGNIZING SELF-CENSORSHIP

Recognizing an act of self-censorship is a difficult task, as to commit an act of self-censorship is not so much an action as a lack thereof. While out-and-out censorship involves an outside party objecting to the inclusion of an item in a library collection, no outside party is involved in cases of self-censorship, which occurs when librarians deliberately or even subconsciously deem a book or other item unsuitable to their collection due to its potentially controversial nature. Whatever challenge is involved in a case of self-censorship is merely assumed, not real (Sloan, 2012).

Because the practice of self-censorship is so quiet and perhaps even well-meaning in a misguided way (after all, nobody likes dealing with challenges, so why not just eliminate the possibility at the gate?), it is quite difficult to notice when it's being committed by oneself or one's colleagues. One key component of self-censorship is fear or second-guessing based on assumptions about possible challenges, rather than actual challenges and their fallout (Hill, 2010). The challenge, in a case of self-censorship, is simply a possibility taking place entirely in the librarian's own mind, making the action of self-censorship something of a preemptive strike against an imaginary potential threat.

Making self-censorship even more difficult to spot is the fact that the assumed challenge might not even be one raised by a community member—it might actually be a collecting librarian who has an issue with the book. Skipping over books and other library items out of personal discomfort with the subject matter is also self-censorship (Sloan, 2012). While it may be simple to write this off as merely an act of selection, there is a difference in intent. Selection is an act of choosing to purchase certain materials from among a larger group, while self-censorship is a deliberate act of rejecting one or more items from the group (Evans & Saponaro, 2005). When engaging in selection activities, librarians are looking for a reason to say *yes*; when engaging in self-censorship, they are looking for a reason to say *no*.

Aside from rejecting certain materials due to their potentially controversial nature, library employees have come up with some chillingly creative methods of keeping books out of the public's hands. The practice of library staff members taking turns checking a book out one by one so patrons never have a chance to browse for it or pick it up as a hold has been noted (Wiegand, 2015). Practices such as keeping a potentially controversial book hidden by removing it from the catalog or claiming it has been lost when it's actually hidden in an office have been reported as well (Hill, 2010).

Self-censorship has surely been going on for as long as libraries have existed (a glance at the old *ALA Catalog* reveals how prevalent libraries' roles as providers of assumed quality and deniers of assumed trash has been throughout the history of American libraries), although the phenomenon has only recently shifted from being a hidden secret to an open one.

Because of its furtive nature, keeping track of self-censorship or collecting data on how often it occurs are tasks that are essentially impossible. At this point, statistics are not collected on instances of self-censorship within library systems, almost certainly due to the near-impossibility of librarians admitting to or accusing one another of this practice (Whelan, 2009a).

The insidious thing about self-censorship is not so much that it can be done without outside parties being aware of it, but that it can be done without even selectors themselves being fully aware of their actions or the reasons behind them. Skipping over a title during the selection process—one of many tasks busy librarians undertake throughout the course of their regular work—without formulating a clear rationalization is simple, and the repercussions are often nonexistent. In many library systems, the bulk of the selection work is done with the input of a vendor. Vendors send lists of recommended books to select from, and librarians select from among the titles those that they believe their communities will benefit from while staying within a specific budget. It is quite simple to simply pass over a title with little more than a fleeting thought about expense or demand—and, with that, the issue is closed before it was ever truly opened. Furthermore, whatever books the vendor has chosen not to include on the list are easily neglected, as they simply aren't seen.

THE DISAPPEARANCE OF *BOY TOY*

In 2007, the YA author Barry Lyga knew that his latest novel, *Boy Toy*, would generate controversy, and he was ready to defend his well-reviewed book about a teenage boy who suffers the social and psychic ramifications of his sexual encounter with a manipulative teacher when he was just 12 years old (Whelan, 2009a; Lyga, 2007). Lyga knew that *Boy Toy* had earned critical praise and was even nominated for the Pennsylvania Library Association's prestigious Carolyn W. Field Award (Colarosa, 2008) and had won the 2007 Cybils (Children's and Young Adult Bloggers' Literary Awards) in the YA novel category (Cybils, 2008).

After so much hype, the silence that followed the publication of *Boy Toy* was startling. Where were the angry mobs? Where were the calls for censorship? Lyga had been ready to speak up for his book and defend its subject matter but hardly anyone seemed to even notice it had been released (Whelan, 2009a).

Was it possible that *Boy Toy* wasn't as controversial as Lyga had expected it to be? The answer, it turned out, was no—the book was indeed quite controversial, and as a result, it simply didn't end up on the shelves of many libraries at all. Librarians feared the shockwaves *Boy Toy* might generate so much that they simply didn't buy it—at least not as much as they tended to purchase other well-reviewed YA novels that didn't deal with the statutory rape of a student by a teacher. Even retail bookstores, if they carried it at all, made a habit of stocking *Boy Toy* in the adult section, even though it was marketed as a YA novel (Whelan, 2009a).

Lyga soon realized that his newest book wasn't being challenged; it was being censored—and by the very people whom he'd most expected to defend the book on the grounds of intellectual freedom. Lyga had known that the book would be edgy, but this level of avoidance was outside the realm of his expectations (Whelan, 2009a).

Critics of *Boy Toy* defended the fact that the book rarely made it to the shelves. A 2009 anonymous Annoyed Librarian column in *Library Journal* ridiculed the idea of the book being self-censored, referred to it as "crap," and spoke out in favor of keeping it away from young minds due to its disturbing content (Annoyed Librarian, 2009).

In the end, *Boy Toy* didn't sell as well as Lyga's previous book, *The Astonishing Adventures of Fanboy and Goth Girl*, but the author, who refused to cave to pressure, continues to write well-reviewed YA novels with edgy content (Lyga, 2016).

Think of the Children

Among the more common themes of censorship, be it internal or external, is the preservation of the safety of children. As has been seen in instances of over-filtering computers and barricading certain children's books behind reference desks or office doors, the protection of children has become a well-intentioned idea gone awry (Hill, 2010). Doing it for the kids makes for a fine short-term ratio-nalization for self-censorship—it even has that smack of moral high ground that comes in so handy in arguments like these—but, in the end, self-censorship is an act of self-preservation, not truly a means of protecting children. To purposefully overlook a book that might cause controversy or upset parents is to make a sweep-ing assumption about both children and parents that may very well not be true. According to the Library Bill of Rights, minors have the same rights as adults in public libraries, and therefore have the right to decide for themselves, with over-sight only from their parents and nobody else, what to read and what to leave on the shelves (ALA, 2006).

Many libraries have begun to add programming around Banned Books Week focusing on speaking with children and teens about their feelings on censorship, banned books, and controversial books. Programs such as these, which take the opposite form of deciding what is best for children without their input, can reveal surprising and useful insights from those around whom all this controversy is cen-tered (Hill, 2010).

BE ALERT TO SELF-CENSORSHIP RED FLAGS

- Second-guessing the purchase of a book or other item based on an assump-tion that someone might find it offensive
- Skipping over certain items due to your own personal discomfort with their subject matter
- Seeking reasons to reject materials rather than reasons to include them
- Using vendor lists exclusively without keeping current on small and inde-pendent presses

---

Common Themes of Self-Censored Titles

While self-censorship can occur for just about any reason, some themes have been identified as common targets. The 2009 *School Library Journal* survey men-tioned earlier revealed that self-censorship is most likely to occur when the mate-rials in question contain themes of sexuality or text containing coarse language. Also, books depicting acts of violence and containing LBGT (lesbian, gay, bisex-ual, and transgender)-themed content were likely to be censored by librarians, as were books dealing with religious issues (Whelan, 2009b).

Sexual Content

Sexual content is the most-often cited reason found for self-censorship, especially when it comes to YA books (Whelan, 2009b). More so than violence, sex is interesting to teens and raises the hackles of parents (Heller & Storms, 2015). During the teen years, many kids stop reading for leisure—and, whether adults like it or not—books with sexual content are often exciting for teens and can help get them back into the habit of reading for fun (Heller & Storms, 2015). Making the public library a safe place for teens to safely explore new subjects in YA books ultimately helps with their development into adulthood (Forman, 2015).

Violence

In YA books especially, but also in adult titles, violence, even when well within the context of a larger story, can cause books to be vulnerable to self-censorship. One recent example is Markus Zusak's 2005 YA/adult fiction crossover bestseller *The Book Thief*, which has been criticized for its realistic depictions of cruelty, violence, and death during the Holocaust (Zusak, 2005). Despite the historical accuracy of *The Book Thief* and other books geared toward YA readers, parents often demand rating systems based simply on the violent content, without regard for the greater themes of these books and their portrayal of important eras in history, worms and all (Hill, 2013).

Profanity

Profanity often gets a free pass in adult books, but YA books haven't been so fortunate. In the past decade or so, rough language has become more common in YA literature, to the dismay of parents who aim to shield their children from swearing (Campbell, 2007). School librarians and public librarians specializing in YA literature are often called upon to walk a fine line between giving teens the gritty drama they desire and keeping parents placated. In the end, of course, trying to please everyone often leads to a scenario in which nobody feels fully content with the result. Public librarians do enjoy more freedom than school librarians in this area, although challenges to YA materials are often quite common at public libraries as well—and wherever fear lurks, so lurks the potential for self-censorship.

LGBT Content

While the mere existence of LGBT (lesbian, gay, bisexual, and transgender) characters in books is often assumed to equate to sexual content (even if the characters don't engage in sexual behaviors), library materials containing LGBT-themed content are in danger of a double-whammy when it comes to self-censorship—the assumption that all LGBT-themed materials contain vivid descriptions of LGBT sex, plus the still-rampant taboo of LGBT themes in and of themselves (Whelan, 2009a). Therefore, books with LGBT content for any intended age are at great risk of self-censorship.

It has been noted that the likelihood of coming out as an LGBT individual with confidence is partly determined by how taboo the topic seemed during one's teen years. Books with LGBT characters and content can do more than just open one's eyes to various sexual identities; they can also be a beacon of hope for those struggling with coming out to their friends and family (Heller & Storms, 2015). These books, therefore, can have a tremendous impact on people's lives. Unfortunately, they are also among the most commonly self-censored books, while also being those that tend to raise the most curiosity (Heller & Storms, 2015).

Religion and Atheism

Religion is rightfully a hot topic in collection development, as most public libraries are municipally run and therefore subject to the First Amendment mandate of separation of church and state.

Whelan (2009b) reports that 16 percent of librarians surveyed reported that books with religious themes make them wary and prone to instances of self-censorship. If dealing with themes of religion is difficult for selectors, the same can certainly be said about atheism and agnosticism.

ACCEPTING AND MOVING BEYOND BIAS

Avoidance and fear very often go hand-in-hand. Those who are afraid of heights aren't likely to spend their time leaning over the edges of tall bridges, just as those who fear backlash or judgment aren't likely to court controversy. Admitting one's biases is a difficult task for anyone, not just librarians. It's natural to avoid or even disparage situations that cause anxiety. To do so is a normal human reaction. Librarians, however, are in a unique situation of having a professional responsibility to move past their fears and biases in order to provide quality service. Like teachers, therapists, and community leaders, the bar is set higher for librarians than it is for laypersons. While coming to terms with one's own biases and the reasons behind them can be uncomfortable, it can also be enlightening and liberating, and is ultimately likely to serve as time and effort well spent.

Fear of Controversy

Without the benefit of quality community assessment procedures and well-written collection development policies, it's all too easy for librarians who perform collection development tasks to assume that their communities simply do not want those books they do not want to purchase. Lack of proof to the contrary is an easy excuse. But even in cases in which a population hasn't been fully studied, it is safe to assume that a well-rounded collection will serve any community better than a skewed one. A balanced collection will have something for everyone, to the greatest extent possible. It's reasonable to assume that a community will have people of various ages, genders, sexual orientations, and educational levels—and also of various sensibilities in terms of what is appropriate and what is not. Erring on the side of caution by failing to collect potentially controversial books does a disservice to those in the community who enjoy a bit of spice in their library selections, or who simply aren't as easily offended as others might be. To self-censor out of fear of controversy fundamentally boils down to deciding to what others should be given access and to what they should be denied access (Moellendick, 2009).

Even for those who fear controversy acutely and allow it to dictate their selections, it might help to know that at the end of the day, even the most censorious, carefully constructed collection of supposedly non-offensive items is still not immune to controversy (McNeil-Nix, 2001). There is simply no telling what someone might object to—and a lack of controversial items could very well be as objectionable as a large collection of them.

A reading of the First Amendment and the Library Bill of Rights should make it clear that censoring out of fear of controversy acts in direct opposition to the professional standards of librarianship.

Fear of Judgment

Any public library collection of quality will have items that represent disparate points of view. Trouble rears its head, though, when librarians believe that their collections represent themselves as people. Librarians often self-censor books they personally find distasteful, but it is more common to self-censor those that they believe community members will find distasteful. The fear of being called upon to defend one's selection choices can feel uncomfortably personal, and this fear may easily seep into collection development choices (Moellendick, 2009).

The thought of facing judgment from community members is fear-provoking enough, but when fear of being judged by one's own higher-ups comes into play, the odds of self-censorship occurring skyrocket. While librarians involved in collection development must be alert to self-censorship, supervisors and library management must be aware of the damage that self-censorship can do as well. Self-censorship is obviously more likely to occur without proper supervision and support. The fear of being judged by one's own supervisors, and of that judgment possibly leading to loss of livelihood or professional reputation, can very easily lead one to engage in self-censorious activities (Evans & Saponaro, 2005).

IT'S NOT JUST LIBRARIES

If librarians are gatekeepers to knowledge, as is often said, then publishers and vendors are gatekeepers to access. When librarians limit themselves to lists provided by their vendors—a common practice that truly does help librarians manage their time and budgets—without keeping up on works put forth by small and alternative presses, a disservice may be done to an entire community.

Just as librarians used to be held to the lofty standards of the *ALA Catalog* and other indexes of recommended books, they are now often limited in terms of the items they purchase by the recommendations of vendors—companies that sell books and other materials to libraries, usually at a discount, with the convenience of condensed lists of recommended titles and a single bill rather than multiple invoices (Wiegand, 2015). Vendors are invaluable when it comes to saving time and money, as well as staying current on upcoming best sellers. That being said, building a comprehensive collection involves looking outside of mainstream sources from time to time.

Particular authors and books tend to be subject not only to self-censorship at an individual library level; it's also often publishers and vendors who keep these books hidden in some aspect. YA authors especially have often reported having to struggle with their publishers about titles, themes, and even specific wording (Whelan, 2009a). With this in mind, it's not difficult to understand why authors may cave to pressure in order to get their books published, albeit at the peril of their literary voice. Even with those books that make it through the publishers' demands, it then becomes up to vendors working with libraries whether or not to include them on their list of recommendations.

It is also common for publishers to request that certain YA books get cleaned up in the form of having sex scenes, profanity, and violent images removed in the editing process so they will be more appealing to YA and school-based librarians, thus being able to make more money for the publisher and author alike (Campbell, 2007).

CHECKLIST: HOW TO KEEP SELF-CENSORSHIP AT BAY IN YOUR LIBRARY

- Talk about it—provide regular staff training and ongoing support regarding self-censorship and intellectual freedom.
- Use mainstream vendor lists but also keep a regularly updated list of small and independent presses to consult—especially those that serve commonly under-represented populations.
- Be sure your own and your employees' knowledge of the Library Bill of Rights and the First Amendment is kept in mind during collection development tasks.
- Use teams to support and hold one another accountable.
- Ask for assistance from the Office for Intellectual Freedom (OIF) and other pro-intellectual freedom groups whenever you need it—these groups are there to help.

WHAT CAN BE DONE

Skewed thought processes lead to skewed collection practices, which in turn lead to skewed collections. Learning to recognize the practice of self-censorship and becoming aware of it both in one's own work and that of others in the field are excellent first steps in helping to push back, but a great deal more can be done to keep this problem at bay and keep collections balanced.

A Proactive Collection Development Policy

As is the case with actual community challenges, self-censorship is less likely to occur in library systems that have clear policies about collection development

(Hill, 2010). Because self-censorship so often happens without the full awareness of collectors or their colleagues, a proactive stance is a sensible starting point for becoming alert to its dangers. A fairly written collection development policy based on the tenets of the Library Bill of Rights and the First Amendment not only helps in cases of actual challenges, it can also be of great value to librarians experiencing doubt or fear about purchasing certain items (ALA OIF, 2010). Knowing that one's library actively supports intellectual freedom and open accessibility helps ease these fears and frees librarians to collect with open minds. Librarians who rely on quality review sources and have strong readers' advisory abilities are also known to be more comfortable with using their skills to select books out of knowledge rather than fear (Hill, 2010). In other words, well-trained and strongly supported librarians are much more likely to purchase items based on their usefulness to the community than to acquiesce to self-censorship out of fear of rocking the boat. On the other hand, poorly trained and unsupported librarians are much more likely to engage in self-censorship. Managers and supervisors play a vital role in this area. The creation of a safe working atmosphere that supports intellectual freedom cannot be overstated. Discussing matters of censorship and intellectual freedom in staff meetings and professional development activities goes a long way toward empowering staff and creating an atmosphere of trust (Mosher, 2010).

Another benefit of thoughtfully written collection development policies is the fact that their review processes and revisions allow the entire library staff to be reminded of and educated on the importance of equitable policies that support the First Amendment and the Library Bill of Rights. This process also allows everyone on staff to know that they are supported in their collection development activities and encouraged to behave ethically (Mosher, 2010).

Use of Small and Alternative Presses

Because self-censorship often begins at the source—the publishers and the vendors who choose from among thousands of new books every month and create lists for librarians to select from—the importance of keeping current with small and alternative presses, who are not nearly as subject to interference and fears of judgment or reprisal as big publishing houses and their allies, cannot be overstated when it comes to building comprehensive collections.

A list of small and alternative presses is provided in the appendix, and, as new presses appear, keeping an ever-changing list handy can be of great assistance to librarians going about the busy work of deciding how to spend their (often meager) budgets fairly and with good representation. True, it makes for a bit of extra work, but the payoff—a more comprehensive and well-thought-out collection—is well worth the burden.

Professional Accountability

Committing acts of self-censorship does more than violate librarianship's professional principles; it also assumes that library patrons—adults and minors alike—are not capable of making decisions for themselves. Being accountable involves advocating for patrons while upholding constitutional law and the guidelines of the Library Bill of Rights. Staying knowledgeable and up-to-date on intellectual freedom issues makes this advocacy feel more comfortable and natural. Furthermore, graduate programs in library and information science have a responsibility to stress professional ethics in their curricula in order to prepare future librarians for the censorship battles they are likely to someday face (Mosher, 2010). Holding a master's degree in any field insinuates a certain level of professional knowledge and capability. In librarianship, therefore, it is perfectly reasonable to assume that those awarded the degree have an understanding of intellectual freedom, the Library Bill of Rights, and the First Amendment. Furthermore, ongoing education, whether self-guided or formal, doesn't seem unreasonable for a field with such close ties to education and social welfare.

Change of Mind-Set

While some public library systems are more supportive of the need to be alert to self-censorship than others, there is nothing stopping librarians from educating themselves on the issue. Selection is, of course, an important part of a collector's job, but equating selection with self-censorship is a commonly held defense. Choosing among books means purchasing some and not purchasing others. This is not the same thing as self-censorship, though. A poorly reviewed book is different than a book that is assumed to be potentially controversial. Selection involves *choosing* thoughtfully from a wide array of resources. Self-censorship involves *rejecting* based on fear of challenges due to an individually held mind-set about what types of books are potentially dangerous and what types of books are not. Viewing self-censorship through the lens of intellectual freedom rather than through the lens of the imagined or true realities of librarians' day-to-day work can help keep ethics in check (Mosher, 2010).

While you must be alert to those materials you feel tempted to reject for the wrong reasons, the same goes for being alert to those you particularly enjoy. For example, a fiction collector who greatly enjoys reading mysteries might be inadvertently skewing the collection by buying many new mystery releases while giving less attention to other genres, thus subtly deeming them less interesting or less important. Everyone has likes and dislikes and to try to deny them would be foolish. The point is to be aware of your own likes and dislikes, and to collect with inclusivity, not personal preference, in mind.

Using Teams Rather Than Independent Selectors

Teams can be made up of librarians working within the same public library or different librarians working within the same community. For example, school librarians have been known to request that their public libraries purchase certain books dealing with issues such as teenage sex that, while possibly not appropriate for a school library, might be of great value to a public library (Heller & Storms, 2015). Libraries at middle and high schools tend to serve smaller segments of age groups than public libraries do, making them somewhat less free to purchase YA books across the board (Shoemaker, 2011). This type of partnership helps teens get the information they want and need in an appropriate environment.

Similarly, librarians working within the same public library system can help one another by mentoring newer collectors, or by reviewing one another's collection decisions in order to help avoid self-censorship. Two pairs of eyes working toward the same goal are invariably better than one—and two librarians both working to avoid self-censorship may well be able to support and challenge each other in this endeavor. Whether or not this type of situation works will certainly depend a great deal on the individual library's organizational culture and the philosophy of its managing bodies, but if it can be done, the benefits are worth the extra time.

The use of teams is helpful when everyone involved is earnestly working toward the goal of inclusivity, but the practice is far from fail-safe. Coworkers, supervisors, and even managers may have vastly different ideals and practices when it comes to self-censorship, even when they do work in teams. If a library's management supports teamwork, but does not truly support efforts to alleviate self-censorship, not much is likely to come from the practice. When this becomes the case, if speaking up brings about a reaction that is either futile or punitive, it may be time to look elsewhere for help.

Reaching Out for Help

The stresses of dealing with self-censorship can be extreme, but there is never a need to go it alone—even for librarians who work in systems that don't support intellectual freedom as well as they could.

Office for Intellectual Freedom

The ALA's OIF is often the first place for librarians to seek support regarding self-censorship concerns and the backlash that may accompany a stance against it (ALA, 2008). Librarians who are dismissed from employment, demoted, or otherwise professionally compromised as a result of involvement with an intellectual freedom issue can ask to make use of the OIF's LeRoy C. Meritt Humanitarian Fund, which provides assistance to librarians in these circumstances (ALA, 2007).

National Coalition against Censorship

The National Coalition against Censorship (NCAC) is a group unrelated to the ALA that deals with censorship concerns. The NCAC offers a page on its website where instances of censorship may be reported anonymously (NCAC, 2016a). The NCAC is also the creator of the Kids Right to Read Project, which offers support to librarians and others dealing with challenges to children's books (NCAC, 2016b). Whether one is dealing with a work atmosphere that supports or encourages actions of self-censorship, or has been subjected to reprisal due to self-censorship opposition, the NCAC is a useful organization to which one may turn for help.

Even (perhaps especially) in library systems that don't offer support and training about how to avoid the pitfalls of self-censorship—or in those that go so far as to encourage it—reaching out for help can provide the support and understanding that is lacking on the local level. Going it alone is never necessary, as plenty of help is available.

Identifying Pro-Censorship Organizations

Just as librarians need to know whom they may call upon for help, it is also wise to be aware of pro-censorship groups in order to keep current on what these organizations are up to. Many politically and religiously conservative groups have spoken or written in defiance of the ALA and intellectual freedom in libraries.

Family Friendly Libraries

Family Friendly Libraries (FFL) is a conservative group created for the purpose of empowering parents to protect their children from libraries that collect items supporting ideas that the group considers contrary to community standards. During the 1990s, FFL took to the media to critique the ALA's missions of diversity, access, and neutrality, claiming that the ALA forced a liberal agenda on library patrons by promoting pro-LGBT materials and also claiming that doing so denied anti-LGBT materials equal visibility (Gaffney, 2014).

FFL leaders have stated that public library collections should focus on pro-family library materials and websites, and they object to selection policies that take a neutral stance on LGBT issues and sex, especially in YA collections. Critics of FFL have stated that the organization's definition of what constitutes a family is very much skewed and seeks to exclude families and individuals who do not meet their strict criteria of what represents morality and family (Davis, 1999).

While FFL does urge its members to get involved as parents and oversee their children's library selections, they object to a great deal of themes common in library materials. LGBT-themed books are frowned upon, as FFL endorses an emphasis on the traditional family, which is defined as being headed by a married man and woman. Books and other library materials containing sexuality are deemed inappropriate for anyone under the age of 18, as FFL members support the idea that minors are particularly vulnerable to psychological damage by being exposed to these themes. FFL urges parents to get politically involved with their communities' public libraries and join trustee boards with the intention of keeping libraries in line with the group's rhetoric (Gounaud, 2016).

Safe Libraries

Safe Libraries is an organization that hosts a website and blog, both of which strongly criticize the ALA, going so far as to deem it terrorist-friendly and anti-child. Safe Libraries members also speak out in favor of Internet filtering in libraries, believing that a lack of filtered computers can easily lead to instances of child pornography (Safe Libraries, 2008; Safe Libraries, 2016).

WISSUP=Wisconsin Speaks Up

Ginny Maziarka, who, along with her husband, organized a challenge against many YA books at the West Bend Memorial Library, as discussed in Chapter 3, has a blog, WISSUP=Wisconsin Speaks Up, which details not only Maziarka's reactions to West Bend Memorial Library's refusal to censor the books she challenged but also her objections to the ALA, the OIF, and others who are perceived as standing in the way of public libraries being controlled by anyone other than local citizens and conservative interest groups (Maziarka, 2014). Although the blog has not been updated for a while, its message remains clear.

TIPS AND TRAPS: AVOIDING SELF-CENSORSHIP

Tips

- When tempted to overlook a book or place it behind a barrier, remember to examine the rationale behind such a decision—does it make sense based on the tenets of intellectual freedom?
- Being a supervisor involves being open with employees about the dangers of self-censorship and keeping alert to its occurrence.
- Be sure to keep current on small and alternative presses to help keep your collection inclusive.

Traps

- A community challenge can happen at any time, for any reason—trying to avoid one is no rationalization for self-censorship.
- Being afraid to examine and work toward moving beyond one's own biases is natural, but librarians have a professional responsibility to do so.
- An organizational culture that promotes self-censorship can make an ethical librarian's job very difficult, but there are organizations to help in these situations—never be afraid to reach out for help when necessary.

WHAT WOULD YOU DO?

Deanna was getting settled into her new job as the branch manager of a small library. As part of her process of getting acclimated, she explored her new surroundings and eventually stumbled upon a cart of books that had recently been weeded and were set to be removed from the library's collection. Curious, Deanna examined the books on the cart. Many of them appeared to be in good shape, but upon further inspection, she couldn't help but notice that many of the titles on the cart were among those that were often considered controversial. There were LGBT-themed books for teens, books about atheism, and several graphic novels featuring violent storylines. Was it possible that Deanna's employees were practicing censorship by weeding?

Deanna contacted the OIF and learned that her situation was not at all unusual. Even when a library has a strong collection development policy which is carefully followed, she learned, its mandates often aren't applied when it comes to weeding. A librarian or other library staff member who has a particular beef with certain books or groups of materials can subtly squelch the offending items by quietly weeding them out, sometimes all at once, and sometimes bit by bit.

While Deanna had strong feelings about self-censorship, she didn't want to come across as overly authoritarian, especially as a new manager in a long-standing system. During a regular staff meeting, she tried to open a dialogue about the practice of selective, censorious weeding. A few staff members agreed with her, but many others objected, saying that the librarians at the other branches were given the freedom to weed as they saw fit. This wasn't how the last manager did things, she was told. It was implied that she was overreacting and micromanaging.

Deanna took this criticism hard, but she wanted to stay true to her values. She initiated a new rule: all weeded items must be eyeballed and given the go-ahead by her. Despite some grumbles, her employees complied. Soon, though, Deanna began to notice that her employees were practicing other methods of self-censorship in ways that were troublingly creative. She discovered that one employee kept certain materials out of circulation by checking them out over and over. She also found materials in staff-only areas and couldn't find their corresponding MARC records in the catalog.

Deanna went to her supervisor, Joe, with this information, hoping for support. Joe shrugged it off, saying that he was tired of dealing with community challenges. "We've had enough trouble with complaints at your branch," he told Deanna. "The staff there had to learn the hard way how to avoid controversy."

Deanna left the meeting feeling torn between wanting to create good relationships with her employees and her ethics. She had already been told by both the staff and the trustees that she was viewed as bossy and overly sensitive. She had worked hard to become a branch manager, and she felt a great deal of pressure to prove herself as a competent leader. But how could she be a good leader if she allowed her staff to do things that were unethical to the profession? She knew she had some hard decisions to make, but she was determined to run her library ethically. If only she knew how to deal with the negative feedback, she thought, she could really turn things around.

QUESTIONS TO CONSIDER

- As a public librarian, if you had concerns about reactions to a book, what methods would you use to determine whether or not it was appropriate for your collection?
- What hints can you think of that might serve as reminders that you're considering giving in to the pressure of self-censoring a book or other item? How might you go about alleviating these pressures?

- Do you feel that books like *Boy Toy* belong in a public library and, if so, in what area of the library—adult, YA, or other? Why?

- If you were a parent of a teenager, how would you go about monitoring (or not monitoring) your child's library selections?

- In a supervisory or managerial position, how would you go about ensuring that your staff understands the importance of being alert to self-censorship?

REFERENCES

American Library Association. (2006, June 30). Library Bill of Rights. Retrieved from http://www.ala.org/advocacy/intfreedom/librarybill

American Library Association. (2007, April 19). The LeRoy C. Merritt Humanitarian Fund. Retrieved from http://www.ala.org/groups/affiliates/relatedgroups/merrittfund/merritthumanitarian

American Library Association. (2008, June 9). Office for Intellectual Freedom. Retrieved from http://www.ala.org/offices/oif

American Library Association Office for Intellectual Freedom. (2010). *Intellectual freedom manual*. Chicago: American Library Association.

Annoyed Librarian. (2009). Librarians "censor" statutory rape book. Retrieved from http://lj.libraryjournal.com/blogs/annoyedlibrarian/2009/02/23/librarians-censor-statutory-rape-book

Campbell, P. (2007). The pottymouth paradox. *Horn Book Magazine, 83*(3), 311–315.

Colarosa, D. (2008). Five books nominated for Carolyn W. Field Award. *Pennsylvania Library Association Bulletin, 63*(5), 17.

Cybils. (2008). The 2007 Cybils winners. Retrieved from http://www.cybils.com/2008/02/the-2007-cybils-2.html

Davis, D. (1999). The not-so-friendly censors: Children's collection development and the family-friendly libraries movement. *Florida Libraries, 42*(4), 62–64.

Evans, G. E., & Saponaro, M. Z. (2005). *Developing library and information center collections*. Westport, CT: Libraries Unlimited.

Fiske, M. (1959). *Book selection and censorship: A study of school and public libraries in California*. Berkeley: University of California Press.

Forman, G. (2015, February 6). Teens crave young adult books on really dark topics (and that's ok). *Time*. Retrieved from http://time.com/3697845/if-i-stay-gayle-forman-young-adult-i-was-here/

Gaffney, L. M. (2014). No longer safe: West Bend, young adult literature, and conservative library activism. *Library Trends, 62*(4), 730–739.

Gounaud, J. (2016). Family Friendly Libraries: Ten ways to create a family friendly library. Retrieved from http://www.ccv.org/issues/harmful-to-children/family-friendly-libraries

Heller, M. J., & Storms, A. (2015). Sex in the library. *Teacher Librarian, 42*(3), 22–25.

Hill, R. (2010). The problem of self-censorship. *School Library Monthly, 27*(2), 9–12.

Hill, R. (2013). Content without context: Context ratings for young adult books. *School Library Monthly, 29*(5), 35–37.

Latham, J. M. (2014). Heat, humility, and hubris: The conundrum of the Fiske Report. *Library Trends, 63*(1), 57–74.

Lyga, B. (2007). *Boy Toy*. Boston, MA: Houghton Mifflin Harcourt.

Lyga, B. (2016). Barry Lyga: Author, reader, recovering comic book geek. Retrieved from http://barrylyga.com

Maziarka, G. (2014, January 9). Your library: No longer a safe place [web log post]. Retrieved from http://wissup.blogspot.com

McNeil-Nix, H. (2001). Family friendly libraries are us. *Journal of Youth Services in Libraries, 14*(2), 17–19.

Moellendick, C.M., (2009). Libraries, censors, and self-censorship. *PNLA Quarterly, 73*(4), 68–76.

Mosher, A.M. (2010). Challenging self-censorship: A 21st century vision for an ethical future. *Library Student Journal, 5*, 13.

National Coalition against Censorship. (2016a). Report censorship. Retrieved from http://ncac.org/report-censorship-page

National Coalition against Censorship. (2016b). Kids Right to Read Project. Retrieved from http://ncac.org/project/the-kids-right-to-read-project

Robbins, L. (2014). Introduction. *Library Trends, 63*(1), 2–10.

Safe Libraries. (2008). Are children safe in public libraries? Retrieved from http://www.safelibraries.org

Safe Libraries. (2016, July 30). Librarians allow kids to borrow BDSM erotica [web log post]. Retrieved from http://safelibraries.blogspot.com

Shoemaker, J. (2011). Nine YA authors talk about intellectual freedom. *Voice of Youth Advocates, 34*(2), 122–129.

Sloan, S. (2012). Regional differences in collecting freethought books in American public libraries: A case of self-censorship? *Library Quarterly, 82*(2), 183–205.

West, C. (1983). The secret garden of censorship: ourselves. *Library Journal, 108*(15), 1651–1653.

Whelan, D.L. (2009a). A dirty little secret [cover story]. *School Library Journal, 55*(2), 26–30.

Whelan, D.L. (2009b). SLJ self-censorship survey. Retrieved from http://www.slj.com/2009/02/collection-development/slj-self-censorship-survey

Wiegand, W. (2015). Part of our lives: A people's history of the American public library. New York: Oxford University Press.

Zusak, M. (2005). *The book thief*. New York: Alfred A. Knopf.

Chapter 8

QUALITY AND DEMAND IN PUBLIC LIBRARIES: WHO DECIDES?

QUALITY VERSUS DEMAND

There was a time, not so long ago, when librarians were considered authorities in what their community members should read, and, often more notably, what they should not read. While the stereotype of the snooty librarian looking down her nose at all but the very best literature may have faded, libraries still deal with issues of quality and demand. Part of a public librarian's role is to provide educational materials for patrons seeking to involve themselves in lifelong learning pursuits, but librarians are also expected to provide materials for entertainment and leisure.

While each public library system is unique in its mission statement and goals, the American Library Association's (ALA's) Library Bill of Rights specifically states that libraries serve to provide resources for interest, information, and enlightenment, and that personal disapproval of library users' tastes has no place in a library setting (ALA, 2006a). Put more simply, libraries exist to serve their patrons by responding to the interests and needs of their community members.

The Changing Role of Public Libraries

As noted in Chapter 1, the downfall of the township library model of the mid-1800s was due, in great part, to the air of elitism community members sensed from their township libraries (Freeman & Hvode, 2003). Being told what was good reading and what was bad reading didn't sit well. The idea of the public having a say in what should be housed on the shelves of public libraries began to take hold.

When the ALA produced its *ALA Catalog*, with 5,000 recommended titles for public libraries, in 1904, the idea behind the publication was to assist librarians in deciding which books were of high enough quality to purchase for their collections (Huynh, 2004). Over a century has passed since the publication of the *ALA Catalog*, and while librarians have, by and large, dropped the elitist attitude of assuming to know what's best for others, the struggle with finding a balance between quality and popularity of books and other library materials is still going on.

Living in the Age of Change

During the first decade of the 21st century, there was a strong push for libraries to stay relevant by becoming more similar in feel to big-name retail bookstores (Huynh, 2004). Coffee carts and comfortable armchairs began to appear in public libraries, replacing the no-food-or-drink rules and disciplinary atmospheres of the past. Now, a decade later, as retail bookstores are closing and eBooks are growing in popularity, there is a push for more downloadable materials. Things are changing so quickly that is often seems that just when libraries get on board with one trend, another one appears, causing them to change track once again.

When libraries are too quick to react to trends, they risk losing sight of their overall mission, but when they fail to take notice of the world around them, they risk becoming irrelevant or outdated. The solution, as the case with most changes, is to have a clear mission, and to make sure new changes fit into that mission (Pakaln, 2014). For example, while simply adding a coffee cart might help make a library appear fashionable and inviting, it would be wise to step back and consider what else can be offered along with coffee. Perhaps the seating area around the coffee cart could be situated so that community information, job flyers, and postings about volunteer opportunities are visible. It's a small difference, but the intent changes with *action* rather than *reaction*. Being fully cognizant of your library's missions and objectives allows you to make decisions about which trends can be made use of most effectively and which would only add the flavor of the month.

Give Them What They Want or Give Them What They Need?

While attitudes and expectations of public libraries have changed, the old question remains: give them what they want or give them what they need—or, more bluntly, what is it believed they need? Keeping up with retail-driven trends can help the profession stay significant in an ever-changing world, but libraries run the risk of losing their distinctiveness when employees are too anxious to jump on the latest bandwagon. Holding fast to librarianship's guiding purposes and professional guidelines can be difficult as trends come and go. Writing and remaining familiar with well thought-out and carefully written mission statements and collection development policies that address the balance between demand and quality are good starting points, as they aid in remembering to maintain libraries' identities as cornerstones of the communities they serve, while also delivering the latest and greatest to their patrons.

Back in 1904, libraries gave the public what they determined, through their own suppositions and by studying such book lists as the *ALA Catalog*, it needed. These days, the pendulum has swung in the opposite direction, and the focus has moved to providing the public with the materials in highest demand (Huynh, 2004). Of course, listening and responding to public wants and needs is a good thing for the profession, the public, and democracy in general. A throwback to the days of librarians supposedly knowing best and forcing their agendas upon their communities would be most unwelcome in this day and age. Questions remain, though. Should public libraries go so far as to refuse to collect classic novels, scientific texts, or scholarly journals if their patrons rarely or never request such items? Would it be just as simple and less expensive to order the novel *Middlemarch* or the movie *Citizen Kane* through interlibrary loan (ILL) service as it would be to purchase it, if patrons request these items perhaps once a year at most? Or does this stance take the commitment to pleasing the public a step too far?

To take this analogy further, how should public libraries handle popular books based on conspiracy theories, yellow journalism, or unproven medical treatments? If they do purchase them, how can they best work to keep their collections balanced?

Obviously, quality and demand are not necessarily mutually exclusive, and one runs the risk of insulting library users when making such implications. Still, librarians are called upon to make decisions about what they will and will not collect—and the result is often the suppression or exclusion of certain genres that tend to be taken less than seriously in the library world. At the risk of disparaging great literature, let she who has never enjoyed a trashy novel on the beach cast the first stone.

QUALITY AND DEMAND REGARDING CHILDREN'S MATERIALS

Children's picture books and chapter books fall across a broad spectrum, from award-winners to classics to barely disguised commercials for the latest movie, television show, or video game. Even with the wealth of well-written and well-reviewed books for kids available, marketing and other blatant commercialism are hardly rare in today's children's books.

Consumerism and Media Influences on Children's Reading Choices

Although quality children's literature is widely available, consumerism has begun to play a large part in the marketing of children's books, and therefore in what materials children tend to look for at their public libraries. A book based on a movie or television show that a child has seen has a different effect on how that child reads the book. The voices and nuances of the characters, for example, won't be up to the child to determine through imagination—she will more likely mimic the way she's experienced that character speak and act on television or on the movie screen (Bickford, 2010). While this is not necessarily harmful in and of itself, it does take a certain level of creativity out of reading and playing (Krashen, 2004).

Corporations have caught on to the idea of marketing books full of subliminal and not-so-subliminal advertising for toys, movies, and the like (Bickford, 2010). A simple search on a public library catalog for children's books involving such corporate characters as Barbie, Dora the Explorer, and just about any Disney character should make this abundantly clear. Nevertheless, many would argue, anything that gets kids reading can't be all bad—and, after all, these are the books children and their parents very often come to the library to find, along with the books they've see in retail chain stores that have caught their children's eye (Genco, 1988). Influences of the media and mass culture will certainly reach all but the most sheltered of children and their parents and guardians as well.

Reaching Reluctant Readers

Despite concerns about quality and influence, mass-marketed and consumer-driven books may just be the very ones that reach reluctant readers and allow them to realize that reading can be an enjoyable experience (Rog & Kropp, 2005).

Reluctant readers are those children who have difficulty reading due to learning difficulties such as dyslexia, environmental factors such as being overscheduled, social factors such as a lack of role models who enjoy reading, or peer pressure such as being told by their friends that reading isn't a cool or worthwhile activity (Findlay, 2014).

Teachers and parents tend to have a hard time reaching reluctant readers, roughly three-quarters of whom are boys, and many of whom have developed strategies to avoid reading both in school and at home—although, in the end, these learned behaviors only serve to prolong the issue instead of solving it at an earlier developmental stage (Rog & Kropp, 2005).

Librarians, teachers, parents, and other adult allies of reluctant readers have the difficult, yet rewarding, responsibility of helping these kids begin to enjoy the experience of reading. While print-centric librarians and other adults might frown on alternative reading techniques, their usefulness is evident. The use of audiobooks can help children who are more auditory than visual in their learning style, while visual learners often appreciate graphic novel adaptations of books over regular print (Snyder, 2014). Using eBook platforms instead of traditional books may appeal to children who enjoy using technology (Maynard, 2010). High-interest, low-vocabulary books, often referred to as Hi/Lo books, are often recommended for children struggling with reading. These books are purposefully written with action-based, age-appropriate plotlines, and are written in short sentences with relatively simple words meant to draw in reluctant readers without going overboard in terms of difficult reading levels (Rog & Kropp, 2005). Supplementing a print collection with these types of alternatives goes a long way toward leveling the playing field for children of differing strengths and challenges.

While there are many reasons why children may become reluctant readers, the overriding solution has been made clear across the board: provide them with a wide variety of options and allow them the control of choosing for themselves (Rog & Kropp, 2005; Findlay, 2014; Snyder, 2014). Public libraries, having such a strong role in the promotion of literacy, could easily be said to have a responsibility to provide young readers with as many of these options as possible and to treat every type of subcollection with as much seriousness as the standard print collection.

Having trouble with reading is difficult and often deeply embarrassing for children. The more choices and autonomy they are offered, the more empowered they are bound to feel. This is an area in which the creativity and open-mindedness of librarians can do wonders toward improving a child's life.

QUALITY AND DEMAND REGARDING YOUNG ADULT MATERIALS

Many complaints about quality versus demand focus heavily on young adult (YA) materials. Parents and other concerned adults tend to fall into one of two camps: those who believe quality and taste are of the essence for teens, and those who believe teens should read anything and everything of interest to them in order to support their developing sense of self (Calkins, 2014).

A few decades ago, YA literature was a different type of genre than it is today. The days of Judy Blume's beloved and often-banned books dealing with first periods, first-time sex, and secretive masturbation, and of S. E. Hinton's *Outsiders*, which depicted teenagers leading lives of violence brought on by their dysfunctional or absent families have given way to a new era of teen issues in YA literature. By 1971, teens were devouring the anonymously written diary, later discovered to be a novel in the form of a diary (Gershowitz, 2013), *Go Ask Alice*, in which a virtuous, awkward teenage girl's life spirals out of control as she descends deeper and deeper into a world of drugs, prostitution, rape, and homelessness, culminating in a fatal overdose (Anonymous, 1971). *Go Ask Alice*, as shocking as it was for its time, was a cautionary tale, and it is often assigned to high school students as required reading. It did, however, set the stage for more sex, more violence, and more shock value in YA books to come.

Taking a stroll around a public library's YA section will reveal many similar plots, characters, and themes. From sensitive, sparkling vampires to young lovers facing terminal illness to fabulously dressed young backstabbers, the high drama of YA literature is what makes it appeal to young readers—and this fact often makes adults feel either appreciative or uneasy.

How Dark Is Too Dark?

In her *Wall Street Journal* article "Darkness Too Visible," Meghan Cox Gurdon (2011) lamented the dark nature of contemporary YA literature, noting the frequent disturbing themes of incest, abduction, domestic violence, and the occult. Depictions of joy, happiness, and morality didn't seem to have a place in YA fiction, claimed Gurdon, but addiction, sexual assault, and pathological violence were all too common for her sensibilities. Sherman Alexie's National Book

Award-winning YA novel *The Absolutely True Diary of a Part-Time Indian*, which remains the most challenged book since 2013 (Crum, 2014), took a substantial grilling in Gurdon's article, along with Suzanne Collins' *The Hunger Games* trilogy, for their depictions of violence; and Cheryl Rainfield's *Scars* was criticized for its sexual-abuse-survivor protagonist's habit of cutting herself as she attempts to remember the identity of her attacker. In a later article, Gurdon (2013) pointed out that if adults write, publish, and market these books, then teens will have no reason to believe that their contents can possibly be harmful. Gurdon stressed that adults are expected to keep children safe in every other area of life, but somehow YA books get a free pass for fear that not allowing kids to read them might be labeled as a discriminatory action, bringing YA literature into the left-versus-right political arena.

Gurdon's 2011 article started something of a firestorm among YA authors, librarians, and other allies of the genre. Alexie, for his part, was especially not amused. Firing back with his own *Wall Street Journal* article, "Why the Best Kids' Books Are Written in Blood," Alexie (2011) compared the events in *The Absolutely True Diary of a Part-Time Indian* to his own difficult childhood, which was rife with poverty, abuse, and self-loathing, and stated his wish that he'd had access to the honesty and bluntness of today's YA books to help him through his own development into adulthood.

Whichever side appeals, it is true that YA fiction often focuses on the dark, the disturbing, and the depressing—to the point where it's even been labeled sick lit, in light of all the characters with physical and mental illnesses. Yesterday's vampires have given way to today's terminal-cancer-ridden or suicidal teenagers (Carey, 2013) in John Green's *The Fault in Our Stars* and Jay Asher's *Thirteen Reasons Why*.

While many adults worry about the potential effects of dark and disturbing YA literature, advocates of the genre stress the viewpoint that adolescence is a life stage marked by intellectual and emotional growth, as well as an increasing proximity to the dangers of the world. This combination of intellectual curiosity and exposure to such dangers as illness, injury, and death may lead teens to try to make sense of their new world by reading about the alarming things they're experiencing—and reading about these very subjects provides a safe way to learn of the world's dangers without directly experiencing them (Forman, 2015).

How Shallow Is Too Shallow?

On the other end of the spectrum from dark and depressing YA books are books like the *Pretty Little Liars* and *Gossip Girl* series, in which popular, rich teens go about their overly dramatic, ultra-privileged lives as if they were Beverly Hills housewives on a reality show. The young characters in these books are impossibly wealthy, and their lives revolve around non-stop scandal in the form of partying, drinking, sleeping around, and serving up revenge to those who have dared to cross them (Gershowitz, 2013).

As is the case with dark themes, parents and other concerned adults often worry about teens reading tales of such debauchery and superficiality—and the fact that the *Gossip Girl* and *Pretty Little Liars* books were both developed into steamy television serials aimed at adolescents and younger adults certainly did little to ease these concerns.

Not all adults scorn shallow YA fiction, though—in fact, there are those who nostalgically look back on their own delightfully trashy teenage reading habits and hope today's teens have as much fun as they did (Gershowitz, 2013).

If dark reading provides a way of exploring new themes safely, then perhaps shallow reading provides a means of escapism and fantasy for teens who don't have all the privileges and drama of the characters in the books they read. It might not be the most intellectually stimulating choice, but, as it's often argued, trashy reading beats no reading at all (Krashen, 2004). If nothing else, perhaps shallow YA books serve as a gateway to Jane Austen novels or other dramatic, character-driven adult writing.

Professional Guidelines

The ALA's Library Bill of Rights stresses the importance of minors having the same intellectual freedom rights as adults and makes it clear that librarians should not block minors from accessing what they choose at their libraries (Morgan, 2010). Put simply, it is not up to librarians to judge what constitutes appropriate reading for anyone else or anyone else's children.

Adolescents and teenagers are different from children and adults in many developmental ways. As children move into adulthood, their cognition changes, and they begin to think about complex issues in new ways. Establishing a sense of self takes time and thought (Calkins, 2014). This can be a troubling time for parents and guardians who may not feel ready to see their kids go through the process of developing into young adulthood. The desire to shield children and adolescents from difficult topics like sex and death can be strong, as can the wish to keep them innocent. With this in mind, is it any wonder why so many challenges issued from concerned parents center on YA books (Calkins, 2014)?

Librarians may or may not agree about whether teens should spend their time reading about dark topics or the fake lives of sensationalistic characters, but neither are they the ones going through difficult developmental changes. Expressing sovereignty through choosing what to read can be an important step toward teens' independence, whether the adults in their lives are ready for it or not. Suppression or elimination of the materials teens want only serves to make them feel unwelcome at their public libraries. Losing the respect of a teen library user often means losing that individual as a library user for life.

QUALITY AND DEMAND REGARDING ADULT MATERIALS

As mentioned in Chapter 2, certain genres of adult materials, such as street lit, romance fiction, and graphic novels tend to be taken less seriously in public libraries' collection development activities.

Adult nonfiction books are also prone to being passed over or self-censored, especially those that contain controversial political or historical ideas, as well as those that tout not-quite-scientific, potentially dangerous, theories.

Holocaust Denial Books

Holocaust denial books, which seek to refute or reinterpret the well-documented history of the slaughter of over six million Jews and others during the Nazi regime of World War II, have caused a great deal of controversy and anxiety among public librarians. Some of these books are written from the perspective that the holocaust never happened, while others admit that it did, but reinterpret historical events to make them seem less monstrous—for example, there are authors who push the idea that the six million figure is far too high and that most of those assumed killed were actually secretly resettled and integrated into other cultures in other countries (Drobnicki, 2014).

Some librarians refuse to collect holocaust denial books, deeming them untrue, hateful propaganda with no scholarly merit and no place on a public library's shelves. Others, citing intellectual freedom, the First Amendment, and the need to represent all points of view, even unsavory or unorthodox ones, do collect these materials with the idea that patrons can read both sides and come to their own conclusions, and trusting that the truth speaks for itself (Drobnicki, 2014). The only thing librarians seem to agree on in this area is that these books make them uncomfortable. What they do about that discomfort varies widely from library to library.

Unproven Medical Science

Books promoting so-called miracle cures and other unproven scientific theories are very popular, especially since the publication of Kevin Trudeau's bestselling *Natural Cures "They" Don't Want You to Know About*. After the success of Trudeau's book, a surge of similar books with provocative-sounding titles hinting at some secret conspiracy, all claiming to reveal secret cures for conditions from menopause to weight gain, occurred, causing debate among public librarians who were torn between giving their communities the books they desired and worrying about the potentially damaging information within (Andriani, 2006). Librarians have been reported to often feel anxious about supplying health-related information to patrons because so many theories, proven and unproven, are readily available on the Web. Furthermore, librarians must contend with the unspoken but often-assumed idea that a librarian, when suggesting certain titles, is somehow vouching for the information contained within. Providing access to materials about hot-topic issues such as vaccinations can be difficult for librarians, who, as laypersons themselves when it comes to medicine, may fear being assumed to be experts, thus possibly causing damage or illness to their patrons (Smith, Hundal, & Keselman, 2014).

Creationism and Evolution

Other materials open to debate about their place in public libraries include those touting intelligent design theories while denying evolution. Creationist groups have been known to donate books on intelligent design to both public and school libraries, only to launch public attacks and accuse the libraries of practicing censorship when the donations are not added to the collections, even if there was already a blend of intelligent design books alongside those on evolution (O'Sullivan & O'Sullivan, 2007). The fact that these donations are made with an attitude of add-this-book-or-else makes selection decisions even more uncomfortable for public librarians. It can be difficult enough to choose from among controversial books without the threat of a challenge attached. Such a threat might frighten a librarian into adding books that don't meet the selection criteria out of fear of controversy, or it might lead to a librarian self-censoring perfectly appropriate books out of righteousness or anger at the bullying undertones of the donation, depending on the beliefs of the librarian in question and the appropriateness of the books.

Professional Responsibilities and the Freedom to Read Statement

Making decisions about controversial materials is difficult, but the ALA offers professional guidelines to make it simpler and to ease fears of complaints or challenges from community members.

The ALA's Freedom to Read Statement (FTRS) goes into great detail about what librarians should keep in mind when developing their collections and is a useful resource for librarians wondering how to solve predicaments such as whether to collect potentially inaccurate scientific materials.

The FTRS states that librarians have a responsibility to keep their collections stocked with materials that reflect diverse points of view, including "those that are unorthodox, unpopular, or considered dangerous by the majority" (ALA, 2006b). This would certainly be true of many books that could be considered historically inaccurate or pushing junk science—and so these books do indeed have a place in a public library collection, and they should ideally be shelved alongside other books dealing with similar issues from varying points of view and theories.

The FTRS also clarifies that librarians do not necessarily endorse every idea they present through their collections, and that to attempt to do so would, in fact, create an ethical conundrum, as it would be an instance of deciding for the public what should and should not be included based on subjective moral standards (ALA, 2006b). Therefore, public library collections are not reflections of librarians' thought processes, moral values, or other personal feelings. Rather, they are reflections of the communities surrounding them—meaning they are diverse, multilayered, and complex.

A thoughtful examination of the issue of quality versus demand through the lens of the FTRS helps librarians understand that they can, in fact, purchase books that the public demands and that are big sellers while still maintaining comprehensive, diverse collections representing a wide range of viewpoints. The patrons at a public library will select what they choose to read from the collections provided. It is not the place of librarians to tell their patrons what to believe, even if it's feared that they may be putting themselves in danger. However, it is absolutely the place of a librarian to offer balanced collections and trust the members of their communities to make the best use of them. Therefore, no suppression or self-censorship is ever necessary or encouraged.

SCIENCE AND PSEUDO-SCIENCE

In 2004, the infomercial marketer and self-proclaimed whistle-blower Kevin Trudeau released a book titled *Natural Cures "They" Don't Want You to Know About*. *The New York Times* bestseller, which is written in a dramatic, even inflammatory, style rife with unnecessary italics, words spelled out all in capital letters, explanation points, and scare quotes (even in the title), blasts traditional medicine and promises a long life of fitness, vibrant health, and a complete lack of illness, so long as the reader follows Trudeau's plan. Throughout the book, Trudeau makes almost-constant use of paranoia-inducing insinuations that valuable medical advice is being suppressed by the medical establishment (Trudeau, 2004).

Trudeau condemns the American Cancer Society, American Heart Association, American Red Cross, and the American Psychiatric Association. These trade organizations, he claims, only serve to sustain and even encourage disease in a never-ending effort to make money. If people stopped getting sick, Trudeau's reasoning goes, these associations would run out of money to conduct research, prescribe medications, and perform new surgeries to treat, but not cure, the diseases they rely upon to stay in business (Trudeau, 2004).

Some of Trudeau's advice is common enough: abstain from smoking, adopt a positive attitude, and reduce stress—although advice on how to accomplish this reduction in stress isn't presented. Beyond this clearly prudent advice, readers are counseled to "use our mind and words to create a healthy alkaline body pH" (Trudeau, 2004, p. 120), "get something to neutralize electromagnetic chaos," (Trudeau, 2004, p. 164), and "get a gentle wind project instrument" (Trudeau, 2004, p. 165), again with no specifics offered on how to go about doing so or even what these statements actually mean or what products these are. Trudeau also advises undergoing 15 colonics in 30 days, submitting to parasitic cleanses, not eating anything that came out of a microwave, wearing white clothing, giving and receiving many hugs, and practicing the religion of Scientology. Despite Trudeau's fantastical claims and passing references to studies, the book contains no bibliography, no references, and no citations (Trudeau, 2004).

Natural Cures "They" Don't Want You to Know About launched a debate among librarians regarding issues of quality versus demand. Some fell on the side of nonjudgmental access to whatever materials the public desires, and others found themselves feeling uncomfortable providing access to a book they strongly felt was full of dangerous lies. Others brought up the fact that the Internet is stuffed with medical advice, good and bad—so how much worse could a book with scientifically unproven theories really be (Thompson & Thompson, 2007)? However one looks at the issue, an enduring question remains: at what point, if any, would a refusal to purchase the book, especially in cases in which it's known to be desired by library users, be considered an act of suppression or even self-censorship?

Natural Cures "They" Don't Want You to Know About is by no means the only book of its kind. Suzanne Somers, the sitcom actress, author, and frequent infomercial hawker, has made wild-seeming claims about people who follow the weight loss plans outlined in her many books losing up to 250 pounds, although Somers does not cite any source material or provide names or identifying details of these supposed success stories (Davis, 2008).

It is entirely true that some people may very well have enjoyed great success following Trudeau's or Somers' advice, but firm scientific research has established over and over again that the odds of such phenomena happening on a regular basis are extremely low (Davis, 2008). Nevertheless, it's easy to feel tempted by the promises of miracle cures purporting to guarantee readers to lose weight, look better, and live long, active, healthy lives. These books are very much in demand, and even those librarians who know through bitter experience that the claims made within are too fantastical to be true very often purchase them for their collections because the public desires them and because they have a tendency to become bestsellers—making their absence only sting more strongly of suppression than it would with less-popular books. The question is: How can librarians striving to keep their patrons satisfied provide for the wants and needs of the public, while creating comprehensive collections that truly reflect diverse opinions and scientific theories?

TIPS AND TRAPS: TRUSTING YOUR PATRONS TO THINK FOR THEMSELVES

Tips

- During reader's advisory interactions, remember that while not all genres of writing are considered quality literature, it is not a librarian's place to decide what is best for someone else to read.

- Teens are going through an important developmental phase, and their reading choices, odd as they may seem, are sure to reflect this.

- Balance is key—a comprehensive, quality collection will reflect different points of view as equally as possible.

> **Traps**
> - The stereotype of the all-knowing librarian doesn't help anyone—keep an open mind about new and varied genres such as street lit.
> - Guiding missions last much longer than trends—when adding a new, exciting service or program, keep in mind the guiding mission behind these additions and avoid adding new services only for the sake of fashion.
> - Offering reader's advisory services to patrons who don't want this type of advice can be seen as condescending and may result in less frequent interaction with patrons, not more.

WHAT WOULD YOU DO?

Diane was amused when two teenage boys came to the reference desk asking for *Mein Kampf.* She took the snickering boys to the stacks and handed them Adolf Hitler's book about his (failed) plans for the future of Germany and the Nazi party. "I hope you read it and learn from it," she told them. Diane was proud to work for a library that contained controversial books. After all, she figured, how else can people be expected to educate themselves?

One of the boys, Connor, came back a week later and returned the book. Diane asked him what he thought of it. "It was dumb," Connor answered. "But my friend Nick really liked it. He's looking for more Nazi books."

"Are you and Connor doing a school project on World War II?" Diane asked.

"Nah," said Connor. "He's just really into that stuff. I think it's stupid, but he thinks that skinhead stuff is cool."

"Well," she told Connor. "I hope he grows out of it."

Nick began coming to the library more often, usually without Connor. His clothing and mannerisms reflected his newfound fascination with neo-Nazism. He wore a jacket with a confederate flag patched on one arm, and his hair was buzzed nearly to the scalp. He asked Diane for books and documentaries on Hitler and specifically requested as many holocaust denial books as possible. Diane, a bit shaken, provided them all, hoping Nick would pass through this phase quickly and learn from it.

One day, Connor came in and asked Diane if she'd seen Nick lately. "He's joined up with some crazy group online," Connor told her. "They're the real deal—violent, racist, out for blood," Connor shook his head. "I'm worried about him," he admitted. "He wasn't always like this, you know. We were best friends. Now I'm worried he's going to do something really bad."

A week later, Diane read about the arson in the paper, realizing with horror that Nick had been the ringleader. He had targeted a synagogue—Diane's synagogue, in fact. She felt her stomach sink thinking of all the materials she had given him, hoping he'd use his head and realize what kind of road he was going down. Now, at 16, Nick was going to be charged as an adult and likely sent to prison for years. Diane wasn't amused any more, the way she had been when she handed the snickering boys *Mein Kampf.* Now she was just angry—at Nick and at herself.

Diane had always believed that information was the road to understanding and acceptance. This was why she had become a librarian. But now she wasn't so sure. Her coworkers and supervisor reassured her that she had been doing her job, and doing it well—it wasn't her fault that some kid made a terrible choice. Diane appreciated their kindness, but she started looking into other careers, realizing that the burden of Nick's crime was too much for her to bear.

QUESTIONS TO CONSIDER

- Do you feel that there are books that may be dangerous to young minds? If so, do you feel public libraries should include them in their collections? Why or why not?
- Do you feel that there are books that are not of high enough quality to be included in a public library collection? Why or why not?
- As a librarian, how would you go about advising and encouraging a parent concerned about his child's reluctant reading?
- If a parent of a teenager came to you asking what her child currently had checked out from the library, how would you respond? Why?

REFERENCES

Alexie, S. (2011, June 9). Why the best kids' books are written in blood. *The Wall Street Journal.* Retrieved from http://blogs.wsj.com/speakeasy/2011/06/09/why-the-best-kids-books-are-written-in-blood/

American Library Association. (2006a, June 30). Library Bill of Rights. Retrieved from http://www.ala.org/advocacy/intfreedom/librarybill

American Library Association. (2006b, July 26). The Freedom to Read Statement. Retrieved from http://www.ala.org/advocacy/intfreedom/statementspols/freedomread statement

Andriani, L. (2006). The Kevin Trudeau effect [cover story]. *Publishers Weekly, 253*(26), 20–21.

Anonymous. (1971). *Go ask Alice.* Englewood Cliffs, NJ: Prentice-Hall.

Bickford, J. (2010). Consumerism: How it impacts play and its presence in library collections. *Children & Libraries: The Journal of the Association for Library Science to Children, 8*(3), 53–56.

Calkins, E. (2014, October 8). The right to read: The how and why of supporting intellectual freedom for teens [web log post]. *In the Library with the Lead Pipe,* 1–8. Retrieved from http://www.inthelibrarywiththeleadpipe.org/2014/the-right-to-read-the-how-and-why-of-supporting-intellectual-freedom-for-teens/

Carey, T. (2013, January 2). The "sick-lit" books aimed at children: It's a disturbing phenomenon. Tales of teenage cancer, self-harm and suicide . . . *The Daily Mail.* Retrieved from http://www.dailymail.co.uk/femail/article-2256356/The-sick-lit-books-aimed-children-Its-disturbing-phenomenon-Tales-teenage-cancer-self-harm-suicide-.html

Crum, M. (2014, September 22). Banned books by the numbers. Retrieved from http://www.huffingtonpost.com/2014/09/22/banned-books-week-infographic_n_5852234.html

Davis, R. J. (2008). *The healthy skeptic: Cutting through the hype about your health.* Berkeley and Los Angeles, CA: University of California Press.

Drobnicki, J. A. (2014). Holocaust denial literature twenty years later: A follow-up investigation of public librarians' attitudes regarding acquisition and access. *Judaica Librarianship 18*, 54–87.

Findlay, D. (2014). Reluctant readers. *Library Sparks, 12*(2), 8–15.

Forman, G. (2015, February 6). Teens crave young adult books on really dark topics (and that's ok). *Time*. Retrieved from http://time.com/3697845/if-i-stay-gayle-forman-young-adult-i-was-here/

Freeman, R. S., & Hvode, D. (2003). The Indiana township library program, 1852–1872: A well selected, circulating library as an educational instrumentality. In R. S Freeman & D. Hvode (eds.), *Libraries to the people: Histories of outreach* (pp. 128–147). Jefferson, NC: McFarland & Co.

Genco, B. A. (1988). Mass market books: Their place in the library. *School Library Journal, 35*(4), 40–41.

Gershowitz, E. (2013). What makes a good "bad" book? *Horn Book Magazine, 89*(4), 84–90.

Gurdon, M. C. (2011, June 4). Darkness too visible. *The Wall Street Journal*. Retrieved from http://www.wsj.com/articles/SB10001424052702303657404576357622592697038

Gurdon, M. C. (2013, July/August 4). The case for good taste in children's books. *Imprimis, 42*(7/8), 1–7.

Huynh, A. (2004). Background essay on collection development, evaluation, and management for public libraries. *Current Studies in Librarianship, 28*(1/2), 19–37.

Krashen, S. (2004). *The power of reading: Insights from the research*. Portsmouth, NH: Libraries Unlimited.

Maynard, S. (2010). The impact of e-Books on young children's reading habits. *Publishing Research Quarterly, 26*(4), 236–248.

Morgan, C. D. (2010). Challenges and issues today. In American Library Association Office for Intellectual Freedom, *Intellectual freedom manual* [Foreword]. Chicago: American Library Association.

O'Sullivan, M. K., & O'Sullivan, C. (2007). Selection or censorship? Libraries and the intelligent design debate. *Library Review, 56*(3), 200–207.

Pakaln, A. (2014). Public libraries: How to save them. *Public Libraries, 53*(4), 7–9.

Rog, L. J., & Kropp, P. (2005). Reaching struggling readers in intermediate grades with books they can and want to read. *School Libraries in Canada, 25*(1), 44–49.

Smith, C. A., Hundal, S., & Keselman, A. (2014). Knowledge gaps among public librarians seeking vaccination information: A qualitative study. *Journal of Consumer Health on the Internet, 18*(1), 44–66.

Snyder, J. (2014). Keep 'em reading. *Library Sparks, 12*(2), 24–27.

Thompson, S.T.C., & Thompson, R. P. (2007, June). Skeptical medical reference: Helping patrons find critical resources for consumer health issues. *Library Philosophy and Practice*. Retrieved from http://www.webpages.uidaho.edu/~mbolin/thompson2.pdf

Trudeau, K. (2004). *Natural cures "they" don't want you to know about*. Elk Grove Village, IL: Alliance Publishing Group.

Chapter 9

WHAT TO DO WHEN COMPLAINTS AND CHALLENGES HAPPEN

WHAT CONSTITUTES A COMMUNITY CHALLENGE?

Considering all the long hours, deeply critical thought, and budgeting logistics that go into collection development, is it any wonder why any whisper of a challenge—whether casual or formal—can raise defenses and cause such high anxiety? Dealing with community challenges is one of the most difficult experiences librarians can face in their careers. Fortunately, though, a wealth of tools exists to help librarians respond effectively and professionally when the appropriateness of materials in their collections is challenged. It may not be anybody's idea of a good time, but with support and information, community challenges can be handled within the professional parameters of librarianship, allowing all parties to come out wiser in the end.

Part of what makes a complaint so nerve-wracking lies in not knowing if it is being issued as a real challenge or if it might simply be a case of a patron expressing distaste for an item or venting frustration about the collection. It can be difficult to gauge whether someone is truly horrified and wishing to take it further or simply having a bad day and needing to blow off a bit of steam. In fact, in many cases, the complainant might not even know for sure what outcome is desired during the heat of the moment. As mentioned in Chapter 5, approximately 90 percent of complaints begin and end at a service desk and never escalate into full-on challenges, mainly due to library employees' customer service skills (Pinnell-Stephens, 2012). A bit of empathy and active listening combined with respectful conversation about library policies and intellectual freedom tenets goes a long way toward helping an upset patron understand the context and policies surrounding a complaint.

The Office for Intellectual Freedom (OIF) deals extensively with community complaints and challenges and offers a great deal of assistance in breaking down the various types of challenges, thus helping keep librarians aware of the different types of concerns they may encounter. Challenges are divided into four categories:

- Expressions of concern
- Written complaints
- Public attacks
- Censorship

When handling a complaint, the first step is to determine what type of challenge is being extended (American Library Association [ALA], 2013a).

Expressions of Concern

The OIF classifies an expression of concern as simply an inquiry that is delivered with an air of judgment (ALA, 2013a). This could be a statement along the lines of "I checked out this book, but I stopped reading it because of all the profanity—why are my tax dollars paying for such nasty books?" or "Why

> When somebody comes in and they start complaining and they're very upset, I think it makes perfect sense to say, 'Oh, I'm so sorry,' because nobody comes to the library in hopes that they'll find something that irritated them.
> —James LaRue, Director, American Library Association Office for Intellectual Freedom and former Library Director of Douglas County (Colorado) Libraries.

do you have so many children's books about divorced families? Traditional families should be represented too." These types of statements may not contain any threats or indications to follow up, but they have overtones of judgment and can cause discomfort and defensiveness. Expressions of concern may or may not lead to further action.

Responding to Expressions of Concern

When faced with an expression of concern, it is imperative to convey that all library users will be taken seriously when they express discomfort with a library item. This is a time to ask questions but not a time to make idle or impetuous promises. Saying "Can you let me know what in particular about this book concerns you?" opens a dialogue and displays concern for the complainant. Conversely, "We'll make sure to change its collection status right away" makes an irrational, knee-jerk promise.

Expressions of concern also open conversations about selection procedures and the collection development policy, while emphasizing the importance of diversity in public library collections (Pekoll & Adams, 2015).

Often, respectful discourse will leave the patron feeling less frustrated and more informed. Remember to always end these conversations by thanking the patron for taking an interest in the public library collection. If the patron wants to take the complaint further, then an explanation of the reconsideration process may be given, along with a copy of the collection development policy and a Request for Reconsideration Form. Afterward, document the interaction and keep the library's management team informed of the situation. No further action is necessary until (and unless) the Request for Reconsideration Form is filled out and submitted (Pekoll & Adams, 2015).

Written Complaints

A written complaint adds an element of formality. In the form of a Request for Reconsideration Form, letter, e-mail, or other written form of communication, this type of complaint challenges the appropriateness of a specific item or group of items (ALA, 2013a). Written complaints may be directed toward a particular librarian or staff member, or to the director, board of trustees, or other managing body of the library. Submitting a written complaint in the form of a Request for Reconsideration Form is a precursor to further action (Pekoll & Adams, 2015), whereas other forms of written complaints may or may not simply be actions with no follow-up expected. If no Request for Reconsideration Form is provided, the complainant should be contacted in a timely and respectful manner to determine whether further action is desired (LaRue, 2007). If the complainant does want to make the complaint formal, the form should be promptly provided.

Responding to Written Complaints

Once a Request for Reconsideration Form has been received, a timely response should be delivered. This includes an acknowledgement of the complainant's wish to have the material in question reconsidered, along with an approximate time line and list of steps that will be taken (Pekoll & Adams, 2015).

A careful review of the complaint comes next. During this review, it should be determined whether the complainant has read or otherwise experienced the item in its entirety, whether the complainant is acting alone or as part of an organized group, and what actions are desired by the complainant. It is also helpful at this stage to review the number of checkouts the item has had and to determine how many other libraries in both local and greater geographic areas own the item, in order to determine its popularity (Pekoll & Adams, 2015). Most important, make no judgments or decisions until the complaint has been reviewed carefully and thoroughly.

Once the complaint and item have been reviewed, it is time for the library's management team to come together to determine if the item actually violates the collection development policy. This is not a time to rush to judgment but to think carefully and thoughtfully about the nature of the complaint as it relates to the collection development policy and the Library Bill of Rights. Follow policy as it is written and remain objective and transparent. If the item meets the selection requirements, it should stay where it was. If it does not, then it must be decided whether it should be moved to another section of the library or, in cases in which policy is clearly breached, removed from the collection (LaRue, 2007; Pekoll & Adams, 2015).

Once a decision is made, a personalized letter (not a form letter) should be sent to the complainant explaining the decision and the appeal process, should the complainant wish to continue with the challenge (Pekoll & Adams, 2015).

The last step, which is very important, is to report the challenge to the OIF in order to assist them in keeping accurate records of challenges (Pekoll & Adams, 2015).

Public Attacks

A public attack isn't necessarily a formal occurrence, but it gets the pot stirring by spreading complaints about the material in question to media outlets or other groups (ALA OIF, 2010; ALA, 2013a). Actions such as starting a social media smear campaign about a library's inclusion of an item, writing letters to the editors of local newspapers, starting inflammatory blogs, or creating other sources of open complaints in an attempt to draw attention and outrage about the item in question would be classified as public attacks.

Ginny and Jim Maziarka's vilification of the West Bend Memorial Library in Wisconsin, as described in Chapter 2, is an example of a public attack. Although it eventually became a formal challenge, the situation began with two people gathering petition signatures, holding community-based meetings, and taking to social media to spread their desire to ban LGBT (lesbian, gay, bisexual, and transgender)-themed books at the library.

Responding to Public Attacks

While expressions of concern and written complaints are easier to deal with, public attacks can be quite another story. The OIF recommends having one spokesperson to represent the library system. This person should have a short, succinct speech ready to deliver to the media or any community organizations about the library's collection development policy and the Library Bill of Rights. This representative should avoid getting into arguments or adopting a defensive strategy of communication. Instead, the focus should be on positive communication about the services the library offers, the people who have been helped, and the allies the library has in the community (ALA, 2013b).

A helpful statement could be a simple "Our library respects the rights of all readers as defined in the Library Bill of Rights and supports inclusiveness and intellectual freedom. We welcome opportunities to communicate with the community about our collection and services, but we do not practice censorship or suppression."

On the other hand, a statement along the lines of "These people don't understand how libraries operate and are just trying to pick a fight" is defensive and catty and would only fan the flames.

Censorship

Outright censorship occurs when an item in a library's collection undergoes a change in status at the hands of someone in authority based on its subject matter

(ALA OIF, 2010). This could take the form of a library director or department manager choosing to move an item from the children's section to the adult section, or electing to place it behind a barrier such as the reference desk or an office door so that people have to specifically ask for it, or even removing it from the collection altogether in order to appease the complainant and alleviate criticism.

Responding to Censorship

While there are recommended methods for dealing with expressions of concern, written complaints, and public attacks, calls for and acts of censorship present a different challenge altogether. Acts of censorship happen within the library, either in response to a challenge or for some other reason, be it real or imagined. While quality, ongoing training, and careful writing of the collection development policy might keep censorship at bay, the fact remains that it does happen, and it does violate the Library Bill of Rights.

If you work for a library that practices censorship, you may wish to report it anonymously to the OIF in order to help keep their database accurate. An open conversation with trusted staff members might be wise, but it also might backfire if the library is unrepentant about practicing suppression. Beyond that, the only choices available are very difficult ones indeed.

Conversely, if you work for a library in which you yourself practice censorship, it can only be recommended that you examine your motives for doing so very carefully and honestly. The good news is that what has been done can very often be undone, and mistakes can be corrected.

HANDLING A CHALLENGE

Despite thorough preparation and well-written policies, a community challenge can arise at any time. Among other reasons, challenges often come up when a patron misunderstands the role of a public library's collection within its larger community. For example, it is often assumed that the library officially endorses the subject matter or theme of every book in its collection, or that certain books are simply bad while others are good, and that people (librarians included) generally agree on what elements constitute this differentiation. It is also often assumed that for every book promoting one side of an issue, there will be another book promoting the opposite side, regardless of how many books may be available to represent each side of the debate (Pinnell-Stephens, 1999; Pinnell-Stephens, 2012).

Another common misunderstanding occurs when parents or members of community organizations make false assumptions about the role of public libraries in regard to minors. There is a common belief that public libraries will not house any materials that parents could potentially find objectionable, or that librarians will not allow minors to check out certain materials. This is, of course, impossible, as every parent holds unique standards of what is and is not appropriate, and public librarians are not able to assume *in loco parentis* status for other people's children (Pinnell-Stephens, 1999; Pinnell-Stephens, 2012). Misunderstandings such as these, paired with the fact that it is quite possible that there might be an actual problem with the material in question, such as where it is housed or labeled, make the probability of a challenge a constant possibility—in fact, public libraries are the second-most challenged type of library, behind school libraries (Evans & Saponaro, 2005).

The Review Process

The review process begins as quickly as possible after a Request for Reconsideration Form is handed over. Ideally, the first step will be a thorough examination of the collection development policy, ensuring that the respondents are as fresh and familiar with it as possible (ALA OIF, 2010). During the review process, whether it's short or drawn-out, the challenged material must be kept in the collection just as it was before the complaint was lodged. It is quite possible that the review process will lead the reviewers to realize that the material is, in fact, inappropriate for the collection as stated in the collection development policy (or it might reveal a gap in the collection development policy that needs to be addressed) and should therefore be either removed or placed in a different area of the library (ALA OIF, 2010), but until and unless this happens, the item should stay exactly where it was. Whether the item stays or goes after careful and thorough review, the complainant must be notified of the decision as soon as possible after it is made, in the form of a personal letter—not an impersonal form letter or anything that may smack thereof (ALA OIF, 2010).

If the complainant expresses dissatisfaction with the result and a desire to continue challenging the material, what comes next may be either one action or a series of actions. Although it is often assumed that the complaint must immediately be brought to the library director or library board, this is not always the most appropriate way to proceed—in fact, the OIF states that a public hearing should not be a routine reaction to a challenge, but a last-resort action (Preer, 2014). There are no legalities requiring libraries to hold hearings in response to challenges and doing so may often be too hasty a first step. Meeting with an individual librarian is often more effective—for example, if the material in question is a picture book, then having the complainant meet one-on-one with the head of the children's department might be the most fitting way to begin a dialogue. At other times, depending on the nature of the complaint, a meeting with the director may be deemed most suitable, or, in other cases, with a young adult (YA) or a technology-oriented librarian (ALA OIF, 2010). Since every challenge and every library is unique, it wouldn't be sensible to follow a strict protocol for every case. There are times, however, when holding a challenge hearing is warranted. A complainant who remains dissatisfied and wants to pursue the matter further has every right to do so and should be advised to initiate the process with a formal written request. In these cases, the existing library policy guide will determine who among the governing members of the library will be present at the hearing (ALA OIF, 2010).

Preparing for a Hearing

Preparation is of the utmost importance before a challenge hearing. If the hearing is scheduled to take place during a regular library board meeting, it should be placed first on the agenda so the complainant and supporters, if any are brought along, don't have to wait through other business before being invited to voice their concerns (LaRue, 2007). Even more advisable is for the meeting to be held outside of regular library board business, as challenge hearings have the potential to be lengthy and contentious (ALA, 2013b). Be sure to fill in your community members ahead of time about the nature of the hearing and invite them to come along to share their feedback. Inviting local media to cover the event is also recommended, as is sending press releases along with copies of the library's collection development policy and the Library Bill of Rights (ALA OIF, 2010; ALA, 2013b). The main point here is to remember that this is a public hearing, not one to be held quietly behind closed doors in a hush-hush environment (ALA, 2013b). Also, in the preparation stage, it helps to decide on a strict beginning and ending time, to avoid having the hearing last into the wee hours (ALA, 2013b). Also, arrange to record the hearing and make the recording available for public viewing as soon as possible afterward (ALA, 2013b). This not only allows for an atmosphere of transparency but helps avoid any misunderstood communication.

A very important part of the preparation process is to make sure all members of the library's governance are familiar and up-to-date with the collection development policy, the specific complaint, the steps already taken, and the reason for the initial decision, which proved unsatisfactory to the complainant. A thorough review of all these elements is advisable during this stage, in order to ensure that any unanswered questions or concerns are resolved before the hearing takes place (ALA OIF, 2010).

The preparation stage is also an ideal time to seek assistance and advice from outside sources, such as your state's intellectual freedom committee as well as the OIF itself, plus local educational organizations, colleges, schools, and anyone else who might be able to offer advice and support (ALA OIF, 2010; ALA, 2013b). The Freedom to Read Foundation (FTRF) also serves as an excellent resource and a good place to obtain legal assistance (Evans & Saponaro, 2012; FTRF, n.d.). There is absolutely no need to go it alone. Community challenges are mentally taxing and emotionally exhausting. Asking for help in advance can, at the very least, boost one's confidence. Even more, it helps in the process of gaining allies, expertise, and support.

During the Hearing

As people enter the room to attend the hearing, they should be handed copies of the library's collection development policy and the Library Bill of Rights. People who wish to speak publically at the hearing for either side may be identified at this time and placed in order on the list of speakers (FTRF, n.d.; ALA OIF, 2010).

It is recommended that the head of the governing body (usually the president of the library board or a designee) be in charge of running the hearing. This person is responsible for establishing that the reason for the meeting is to hear both sides of the issue and to declare that a decision will be made afterward. It should be stated that the decision will be announced at either the next board meeting on the regular calendar or an alternate time. In either case, the time and place of the announcement should be stated. Both sides of the issue may then be presented, and speakers may be invited to state their support for either side, while being held to the predetermined time limit (ALA OIF, 2010; ALA, 2013b).

While all of this may seem overly formal or simplistic, things can quickly become heated for all of the involved parties. Throughout the hearing, no matter how uncomfortable things become, it is imperative to maintain a calm demeanor and to remember to be courteous and willing to listen to all parties with genuine concern. Meeting negative comments about the library's collection with positive comments about intellectual freedom in a composed and friendly manner allows everyone involved with the hearing to understand the library's objective stance (ALA, 2013b). Simply reminding the parties at the hearing that the position of a collector is positive in nature—seeking a *yes* answer, while the complainant is seeking a negative, or a *no* answer—helps in maintaining confidence under pressure (Evans & Saponaro, 2012), as does basing responses and questions on professional judgments rather than value judgments and being actively accountable to this professional standard (ALA OIF, 2010).

After the Hearing

The governing body may come to a decision quickly, or a bit of time might be needed to think things over. Either way, the decision should not be announced until the predetermined time and place. At this next meeting, the decision may be announced and the library policy should be gone over once again, regardless of the decision. After this, the reasons for the decision should be clearly and concisely explained, while making it understood that the decision is now final (Evans & Saponaro, 2005). If the complainant wishes to continue the process further, it will typically then become a formal legal proceeding, with the library playing a much smaller and less visible role, as the process will now involve lawyers, judges, and an examination of the law rather than the library's policies (Evans & Saponaro, 2012).

COMMUNICATION GUIDELINES

Despite preparation and planning, all but the most Zen librarian involved in the process of a challenge will most likely feel a range of difficult emotions when dealing with a community challenge. While no words of wisdom can adequately prepare anyone for the stress of a challenge, it is helpful to turn to the advice of experts in the fields of librarianship and communication to keep a sense of professional cool under the pressure of a challenge.

Understanding and Managing Defensiveness

Because librarians generally take their work seriously and take pride in their collections, the shock of a challenge can feel like a personal attack, even when it isn't meant to be. While it's understandable that your first instinct may be to voice reasons, justifications, and comebacks, your time is better spent taking a moment to breathe and remember that the complainant is actually judging the material in question, not the collector. Even the most perfect comeback won't resonate with a complainant who is upset. Taking a pause, remembering that the complaint is not personal, and validating the complainant's feelings is a professional and respectful way of handling stressful confrontations (Rubin, 2011).

Think back to the last time your feelings were aflame—did you want your concerns to be heard and validated during that moment, or did you want to be lectured, or even worse, proven wrong? Sliding into defensiveness is not only unhelpful to everyone involved, it is also counterproductive to the complainant's right to petition the government for a redress of grievances (ALA OIF, 2010).

APOLOGIES AND RESPONSIBILITIES

Apologizing can be a difficult thing, because it can feel like acquiescing or agreeing with something you don't actually agree with. However, a kind apology for a complainant's upset feelings leaves responsibility out of the equation. "I'm so sorry you're upset by this" is a vastly different statement than "I'm so sorry I upset you." "I know you're feeling impatient and I'm sorry the process takes so long" is not synonymous with "I'm sorry I'm dragging this out." Apologies should never be offered insincerely, but understanding and empathizing with another person's concerns is a professional and mature stance that is virtually guaranteed to make a tense situation more bearable for all parties involved.

Active Listening

There's an old adage about humans having two ears and just one mouth, and how this implies that they are better suited for listening than speaking. While this may be true, sometimes those mouths need to be reminded to let the ears in on the action. Active listening, sometimes known as effective listening, is a learned skill that helps people in all situations put aside their defenses and focus solely on hearing the details of what the other party has to say. When tensions are high and emotions are surfacing, active listening does not necessarily occur naturally. This is what makes it a skill requiring practice, not a reflex.

The common habit of half-listening while organizing one's thoughts into comebacks and statements to the contrary is not active listening, but selective listening, and often only manages to leave one party offended and the other party frustrated by creating a situation in which neither party feels respected or validated. Paying deep attention, showing genuine concern, and asking thoughtful, nonjudgmental questions in an attempt to truly understand and appreciate where the other person is coming from constitutes true active listening. Silences and long pauses are quite alright, as they allow time to think, to empathize, and to let listeners know that their words are being processed (Mosley, Tucker, & Van Winkle, 2014). There is no need to fill the air with chatter—simply focusing and allowing the speaker to be heard without judgment or criticism is the key (Kennett, 2014).

Expressing Gratitude

When dealing with a community challenge, active listening serves as a valuable tool throughout the entire process. Listening attentively is not at all synonymous with caving or agreeing never to state one's own points—it is simply a method of handling a potentially contentious issue in a professional and respectful manner. In instances of community challenges, sincerely thank your complainant, who, after all, is actively engaging with the library and playing an enthusiastic role in its collection. How refreshing it would be if all community members were so involved with their public libraries. Whether the concern is misguided or valid is irrelevant at this stage in the communication process. Thanking the complainant simply expresses that the time and attention paid to the library collection are appreciated (LaRue, 2007).

Restating and Paraphrasing

A substantial part of active listening is letting complainants know that their words have been heard and that their point of view has been understood. This can be done by restating concerns using different wording. Simply parroting back the complainant's own words can come across as sarcastic or thoughtless, but using your own words to convey your understanding does the opposite. When done thoughtfully, paraphrasing indicates that you have heard and understood both the feelings and the content behind the complainant's words (Rubin, 2011). For example, it may help to meet a strongly worded "How could you allow this trash onto your shelves?" with "I'm hearing that you feel this book is inappropriate for the library and that you're wondering why we purchased it for the collection—is that correct?" Restating and paraphrasing lower the tone, while allowing complainants to know that their concerns have been heard and processed. It also allows complainants a chance to clarify their concerns if they are restated in a manner in which they disagree. Fully understanding a complainant's position serves as the first step in the creation of a dialogue (LaRue, 2007).

Body Language

Active listening involves more than just listening and speaking. Your own body language can express quite a lot. Maintain an open facial expression and regular eye contact, and avoid crossing your arms, which sends a message that you are closed off both physically and mentally. Maintain an open posture while paying attention with your whole body. Lean a bit forward, but respect the complainant's personal space—and never step toward an angry person, as this can come across as an act of intimidation (Mosley et al., 2014).

Cultural Sensitivity

Body language appropriateness varies from culture to culture, so pay close attention to any clues about what level of personal space is appropriate. Back off a bit if you sense tension about your proximity to the complainant. If language is a barrier, using an interpreter may help the conversation flow with more ease. At the very least, avoid using jargon that could get lost in translation (Mosley et al., 2014).

Responding to Concerns

Once a complainant's point of view is fully understood, both parties can speak or write with clarity. In this stage, it is essential to respond to the concerns that have been brought up, not to the person as an individual. Anything that smacks of a personal slight will very likely dismantle the process of effective dialoging. It can take time and a good amount of additional active listening and restating rounds to get to the true heart of the matter (LaRue, 2007). Perhaps a complainant first expressed concern over a book that was seen as inappropriate for teens due to depictions of violence. Keep in mind that it can take some time and effort to get to the issue behind the issue. For example, in this case, the complainant may want the book relocated to the adult section or have it removed altogether, or it could be that the complainant thinks the item should have a label or warning attached. Acknowledging these expectations does not necessarily constitute accepting them or agreeing to take the desired action. Once the true nature of the concern is understood, it can be addressed within the professional guidelines of librarianship. This is also an ideal time to clarify the library's collection development policy as well as the tenets of intellectual freedom, the Library Bill of Rights, and the First Amendment (LaRue, 2007), since the complainant needs to have an understanding of these as the process moves on into the development of an action plan.

Action Plan

Once both parties understand the concern and the professional parameters surrounding it, the time has come to speak about the action the library will take, or the lack thereof. This will surely vary in each unique instance, but some common actions include moving the item in question from one section to another, if it was analyzed and decided that it actually is more fitting for, say, the adult collection than the YA section; keeping the item in its current area after analysis and a decision that it was, in fact, adequately placed; keeping the item, but purchasing other items to round out the collection in order to more adequately represent other points of view; or, if absolutely necessary and appropriate from the library's point of view and not as an appeasement in the face of pressure, withdrawing the item from the collection altogether (LaRue, 2007).

Chances are strong that the problem won't be something that can be solved right away, so be sure to explain the timeline to the complainant and to follow up. Promising to send an explanation in writing is often recommended as a professional courtesy, so remember to send these in a timely manner (Rubin, 2011).

While a complainant might request that some sort of warning label be placed on the offending item, and while this might, in fact, seem like a good solution, keep in mind that agreeing to do this can create a slippery slope. Librarians label their items by cataloging them and placing them in a certain section of the overall collection. To do more than that is to state, openly or subtly, that these general and nonjudgmental collection areas are not enough, and that it is necessary to break down subcollections into even smaller groupings. This is not only pointless if the item is placed in the correct subcollection, but it sets the stage for more complaints and more acquiescing, potentially leading to libraries consisting of collections divided into meaningless mini-collections based on personal feelings rather than solid cataloging (LaRue, 2007).

Explaining the Alternatives

Once all of these steps have been completed to the best of the library's ability and the complainant has been informed of the resolution or lack of resolution, the complainant may decide to accept or appeal the decision. If the resolution is not acceptable to the complainant, the library's designee has the responsibility of explaining how to go about the appeal process should this be the desired course of action (Pekoll & Adams, 2015). Respectfully explaining that the complainant may take the issue to the library board or whatever governing body the library in question defers to, and how to contact this group, is an appropriate response in this area of communication (LaRue, 2007).

Expressing Gratitude, Round Two

Whether this dialogue has taken place in person, by writing, by e-mail, or whatever other means, it always helps to finish on another earnest note of thanks. This takes the communication cycle full circle and ends it on a respectful, professional note (LaRue, 2007).

WHY SO HOSTILE? TEN TIPS FOR DEALING WITH THE EMOTIONAL OR ANGRY PATRON

- Listen first, think second, speak third—you can't understand someone's point of view without hearing the whole story.
- Keep in mind that, even when upset, the complainant is engaging with the community by bringing concerns to your attention—and remember to express thanks for that involvement.

- You don't have to agree with a person to empathize—statements like "I see that this is very important to you" and "I understand your concern" help align you with the complainant and can go a long way toward finding common ground.

- Paraphrase the complainant's concerns back to be sure you fully understand—try something along the lines of "I'm hearing that you feel this book is inappropriate and possibly dangerous for an area where children congregate—is that correct?" and be open to hearing a clarification.

- If the complainant begins to use a raised voice, keep your own voice low and steady—this helps diffuse strong emotions and aids in maintaining your professionalism.

- Avoid the temptation to provide an instantaneous solution—assure the complainant that the concerns brought forth will be addressed through the library's formal channels, and express appreciation again for having shared them with you.

- Ask for help when you need it—if you sense that you're in danger or if you feel you can't maintain your professional cool, politely excuse yourself and find a supervisor or trusted coworker to speak with the complainant—and do the same for your colleagues when they need your help.

- If you're speaking on the phone, never hang up on the caller or abruptly end the call—if you need a break to collect yourself, respectfully place the caller on hold until you feel calmer, or call upon a trusted supervisor or coworker to pick up where you left off.

- Threats and intimidations are never okay—don't hesitate to call the authorities if someone implies that harm will be done to you or your livelihood.

- Don't take the law into your own hands—channel any legal questions or threats to the proper source—usually your library's management or your city's attorney.

REQUESTING ASSISTANCE FROM THE OIF

Every challenge is unique, and every complainant is an individual. There are surely times when librarians use every tool at their disposal only to still feel left floundering. The OIF spends significant time and effort helping librarians handle challenges effectively and fairly. Their website has information on how to contact them for assistance (ALA, 2013c).

Even if a challenge is being handled without assistance from the OIF, it is strongly recommended that the challenge be reported. The OIF has been keeping a database of challenged materials since 1990. The office relies on media reports and those submitted by individual librarians to keep this database current. These reports are entirely confidential, and they help the OIF compile lists of frequently challenged books for each year's Banned Books Week (ALA, 2013c). Reporting of challenges, big or small, allows the OIF to keep accurate records on intellectual freedom issues across the county, benefitting the entire profession.

TIPS AND TRAPS: HANDLING COMMUNITY CHALLENGES CONSTRUCTIVELY

Tips

- Keep in mind the importance of maintaining openness to challenges—respectful conversations begin with asking questions and listening carefully.

- Active listening is a skill that takes practice—work on applying it in other areas of life, and it will come easier in your professional duties.

- Public library patrons who express concerns about the collection are playing an active role in their library and exercising their right to file complaints if they feel such action is warranted—thanking them for this involvement is always a good starting point.

Traps

- Avoid judgmental tones when dealing with community challenges—remember to appreciate that complainants are being engaged and involved with their public libraries.

- Actions speak louder than words—keep on guard for defensive or antagonistic body language when speaking with complainants about their concerns.

- Moving, blocking, or changing the status of a challenged item is never appropriate until or unless a formal decision been finalized.

CONCLUSION AND FURTHER THINKING

Librarians, as professionals in a service-based occupation, are known for having strong customer service skills. Unfortunately, sometimes this focus on patrons' needs falls by the wayside when challenges to library collections are encountered. Just as librarians may not understand the intricacies of other professions, it would be presumptuous to assume or expect library users to have a deep understanding of collection development and intellectual freedom tenets like those in the profession hold close to their hearts.

Respectful dialogue, thoughtful explanations of the Library Bill of Rights, and active listening are excellent tools when it comes to both educating the public about the professional guidelines of librarianship in any type of challenge and to creating constructive conversations with communities and allies.

WHAT WOULD YOU DO?

As a concerned mother of twin preschoolers, Tanya was alarmed to find DVDs and books about human reproduction in her public library's children's room, well within reach of little hands. She herself didn't mind all that much, but she knew other parents who might not be quite so open-minded.

Tanya took one DVD and one book to the children's reference librarian, Sam, and asked about their presence. Sam, who had taken great pains to make sure the library's collection development policy had a section about inclusiveness and parents' responsibility to monitor their children, immediately responded with a terse lecture about how public libraries do not have *in loco parentis* status and how children's materials are not to be sequestered.

"Hey, I'm just asking a question here," Tanya replied, feeling a bit patronized. "There's no need to get snippy or throw Latin phrases at me. I'm just thinking there might be a better way to display these things."

"Well, there isn't," said Sam, keeping his eyes on his computer monitor while he spoke. These parents who expected the library to babysit their kids really got under his skin, and he was tired of having to explain intellectual freedom to every helicopter parent he encountered. "You can fill out a complaint form if you want, but what you're suggesting goes against our policy."

"Sure, I'll fill out a form," Tanya said. Sam shrugged and handed it over, and Tanya left, shaking her head in frustration. *What a snooty librarian*, she thought.

That night, Tanya filled out the Request for Reconsideration Form, and the next day, she showed it to her pastor to get his input. The pastor agreed that the library's policy and Sam's attitude were unsafe for children and should be challenged. He even added some comments of his own to the form. Tanya thought the pastor was making more of the situation than it really called for—after all, her concern was a minor one in the grand scheme of things. But she figured her pastor may have a point, and she had already rocked one boat that week—why make it two?

Within a few days, Tanya's pastor called the library and made an appointment to speak on her behalf to someone in charge. Tanya went along, although all she really wanted was for someone to hear her concerns. She wasn't interested in getting into a debate with her public library, where she took her kids at least once a week. The head of the children's department spoke with Tanya and her pastor, apologized for Sam's attitude, and promised to talk with him about his customer service skills.

Tanya was pleased with this, and decided to take it no further. Her pastor, however, had different ideas. Before long, the pastor was involved in a very public and antagonistic challenge with the library, bringing new publicity and new members to his church. Tanya, self-conscious and abashed about her role in the debacle, found another church and stopped taking her kids to the library.

QUESTIONS TO CONSIDER

- What methods do you use to keep a cool head in intense situations, and how would you employ these during a community challenge?
- Do you feel that there are times when it is best to compromise on a challenge quietly and quickly in order to avoid controversy? Why or why not?
- If faced with a statement of concern, what would you have in your librarian's bag of tricks to help diffuse the situation?

- What examples of specific wording for collection development policies can you think of that could help quell a challenge?
- In your community, what organizations can you think of that might serve as allies for your public library's intellectual freedom activities?

REFERENCES

American Library Association. (2013a, March 26). Challenges to library materials. Retrieved from http://www.ala.org/bbooks/challengedmaterials

American Library Association. (2013b, March 26). Conducting a challenge hearing. Retrieved from http://www.ala.org/bbooks/challengedmaterials/support/hearing

American Library Association. (2013c, March 26). Reporting a challenge. Retrieved from http://www.ala.org/bbooks/challengedmaterials/reporting

American Library Association Office for Intellectual Freedom. (2010). *Intellectual freedom manual*. Chicago: American Library Association.

Evans, G. E., & Saponaro, M. Z. (2005). *Developing library and information center collections*. Westport, CT: Libraries Unlimited.

Evans, G. E., & Saponaro, M. Z. (2012). *Collection management basics*. Santa Barbara, CA: Libraries Unlimited.

Freedom to Read Foundation. (n.d.). About FTRF. Retrieved from http://www.ftrf.org/?page=About

Kennett, M. (2014, November 1).Wise words: Self coach. . .effective listening. *Management Today, 60,* 52.

LaRue, J. (2007). *The new inquisition: Understanding and managing intellectual freedom challenges*. Westport, CT: Libraries Unlimited.

Mosley, S., Tucker, D. C., & Van Winkle, S. (2014). *Crash course in dealing with difficult library customers*. Santa Barbara, CA: Libraries Unlimited.

Pekoll, K., & Adams, H. R. (2015). How to respond to challenges and concerns about library resources. In T. Magi & M. Garnar (eds.), *Intellectual Freedom Manual* (pp. 83–92). Chicago: ALA Editions, an imprint of the American Library Association.

Pinnell-Stephens, J. (1999, June). Libraries: A misunderstood American value. *American Libraries, 30*(6), 76.

Pinnell-Stephens, J. (2012). *Protecting intellectual freedom in your public library*. Chicago: American Library Association.

Preer, J. (2014). Prepare to be challenged! *Library Trends, 62*(4), 759–770.

Rubin, J. (2011). *Defusing the angry patron: A how-to-do-it manual for librarians*. New York: Neal Schuman Publishers, Inc.

EPILOGUE

Into the Future

CURRENT TRENDS IN CENSORSHIP AND INTELLECTUAL FREEDOM

The results of the July 2015 Harris Poll, referenced in Chapter 4, were alarming to the Office for Intellectual Freedom (OIF) and other proponents of intellectual freedom. The findings of the poll indicated that conservative, pro-censorship attitudes were on the rise, especially in subject areas of religion and atheism, violence, witchcraft, and even vampires. The Harris Poll results were troubling, as they proved that acceptance of book-banning was on the rise since the previous poll, in 2011 (Harris Poll, 2015).

Perhaps even more disturbing than the Harris Poll results is the fact that more and more often, challenges are being issued regarding books with characters who are not white or who are LGBT (lesbian, gay, bisexual, and transgender)-identified (Issues and Trends, 2016). Diversity of characters, it seems, leaves books especially vulnerable to challenges.

There is good news, however. While public opinions about book-banning and diversity in library materials may be troubling, the number of reported challenges has gone down. The OIF reports that between 1990 and 1999, 6,288 people initiated challenges (American Library Association [ALA], 2013a); between 2000 and 2009, the number was down to 5,403 (ALA, 2013b). While these numbers must be taken with a grain of salt, as it is estimated that as many as 85 percent of challenges go unreported (ALA, 2013c), any drop in the number of challenges is a step in the right direction.

The other good news is that many recent high-profile challenges have been met with staunch refusals by both libraries and community members to cave to pressure and remove books in the face of a challenge. While the Harris Poll results indicate that certain individuals and groups are advocating for censorship, recent headlines and news stories tell a different story.

Recent Failed Challenges

My Princess Boy and *This Day in June*

In 2015, a high-profile challenge occurred in Hood County, Texas, surrounding the books *My Princess Boy* by Cheryl Kilodavis and *This Day in June* by Gayle E. Pitman. Both are children's books featuring LGBT characters, and both were housed accordingly, in the children's section of the public library. The challengers insisted that the books should be moved from the children's section or banned from the library altogether due to their pro-LGBT stance. The library director, Courtney Kincaid, following a contentious public hearing, refused to change the status of the books. Not only was Kincaid not vilified for her decision, she was widely praised for it. Kincaid was awarded the ALA's "I Love my Librarian" award after being nominated by members of her community for her commitment to intellectual freedom in the face of a difficult challenge (Issues and Trends, 2016).

The Immortal Life of Henrietta Lacks

Another well-known 2015 challenge was led by Jackie Sims, a mother in Knoxville, Tennessee, who was upset by the inclusion of Rebecca Skloot's book *The Immortal Life of Henrietta Lacks* on her 15-year-old son's summer reading list. This nonfiction book tells the tale of a poor African American woman whose cervical cancer cells contributed to many major scientific achievements, including the polio vaccine and in-vitro fertilization, without the consent or knowledge of Lacks or her family (Issues and Trends, 2016). Ms. Sims claimed *The Immortal Life of Henrietta Lacks* was overly graphic for teenagers, even labeling it pornographic. Again, the community widely supported keeping the book on the school's summer reading list, and the school board steadfastly refused to remove the book from the summer reading list (Taylor, 2015; Issues and Trends, 2016). The challenge was reported, with an obvious focus on the foolishness of book-banning, on such high-profile news blogs as the *Huffington Post*, Salon, and Jezebel (Merlan, 2015; Silman, 2015; Taylor, 2015).

What Is Changing?

This rising trend of challenges being squelched and libraries being supported may be due in part to the popularity of blogs and social media, which help news spread fast and allow people to share their thoughts in comments, thus spreading ideas about censorship and its dangers.

Challenges may be slow to dwindle but responses to them are more and more often being met not with acquiescence but with an understanding of intellectual freedom tenets, the First Amendment, and the Library Bill of Rights. As this trend continues, attempts at book-banning and other forms of censorship are likely to become less common, as communities will have more opportunities to learn about the responsibilities and ethics their libraries are held to.

PROFESSIONAL REALITIES AND REAL-LIFE CHOICES: A SUMMARY

Knowing What Items Are Likely to Be Challenged

As a librarian, you have a responsibility to be familiar and confident with your collection, and part of this means knowing which items are particularly vulnerable to censorship attempts. Understanding this is *not* a reason to avoid purchasing these items, as that would be self-censorship. Instead, understanding what elements of your collection are at risk allows you to defend them and keep them on the shelves in their proper place.

As you have learned, materials dealing with sexual or violent themes, LGBT themes, religion and atheism, and the occult are vulnerable to challenges, especially those materials that are intended for children or teens.

- Never attach labels to materials or catalog records indicating that an item contains sexual content, violence, or anything else that could be construed as a value judgment or warning—allow the item to speak for itself.

- Keep all materials where they belong: children's books on the children's shelves, young adult (YA) books on the YA shelves, and adult books on the adult shelves—moving items to areas that don't reflect their audience is unethical and tantamount to hiding or barricading them.

- Never keep items behind barriers, such as desks or office doors, causing people to have to ask for them, as this creates a chilling effect and makes the item much less likely to be used—this is the opposite of making your collection useful and available and is a dangerous step on the road to practicing self-censorship.

CIPA and Filtering

Despite the fact that almost all public libraries in the United States filter their computers, the fact remains that doing so is a choice, albeit a loaded one. You yourself, however, might not be able to make that choice if you work under a management structure that has made its own decision or if you cannot operate effectively without the E-rate benefits attached to filtering.

If your library chooses to filter its computers, be wary of the dangers of standing back and allowing filtering software to make decisions about obscenity.

- You are the librarian, and the filter is merely a tool—don't allow an inanimate object to override your human authority or judgment.

- Never depend solely on filtering software to take the decision-making about what is and is not obscene out of your hands—librarians are the very people who are most invested in, and knowledgeable about, their public computers.

- Empower your staff and communicate with your colleagues about keeping alert and aware of how patrons use their library's public computers—this allows for better control and awareness of how these services are being used.

- If possible, use URL-based filtering software, which tends to be less problematic than software systems that use keywords to determine which sites to filter.

Media Materials

Although the Library Bill of Rights specifically states that minors have the same rights as adults in terms of library use, this fact is often overlooked, especially when it comes to movies and video games. Ratings for movies and video games are created by private organizations, and their findings are not legally binding and do not apply to public institutions such as libraries. Despite this, the practice of denying media with certain ratings to minors is very common.

- While creating juvenile-only cards that allow parents to determine what movie and game ratings their children may access takes the pressure off librarians and creates a convenience, it can also be legally problematic.

- Ratings for movies and video games are created by private organizations, and they have no legal application to public institutions such as libraries.

- Do your part to educate parents on the limitations of the law and your own limitations as a librarian.

- Always keep catalog records free of outside ratings—they have nothing to do with standard library subject headings.

- Never assume that certain items are more prone to theft, as this may lead to items such as rap and hip-hop CDs being more heavily guarded than other materials, creating the possibility of singling out certain library users and making them feel unwelcome.

- Create a welcoming atmosphere and ask your patrons for their input about media materials—this can lead to a reduction in theft and an air of openness.

Creating Policies and Training to Prevent and Prepare for Challenges

The time it takes to write a comprehensive collection development policy is never wasted time. Should a challenge arise, your policy can make or break your case. The same goes for employee training. Well-trained and supported front-line employees are more likely than anyone else to prevent challenges.

- Writing a collection development policy alone is never wise—when the whole library staff is involved, employees are more likely to feel a sense of ownership and have confidence when discussing intellectual freedom and censorship with patrons.

- Do not write the policy and then leave it as is indefinitely—regular review and revision are essential.

- Make it clear in your Request for Reconsideration Form that the burden of proving that an item is inappropriate for your collection is on the complainant—simply voicing a complaint does not warrant any kind of meeting or resolution if the complainant can't demonstrate how the item fails to meet the standards of the collection development policy.

- Train your staff and talk to your colleagues about active listening and trust them to dialogue effectively with patrons.

- Involve trustees, Friends of the Library volunteers, and other stakeholders in the writing and revision of the collection development policy—the more they know, the better they will represent your library's stance on intellectual freedom.

Facts and Figures

Most public libraries will undergo a community needs assessment at some point in order to get a snapshot of their community members' wants, needs, and demands. The main point to remember is that it is not only the majority that needs to be understood and served but also subcommunities and individuals who don't fit neatly into boxes. When libraries rely solely on statistics, they run the risk of missing out on the nuances and quirks that make up a true community and its various subcommunities.

The needs of the majority are, of course, very important, but meeting these needs while neglecting those of smaller groups leaves a substantial segment of the population unrecognized and underserved.

- One assessment will capture only one moment in time, but communities are in a constant state of flux, so be sure to follow-up with new assessments regularly—assessments must be dynamic and ongoing in order to collect and maintain true data.
- Follow-up assessments and longitudinal studies allow libraries to understand the communities they serve even as those communities undergo changes.
- Assessing the wants, needs, and demands of subcommunities, such as LGBT populations, seniors, people with disabilities, and those who don't speak English as a first language can reveal powerful data to be used in programming and collection development.
- Don't be afraid to ask the hard questions of those who do not use your library—this is an opportunity to improve and make your library more open to people who might have felt unwelcome or even discriminated against in the past.
- Community assessments can identify potential partners and keep librarians from reinventing the wheel—if certain services are already offered in your community, partnering up may be a good way to expand these services.

Avoiding Self-Censorship

Self-censorship is likely the most insidious form of censorship there is. Because of its furtive nature, it is almost impossible to recognize and even more difficult to conquer. Issues of self-censorship have been gaining more attention lately, and librarians are more and more often being challenged to examine their own biases and those of the employees they supervise.

Being alert to these trends in self-censorship helps librarians in their collection development tasks. Simply knowing that books and other items with sexual content, violence, profanity, LGBT themes, and religious or atheistic perspectives are especially susceptible to self-censorship is a strong first step in recognizing and refusing to participate in the process.

Librarians who are well-trained and strongly supported are much less likely to engage in self-censorship than those who have reason to fear that their decisions will be judged by higher-ups. Supervisors and managers have a crucial responsibility in this area.

- Be sure that diversity and its adversary—self-censorship—are addressed in your collection development policy.
- Fear of being judged can lead to self-censorship, so remember: you are a professional and you are held to high professional standards—worrying about what people will think of you is no reason to refuse to purchase certain materials.
- Purchasing a book does not necessarily mean you endorse the ideas or materials within—it means you are collecting fairly and responsibly.
- Keep alert to small and alternative presses to make sure your collection reflects diversity.
- Use teams of collectors or pairs of mentors and protégées with common goals of avoiding self-censorship and increasing inclusivity—this boosts morale and creates an organizational culture based on ethics and professionalism.
- If you feel unsupported or even threatened regarding the items you purchase for your library, contact the OIF at www.ala.org/offices/OIF or the National Coalition against Censorship at www.ncac.org for help and advice.

Questions of Quality and Demand

Librarians and other bookish types have long had a tendency to look down their noses at less-than-serious genres such as street lit and romance fiction, although this only serves to alienate potential patrons. Remember that some genres tend to serve as gateway reading for readers working their way up the ladder of serious reading. Also keep in mind that there are those patrons who simply like what they like and don't have a desire to move on to more serious literature—and this is perfectly fine.

- Help decrease judgment about certain genres by exploring them, getting to know them, and engaging in discussions with your patrons who enjoy them—this may open your eyes to the joys of different types of reading, and it helps make your library a friendlier place.
- While parents and other adults often voice strong feelings about what makes quality children's literature, having materials available in a variety of formats is of great value to children—especially those who struggle with reading.
- The most often-challenged books are those meant for teens, especially when they're edgy or dark—but remember that these books appeal greatly to teen readers, who are at an age when reading rates often drop off significantly.
- Because the ALA is committed to providing the same rights to children and teens as adults, it is not the role of libraries to limit what minors may browse and check out—be sure all books are shelved properly and not hidden behind barriers.
- Books touting so-called miracle cures and other pseudoscience might seem dangerous to purchase for a library collection, as librarians may worry that their patrons will believe everything they read or think that every book is well-researched and scientifically valid—however, a look at the Freedom to Read Statement, which makes it clear that librarians do not necessarily endorse every book they purchase and that they trust their readers to make their own decisions, can help calm this fear.

- The goal of public libraries is to provide materials to educate and entertain their communities without judgments or biases—librarians provide access; the public takes it from there.

Handling Community Challenges

Sooner or later, most public librarians will have to deal with a community challenge to an item or group of items in their collection. Being prepared is the best means to handling challenges respectfully and professionally.

- Nothing beats prevention when it comes to quelling community challenges—a well-written and regularly reviewed policy, clearly defined chains of command, and regular training on intellectual freedom and communication for staff, trustees, and stakeholders allow everyone involved with the library to understand the dynamics of challenges.
- Allow front-line employees to explain policies and the reasons behind them—this often leads to polite, respectful conversations about concerns and policies which can cool potential challenges and keep them from getting out of control.
- If a complainant will not be calmed or will not accept your library's policies and their reasons to be, ask the complainant to fill out a form explaining his concerns, but never make rash promises or indicate that the offending item will be moved or deleted—explain that the complaint will be examined and the decision will be shared with the complainant once it is made.
- Until a decision is reached, the item must not be moved, barricaded, or hidden—it must stay where it was until and unless the librarians responsible for the review decide that it was truly inappropriate for either the library or a certain area within.
- If the complainant goes as far as to request a hearing, remain professional and respectful of the complainant and his concerns, listen carefully and without judgment, and consider disparate points of view—all under the lens of intellectual freedom.
- Learning and practicing active listening skills can help cool the flames on both sides of the debate—remember that the complainant is engaging with his library and sharing his concerns and that these are actions librarians characteristically would like to see more of.
- Be civil and professional—begin and end every interaction by sincerely thanking the complainant for being involved and concerned about his public library.

What Does the Future Hold?

It is impossible to tell what issues may arise in the future of public librarianship, censorship, and intellectual freedom, but taking a look at today's challenges and confronting them serves to avoid having history repeat itself. Issues librarians face today have to do not just with censorship but also with inclusivity, serving the historically underserved, and closing the digital divide.

INCLUSIVITY, THE UNDERSERVED, AND INTELLECTUAL FREEDOM

Equal access for historically underserved individuals and communities is gaining attention as public libraries move into the future. Comprehensive collections and programs should be aimed at all members of the community. Underserved demographics have a history of missing out on important services, and it is past time for this to change.

Minors

A look around the average public library wouldn't indicate that children and teens are underserved, but it is often forgotten that their rights in libraries are meant to be equal to those of adults (ALA OIF, 2015). When a child is not permitted to check out a movie due to its MPAA (Motion Picture Association of America) rating or access a book from a restricted shelf, that child's rights are not in alignment with those of adult patrons.

This being said, the fact remains that the majority of Americans believe that librarians do, in fact, bear a responsibility for preventing minors from accessing materials that could be harmful to them, although there doesn't appear to be much of a consensus about what exactly warrants harmfulness.

With this being the case, it is wise to keep patrons of all ages advised through as many channels as possible of what can and cannot be done about limiting the library rights of minors.

- The Library Bill of Rights specifically states that minors have the same rights as adults, but this is rarely known or fully understood by adults—so do your part by initiating conversations with parents, posting the Library Bill of Rights prominently in your library, and conveying the importance of minors' rights to patrons and stakeholders.

- If you have the authority to do so, eliminate juvenile-only cards and restrictions on movies and video games based on MPAA or ESRB (Entertainment Software Rating Board) ratings—and if you don't have that authority, consider questioning the reasoning behind the policy.

Physically and Developmentally Disabled Patrons

As community hubs, public libraries must create welcoming spaces for everyone. This means having such things as assistive technology and interactive devices for children and adults with disabilities as standard features of your public library (Williams, 2016).

In addition to proactive collection development policies, ongoing training and support for staff who have questions or experience discomfort about serving people with disabilities of any kind has proved very helpful (Holmes, 2008). Some people have had very limited contact with disabled people and may be at a loss about how to communicate with them. Training and education are of great help in this area.

- Assistive technology such as text-to-speech equipment and magnification devices, as well as large print books for all ages, are not luxuries—they are necessities for many patrons.
- Include audio and large print books, as well as Hi/Lo (high content, low reading level) materials in your collection budget for patrons with developmental disabilities and reading difficulties.

LGBT Patrons and Allies

Inclusivity involves having collections representative of all segments of the community, including LGBT patrons of all ages and their allies. The LGBT community needs not only books featuring LGBT characters but materials containing information specific to the community, such as candid information about sexual health (Rauch, 2011). Books about LGBT parenting and growing up LGBT are necessary for this demographic as well (Heller & Storms, 2015; Naidoo, 2013).

- Check the GLBTRT (Gay, Lesbian, Bisexual, and Transgender Round Table) website frequently at www.ala.org/glbtrt to read book reviews and keep current on Stonewall Award winners—and make sure they're well-represented in your collection.
- Order a GLSEN (Gay, Lesbian, and Straight Education Network) Safe Space kit and post Safe Space stickers in your library to indicate that it is a welcoming place for LGBT students and their allies (find these resources at www.glsen.org/safespace)—and walk the walk by being friendly and open with your LGBT patrons, openly advocating for positive change for the LGBT community, and never tolerating discrimination or bullying in your library.

Small and Rural Library Patrons

A discussion of underserved demographics wouldn't be complete without a mention of small and rural libraries, which often must get by with very few employees and a significant deficiency of staff members with MLIS degrees. Budgets at rural and small libraries tend to be significantly lower than those of their larger counterparts, and hours of operation average about 20 hours a week. Pay and benefits tend to be low as well (Fischer, 2015).

The good news is that staff creativity has led many small and rural library employees to discover new funding sources to improve fiscal conditions. Also, these employees report a high level of satisfaction with their work and love of their communities, despite the many challenges they face. But the bad news is that staffing and budgets are still serious issues for small and rural libraries that need to be resolved as librarianship moves into the future (Fischer, 2015). Another issue with small and rural libraries is that their limited budgets and geographic restrictions often make the provision of eBooks and high-speed broadband connectivity difficult, despite strong community interest in such services (Aspen Institute, 2014).

- Support small and rural libraries by working with consortiums made up of both large and small libraries—share your resources as much as possible, especially digital collections that large and urban libraries are able to offer.
- If you work in a small or rural library, explore grant opportunities and fellowships to beef up your funding.
- Support and publicize online MLIS programs to help small and rural libraries educate their staff and increase their numbers of employees with MLIS degrees.

The Digital Divide

As the digital divide slowly closes, libraries are becoming a blend of physical and digital space, with the digital portion being as interactive, engaging, and valuable as the physical buildings and their holdings. Social interactions such as book clubs and classes may be offered in both live and online formats, bringing the library's community presence into both milieus (Hildreth & Sullivan, 2015). Many libraries are beginning to offer cutting-edge technology experiences to their patrons, from 3-D printing projects to day camps for children and teens eager to experience technology-related projects (What Trends May Come, 2016).

Between partnerships and programs, more and more public librarians are supplying mentorship opportunities to help young people increase their digital literacy (Issues and Trends, 2016). Even with all this progress, there is much more to be done before the digital divide closes once and for all.

- Encourage your community leaders to join in the vision and execution of a digitally connected world for all, and do your own part as well—as society shifts and becomes more and more connected, there is no better time for public libraries and their partners to help close the gap.
- Explore grants and partnerships designed to offer experiences with new technology to patrons of all ages and incomes.
- Keep in mind that a significant number of children and teens are growing up without access to digital resources or high-speed connectivity, and that this imbalance very often correlates with low socioeconomic status—work toward leveling the playing field in this area by partnering with community organizations to bring technology into libraries and teach kids how to make the best use of it.

POSITIVE TRENDS: STEPS IN THE RIGHT DIRECTION

Partnerships with School Libraries

Partnerships between public libraries and school libraries have had a great deal of success when it comes to allowing kids to read what they want to read. School libraries not only face budget crises more often than public libraries do, but they also are under much more pressure to keep potentially controversial books off the shelves (Wolfe & Reuling, 2015).

"Off the shelves" doesn't always mean that school libraries don't purchase potentially controversial books. Often, these books end up in restricted areas—behind barriers or in counseling or other offices behind closed doors—actions public librarians should never take, since they don't have *in loco parentis* status. Partnerships between school and public libraries can get students the books they want and need without the discomfort of facing the roadblocks set up by their schools (Doyle, 2015).

A Focus on Diversity

Diversity and equity have long been important for public libraries, but these themes are gaining more attention as libraries move into the future. During 2016's Banned Books Week, the OIF focused on diversity and posted a list of books with diverse themes that have a history of challenges and bans (ALA, 2016). Understanding and embracing diversity involves much more than simply reading about people of different backgrounds than your own. It means providing quality library services to populations that have typically been underserved.

Embracing diversity can include having subcollections in different languages for people who don't speak English as their first language. It can include collecting genres such as street lit and fotonovellas for African American and Hispanic patrons (not that these genres cannot be enjoyed by patrons of any background).

Finally, a commitment to diversity involves collecting and being ready to defend books with diverse characters and themes, which are all too often subject to challenges and banning attempts (ALA, 2016). A diverse collection represents a focus on inclusivity and equity as important elements of librarianship.

Teamwork, Training, and Innovation

When it comes to complaints and potential challenges, front-line library employees are usually the first to respond. Quality training and trust in your employees' ability to speak with irate patrons with respect and authority is absolutely necessary but so is involving all staff members in developing innovative ideas and sharing their collective wisdom. A well-trained staff is one that is empowered by its administration to act appropriately when challenged, and a trusted staff is one that feels comfortable bringing new ideas into the fray. Library managers must not only encourage and support new ideas from their front-line employees but also execute them and give credit to those who brought them forward (King, 2015). Trust in your staff helps quell complaints and keeps them from becoming full-on challenges.

When it comes to public library management, experience and education are vital but so are the qualities that make a good librarian—commitment to community service, teamwork, collaboration, and a dedication to social justice (LaGuardia, 2015).

Patron Privacy

Despite the enactment of Children's Internet Protection Act (CIPA), privacy remains an important issue for library employees and patrons alike. Ventures such as the Library Freedom Project have brought attention to privacy concerns for library patrons, advocating for Tor exit relays, which keep Web searches anonymous. The Library Freedom Project has been successful in advocating for library patron privacy, even in the face of pressure from the Department of Homeland Security (What Trends May Come, 2016). Libraries that use filters can offer Tor Browser and Tor exit relays, making patrons' searches much more confidential (Macrina, 2016). Public libraries have a responsibility to stay current on new options like these to keep patron searches and records private.

Libraries Transform

The ALA launched the Libraries Transform campaign in 2015, with the goal of raising public awareness of the importance of libraries. In an era in which libraries are seen by some as obsolete or old-fashioned, this campaign works to remind those who create public policies and raise funding that libraries are much more than they used to be and also stresses the importance of keeping the core values of librarianship (and therefore the antitheses of censorship) strong—privacy, confidentiality, equity, and free access. It's about what libraries can do *for* their communities as well as *with* them (Feldman, 2016; Issues and Trends, 2016). Libraries Transform identifies privacy, income equality, and connected learning as just a few of the trends libraries are working on promoting (Trends, 2015). Initiatives and campaigns such as Libraries Transform are keeping libraries current and innovative.

YOU'LL NEVER WALK ALONE

Librarianship is a profession with a great deal of support. Sooner or later, you will likely find yourself in a tight spot. When this happens, remember to examine your situation under the lens of the Library Bill of Rights, the Freedom to Read Statement, and the First Amendment. If the answer doesn't become clear, there are people and organizations to help you come to an informed, ethical decision. Contact the OIF and ask for assistance. Send an e-mail to the ALA's Social Responsibilities Round Table. Get in touch with the National Coalition against Censorship. Above all, know that facing a difficult task alone is never necessary in librarianship.

LOOKING TO THE FUTURE

What will the future of censorship in public libraries look like? In many ways, the answer depends on the actions of librarians today. Having an understanding of the history of censorship and intellectual freedom challenges helps keep them from being repeated but new concerns have a way of cropping up as old ones fade away.

Librarianship is a profession built on ethics and equity, and librarians therefore have a duty to behave ethically and fairly. Fighting censorship is important work, although it is slow-going—and this is why preventing challenges through strong policies, ongoing training, and a mind-set of inclusivity is so important.

Learning from the past and confronting today's issues will make the challenges of the future less problematic to understand and confront. Librarianship in the United States has come a long way in a short time. Many great steps have been taken. Knowing how far we have come, conquering censorship while promoting intellectual freedom seems less a pipe dream than one more step in the right direction.

REFERENCES

American Library Association. (2013a, September 6). Number of challenges by reasons, initiator & institution, 1990–1999. Retrieved from http://www.ala.org/bbooks/frequentlychallengedbooks/statistics/1990–99

American Library Association. (2013b, September 6). Number of challenges by reasons, initiator & institution, 2000–1009. Retrieved from http://www.ala.org/bbooks/frequentlychallengedbooks/statistics/2000–09#reasons2000

American Library Association. (2013c, March 26). Frequently challenged books. Retrieved from http://www.ala.org/bbooks/frequentlychallengedbooks

American Library Association. (2015). Trends. Retrieved from http://www.ilovelibraries.org/librariestransform/trends

American Library Association. (2016, August 5). Frequently challenged books with diverse content. Retrieved from http://www.ala.org/bbooks/frequentlychallengedbooks/diverse

American Library Association Office for Intellectual Freedom. (2015). *Intellectual freedom manual*. Chicago: ALA Editions, an imprint of the American Library Association.

Aspen Institute. (2014, October) Rising to the challenge: Re-envisioning public libraries. Retrieved from https://assets.aspeninstitute.org/content/uploads/files/content/docs/pubs/AspenLibrariesReport.pdf

Banned Books Week. (2016). Celebrating the freedom to read: September 25-October 1, 2016. Retrieved from http://www.bannedbooksweek.org/

Doyle, M. (2015). Rethinking the "restricted" shelf. *Knowledge Quest, 44*(1), 72–73.

Feldman, S. (2016). President's message. Libraries Transform. *American Libraries, 47*(1/2), 6.

Fischer, R. K. (2015). Rural and small town library challenges. *Public Library Quarterly, 34*(4), 354–371.

Harris Poll. (2015, July 8). Adults are more likely to believe there are books that should be banned than movies, television shows, or video games. Retrieved from http://www.theharrispoll.com/health-and-life/Censorship_2015.html

Hildreth, S., & Sullivan, M. (2015). Rising to the challenge: Re-envisioning public libraries. *Journal of Library Administration, 55*(8), 647–657.

Holmes, J. L. (2008). Patrons with developmental disabilities: A needs assessment survey. *New Library World, 109*(11/12), 533–545.

Issues and Trends. (2016). *American Libraries*, Special Issue, 14–19.

King, K. (2015). The future's so bright I gotta wear shades. *Public Libraries, 54*(3), 22–23.

Heller, M. J., & Storms, A. (2015). Sex in the library. *Teacher Librarian, 42*(3), 22–25.

LaGuardia, C. (2015). Where are we headed? An unscientific study. *Library Journal, 140*(19), 14.

Macrina, A. (2016). Protecting patron privacy. *Library Journal, 141*(12), 38–39.

Merlan, A. (2015). Mother says book on cancer cell research is too "pornographic" for son's school [web log post]. Retrieved from http://jezebel.com/mother-says-book-on-stem-cell-research-is-too-pornograp-1729541630

Naidoo, Jamie Campbell. (2013). Over the rainbow and under the radar. *Children & Libraries: The Journal of the Association for Library Service to Children, 11*(3), 34–40.

Rauch, E.W. (2011). GLBTQ collections are for every library serving teens! *Teacher Librarian, 39*(1), 13–16.

Silman, A. (2015). Tennessee mom wants "pornographic" Henrietta Lacks book banned from shelves [web log post]. Retrieved from http://www.salon.com/2015/09/09/tennessee_mom_wants_pornographic_henrietta_lacks_book_banned_from_schools/

Taylor, D. (2015). Tennessee mom calls book on cervical cancer cells "pornographic" [web log post]. Retrieved from http://www.huffingtonpost.com/entry/mom-cells-book-pornographic_us_55ef1340e4b002d5c076c412

What trends may come in 2016. (2015). *Information Today, 32*(10), Cover-25.

Williams, T. (2016). Inclusivity in any library. *American Libraries, 47*(6), 28.

Wolfe, S., & Reuling, L. (2015). Repurposing for the future: A library story. *Teacher Librarian 43*(1), 25–29.

APPENDIX A

Where to Turn: A Source List of LGBT-Friendly Books and Other Materials

WEBSITES

GLBTRT Website (www.glbtrt.ala.org)

The website of the ALA's Gay, Lesbian, Bisexual, and Transgender Round Table provides current reviews of new LGBT-themed books, plus comprehensive, frequently updated booklists in a variety of subject areas. The GLBTRT also offers a subscription to their blog to help librarians stay current on new LGBT-themed book reviews shortly after publication. One may also subscribe to the GLBTRT on Facebook, Twitter, and various other social media.

Goodreads' LGBT Book Lists (www.goodreads.com/list/tag/lgbt)

Goodreads, Amazon's popular social cataloging website, provides lists of LGBT books in many genres, including fantasy, romance, humor, historical fiction, and fiction in which a character has a disability. There is something for everyone here.

Lambda Literary Foundation Website (www.lambdaliterary.org)

The Lambda Literary Foundation works to advocate for LGBT-themed literature as an imperative part of LGBT culture and history. Click on the Reviews tab to access current reviews of LGBT-themed materials in the genres of general fiction, biography/memoir, poetry, nonfiction, YA, illustrated books, anthology, erotica, romance, mystery, speculative, drama, and film. Click on the Lammys tab to see the current finalists and previous winners of the Lammy awards in a variety of genres.

Over the Rainbow Books (www.glbtrt.ala.org/overtherainbow)

The GLBTRT website offers information about current and past Over the Rainbow selections. At the end of each year, the GLBTRT announces their top 10 Over the Rainbow books, plus their lists of final bibliographies—recommendations in the areas of art, drama, fiction, mystery, short stories, graphic narrative, nonfiction, biography/memoir, essays, and poetry.

Rainbow Books (www.glbtrt.ala.org/rainbowbooks)

> The GLBTRT website offers ongoing information on their current and past recommendations of children's and YA Rainbow Books, which can be used to build and sustain quality children's and YA collections.

Stonewall Award Books (www.ala.org/glbtrt/award)

> The coveted Stonewall Book Awards have been going strong since 1971. Becoming familiar with current and past Stonewall Award books is a recommended starting point for building any comprehensive LGBT collection. To win this award, a book must be found to be of exceptional value to the LGBT experience.

BOOKS

Gay and Lesbian History for Kids: The Century-Long Struggle for LGBT Rights, with 21 Activities by Jerome Pohlen. Chicago: Chicago Review Press, 2015.

> Intended for children in grades 4 and up, this history and activity book examines LGBT rights era by era, focusing mainly on the twentieth century. Appropriate for classrooms, school libraries, public libraries, and homeschooling collections, the book includes fun, educational activities to help children understand LGBT history in an applied and enjoyable manner.

Gay, Lesbian, Bisexual, Transgender and Questioning Teen Literature: A Guide to Reading Interests by Carlisle K. Webber. Santa Barbara, CA: Libraries Unlimited, 2010.

> LGBT teens and the librarians who serve them can benefit from the wide-ranging reading suggestions this book offers. It offers a wide range of fiction and nonfiction recommendations marked with codes for awards, reading levels, and age appropriateness due to sexual context. The author also gives due attention to alternative reading formats for teen readers and stresses the importance of quality readers' advisory and collection development for this often-underserved demographic.

Gay, Lesbian, Bisexual, and Transgendered Literature: A Genre Guide by Ellen Bosman, John P. Bradford, & Robert B. Marks Ridinger. Westport, CT: Libraries Unlimited, 2008.

> This comprehensive book provides historical facts and practical advice for librarians involved in collection development and readers' advisory, as well as over 1,000 recommended titles and read-alike suggestions covering genres of romance, science fiction, horror, mystery, graphic novels, coming out stories, memoirs, biographies, and much more.

Rainbow Family Connections: Selecting and Using Children's Books with Lesbian, Gay, Bisexual, Transgender and Queer Content by Jamie Campbell Naidoo. Santa Barbara, CA: Libraries Unlimited, 2012.

> This comprehensive book helps readers understand the particular dynamics of LGBT families, how libraries play a role in their reading selections, an overview of children's LGBT-themed books, past awards, and wide-ranging lists of both picture books and chapter books for children, plus recommendations of informational books for librarians, educators, and parents.

Serving Lesbian, Gay, Bisexual, Transgender, and Questioning Teens: A How-To-Do-It Manual for Librarians **by Hillas J. Martin & James R. Murdock. New York: Neal-Schuman Publishers, 2007.**

Although it's getting a bit dated, this manual still provides librarians with a wealth of resources and information about how to serve the teen LGBT demographic effectively and proactively. An expansive bibliography is included, which would serve any public library collection well.

Top 250 LGBT Books for Teens: Coming Out, Being Out, and the Search for Community **by Michael Cart & Christine Jenkins. Chicago: American Library Association, 2015.**

This summary of recommended books for LGBT teens and their allies provides well-researched recommendations for any public library's LGBT teen collection. Genres covered include fiction, nonfiction, graphic novels, and classics for middle- and high school-aged readers. Information on programming, special services, and other methods for reaching LGBT teens is included. This book is up-to-date and useful for LGBT young adults, librarians, teachers, parents, and other allies.

A World of Rainbow Families **by Jamie Campbell Naidoo. Santa Barbara, CA: Libraries Unlimited, 2016.**

This resource serves as a guide and collection development tool for librarians looking for the latest and greatest in LGBT-themed books and media for children.

PUBLISHING HOUSES

Arktoi Books (www.arktoi.com)

This highly selective publishing house, an imprint of Chicago's Red Hen Press, specializes in high-quality works of fiction, nonfiction, and poetry by lesbian writers.

Bold Strokes Books (www.boldstrokesbooks.com)

Focusing on younger readers, this publisher specializes in LGBT-themed books and features books for both YA and new adult (ages 18–25) readers.

Dreamspinner Press (www.dreamspinnerpress.com)

Dreamspinner publishes gay male romance books, including the genres of fantasy, coming-of-age, science fiction, and books featuring transgender characters. Their easy-to-use, interactive website is a bonus feature.

Harrington Park Press (www.harringtonparkpress.com)

Highly selective and academic, Harrington Park specializes in academic and scholarly LGBT-themed books.

Lethe Press (www.lethepressbooks.com)

Lethe Press specializes in offering multiple genres of LGBT-themed books, including speculative, occult, and supernatural fiction.

Queerteen Press (www.queerteen-press.com)

Queerteen specializes in YA eBooks. Among other genres, they are known for publishing action/adventure, science fiction, and horror books.

Redbone Press (www.redbonepress.com)
Deeply committed to diversity, Redbone specializes in books written by black lesbians and gay men.

Sibling Rivalry Press (www.siblingrivalrypress.com)
This Little Rock, Arkansas, press publishes high-quality poetry books, including Lambda winners.

Transgress Press (www.transgresspress.com)
This socially conscious publisher of transgender-themed books donates 40 percent of their book sale profits to groups serving disadvantaged communities and environmental causes.

BOOK FAIRS

OutWrite Book Fair (www.thedccenter.org/outwritedc.com)
Held every summer in Washington, D.C., OutWrite offers readings, workshops, poetry readings, book sales, and exhibitors centering on LGBT writing. For those who can't make it there in person, the website has a blog and a wealth of information.

Rainbow Book Fair (www.rainbowbookfair.org)
Held every spring in New York City, this book fair includes exhibitors, author panels, and readings by distinguished writers of LGBT-themed books. Experience it in person or check out their website for helpful information.

APPENDIX B

Where to Turn: A Sampling of Small and Alternative Presses

LITERARY FICTION, NONFICTION, SHORT STORIES, AND POETRY

Coffee House Press (www.coffeehousepress.org)
This well-known independent press began as a poetry magazine and grew into a nonprofit literary publisher advocating for books reflecting diversity and the American experience.

Dzanc Books (http://www.dzancbooks.org)
This nonprofit press not only publishes fiction, nonfiction, and poetry by new writers in both print and eBooks formats but also partners with public schools through their writer-in-residence program, and coordinates the Disquiet International Literary Program writers' conference.

Graywolf Press (www.graywolfpress.org)
Based in Minnesota, Graywolf Press is a nonprofit literary publisher distributing works of fiction, nonfiction, and poetry. The press has published several award-winning books, and offers prizes and a writer residency program.

New Directions Press (http://www.ndbooks.com)
New Directions was formed in 1936 and is known as one of the oldest and most well-regarded independent presses in the country.

The New Press (www.thenewpress.com)
The socially conscious New Press specializes in books that contribute to discussions and understanding of democratic values. The prestigious New Press Social Justice Awards have been in place since 2010.

OR Books (www.orbooks.com)

This newer independent press is highly selective and progressive. OR Books offers a fast turnaround publishing timeframe so authors can write about current political or cultural events as they're occurring.

Seven Stories Press (www.sevenstories.com)

Seven Stories publishes mainly nonfiction dealing with political and cultural issues.

Tyrant Books (www.nytyrant.com/books)

Widely praised by critics including the *Los Angeles Review of Books*, this small press specializes in edgy fiction.

TRANSLATIONS

Archipelago Books (www.archipelagobooks.org)

This small press offers quality translations of classics and contemporary books from all over the world.

Europa Editions (www.europaeditions.com)

Based in Italy, Europa is dedicated to bringing books from other cultures to all readers through translation and recognition.

Wakefield Press (www.wakefieldpress.com)

Wakefield is committed to the translation of overlooked books, available in an affordable paperback format.

STREET LIT

G-Unit Books (www.simonandschuster.com/series/G-UNIT)

Founded by the rapper 50 Cent, this imprint of Simon & Schuster specializes in street lit and edgy, urban fiction for teens and adults.

Triple Crown Publications (www.triplecrownpublications.com)

Triple Crown is the leading publisher of street lit and urban-themed fiction, offering works by authors such as Vickie Stringer and Nikki Turner.

CHILDREN'S AND YA BOOKS

Candlewick Press (www.candlewick.com)

Candlewick is an independent publisher of children's books, many of which have received awards and critical acclaim. Librarians can use free discussion guides, activity suggestions, and story-time kits available on their website.

Barefoot Books (www.barefootbooks.com)

This press and online store offers books for children and teens focusing on cultural and emotional literacy.

Children's Book Press (www.leeandlow.com/imprints/4)

An imprint of Lee & Low, this press specializes in children's books written by authors of color and featuring characters of varied cultures and ethnicities. Many award-winning books have come from Children's Book Press.

Dawn Publications (www.dawnpub.com)

This press publishes children's and YA books with themes of nature. The website includes activities for teachers and librarians.

Just Us Books (www.justusbooksonlinestore.com)

Just Us is a publisher of books for children and teens focusing on African American culture and history.

Triangle Square Books (www.sevenstories.com/trianglesquare)

Seven Stories Press offers children's and YA books through their Triangle Square young readers' books, featuring cultural diversity and humor.

INDEX

About the Author

JENNIFER DOWNEY, MLIS, is reference librarian at Rancho Cucamonga Public Library. She holds a Master of Library and Information Science from San Jose State University as well as a Master of Science in counseling from Canisius College. Prior to her library career, she spent 10 years as a social worker, providing services to at-risk children and families. Downey is the winner of the 2005 Progressive Librarians Guild's Miriam Braverman Prize and has been awarded several grants, allowing her to enhance public library services to underrepresented groups.